1

Cabbages and Kings.

Best Wishes,
Mary Chiappe.

Cabbages and Kings.

BY

MARY CHIAPPE.

Published by HKB Press, 139 The Ryde, Hatfield, Herts AL9 5DP.

Typeset and printed by Tipografía la Nueva, Tarifa, S.C.A.
Calle Arapiles, 11-A, 11380 Tarifa, Cadiz, Spain.

Copyright: © Mary Chiappe 2006.

ISBN 0-9552503-2-3   and   987-0-9552503-2-3

ACNOWLEDGEMENTS:

My thanks to Clive Power for encouraging me to publish the book; to Sam Benady for his very helpful advice on the question of printing; to Dorothy Prior for invaluable help with preparing the typescript.

On reading over these articles I am aware of how much I am indebted to any number of magazines and newspapers I have read, television programmes I have watched, and books that have made a deep impact on me: I am grateful to them all, and especially to Karen Armstrong whose book, "The Gospel According to Woman", helped me understand a great deal about woman's place as it developed in Christian Europe, and to Bill Bryson's "A Short History of Nearly Everything".

And, not least, my thanks to the "Gibraltar Chronicle" for permission to publish these articles;

    – and my thanks also to the Gibraltar Government Ministry of Culture for its help.

CONTENTS.

FURTHER DIMENSIONS.

CHRISTINA THE ASTONISHING.

Sitting on top of my computer screen is the small figure of a bishop. In one hand he holds aloft a laptop and from the other hand dangles a mouse. It's St Isidore of Pelusium who died around 450 AD and obviously never touched a computer in his life, though he appears to be patron saint of IT. He did, however, write an awful lot of letters: 10,000 "in his lifetime" as the book says.

"Why, 'in his lifetime'?" I thought; he could hardly have carried on writing posthumously, could he? And, "What book, 'says'?" I hear you ask. I refer to the pocket "Dictionary of Saints" that makes intriguing to inspiring to hilarious reading. Pride of place goes, for me, to Christina the Astonishing, 1150 - 1224. It would appear that she died as a result of an epileptic attack at the age of twenty-one, but during the mass that was being said for the repose of her soul, just prior to burial, she suddenly took off and soared to the roof of the church. Thank goodness they hadn't battened down the hatches is all I can say. The priest ordered her down and she obliged. She *then* lived the rest of her life - a life of poverty and prayer - and reputedly went from strength to strength after her first un-powered flight. Sadly, she couldn't stand the odour of human beings and tried everything to escape human contact: she climbed trees, flew up into the rafters of churches and (this is my favourite) "hid in ovens". My "Dictionary of Saints" adds laconically that she "was thought by some to be insane, but venerated by others". Hmm.

I think she was a sister-in-the-spirit to St Simeon Stylites, a shepherd boy born in 390 AD who had a vision that foretold his later life on pillars. Yes: read on. He entered a monastery that he left after two years because life there was not harsh enough. He moved on to the strict monastery at Heliodorus from which he was expelled for practising mortifications that even they considered excessive. So he became a lonely hermit, but his reputation for holiness spread and attracted many followers....*so*, to escape them, he took up residence at the top of a home-made wooden pillar that stood ten feet high. Popularity has its inbuilt penalties and as time passed the crowds grew larger and consequently he moved to ever-higher pillars. By the time he died at the age of 105 the last pillar was sixty feet high. These pillars never had a diameter of more than two metres. He hardly ate and "he slept little, if at all", and what he wanted was to avoid people. Hmmm.

Neither Christina nor Simeon seems to have been too keen on the human race that each was presumably praying for, wouldn't you say? Maybe real mortification for them would have involved asking ordinary people to tea and passing round the cucumber sandwiches and fairy cakes?

Defining sanctity is not easy, any more than defining normality or lunacy or love is easy. Words like "holy…devout…sanctified…godly" all take you round in a circle. Each age has its own ideas about the matter and saints probably reflect the age that saw their canonization as much, at least, as the age they lived in; and there doesn't really appear to be any immutable and objective yardstick employed. In the very early Christian church, with emperors like Nero around, martyrdom was very much on the cards. There is a supposedly autobiographical account by St Perpetua of her captivity. She was a young matron, pregnant, who had a series of dreams while in prison. They helped her come to terms with the death that awaited her in the amphitheatre at the public games.

In her last dream she saw herself as a male athlete, stripped naked and anointed with oil by her friends and facing a towering Egyptian in the arena. She described an exhilarating fight that included kick-boxing and she awoke knowing that she would overcome. The day after she gave birth she was cast into the arena and was gored to death. Unlike records of later saints, she was a mother, not a virgin, who went through the very normal process of dreaming a solution to her situation. She didn't want to suffer: she was trying to find the courage to face a very unpleasant death.

Autobiography, biography or fiction? It doesn't really matter because what is relevant is the ideology that gave birth to the attitude - the physically weak and vulnerable can triumph over fear and can face the might of the Roman Empire. As the Roman Empire changed, so did the fear of martyrdom recede and we have such saints as the virginal Martina. Now she is *not* in my dictionary though I've read of her, and others like her, and she typifies an attitude to martyrdom that can make you feel unwell. She was slashed all over, drawn, staked down and set on fire with burning oil. The next day she was up early, well before her torturers, raring to go again. She is one of those virgin martyrs who had their breasts torn off with hot pincers, were thrown into brothels (with monotonous regularity) and were inevitably saved from defilement by a statuary angel. Fact or fiction? Again, what matters is the attitude it reveals. Gone is the young mother who fears death and struggles to keep the faith and die with dignity. Instead we have the virgin, fearless, whose chronicler can give full rein to a prurient interest in torture and potential sexual assault. He clearly has little idea about how the body reacts to substances like boiling oil, and couldn't care less because he wants to make a point about the power of God. His virgin martyrs are not just fearless, they practically engineer their own deaths by being abominably rude to the local prefect, consul or whoever till the provocation becomes impossible to ignore. They ask for it and get it!

And hundreds of years later, any young woman seeking sanctity could only enter an enclosed order of nuns, never leaving the convent or having contact with the outside world thanks to Pope Boniface VII's decree on the issue. Over 200 years after that, Mary Ward founded the Institute of the Blessed Virgin Mary, an order that went outside convent walls to serve the world. Gibraltar's Loreto nuns belong to this order, but Mary Ward saw her organization suppressed by order of Pope Urban VII because the work she was already carrying out successfully, did not suit the "weakness of (the) sex, womanly modesty and virginal purity". So there. And she hasn't been canonized yet. On the other hand, St Margaret Mary has made it. She once tied a chain so tightly round her waist that it pulled the flesh away with it when removed. She could say that suffering was, "This food, so delightful to my taste that He (Christ) never said, 'Enough!'" Hmmmmmm.

The voice of Christ? The voice of a woman? The voice of masochism?...of a biographer?...of a point in time?

Looking at the positive side, I suppose there are holy folk to suit every taste. There was Thecla who worked with St Paul, then dispensed with him and baptized herself before carrying on with her missionary work. Northumbria gave us St Hild who ruled over both monks and nuns in her monastic house. It also gave us Willehad, Willibald and Willibrord. They seem pretty average. Willehad had to flee from the environs of Utrecht. What had Willehad done to the pagans? Well, Willehad had burnt their temples, had he. And Willibald (d. 786), a great traveller, wrote what can be classified as the first travel book in English, "Hodoeporicon"…but I've included them principally because I can't resist the names - great if you have triplets!

As for St Isidore, he hasn't managed to save me from major virus or pernicious worm, but he's company and I like the natty pair of specs he wears.

25th June, 2004.

WE WILL HAVE MIRACLES.

This week I'm planning to found a new religion. You see, between you and me, I have seen The Way. It happened when I was sorting out the address book. Yes, revelation can come at any time. I worked out that I have almost always lived at number forty-something. It's number 44 today; it was 46 before that, 45 in UK, 46 when I was a child. One of my daughters lives at No. 45 and my brother lives at No. 244. Let's face it: is that a sign or is it a sign? And half of four is two. I found myself listing birth dates and anniversaries and, what did I find? There they were, all the twos: 2nd, 12th, 20th, 21st, 23rd, 24th, 25th, 26th, 27th, 28th, 29th, and listen to this - 22nd appeared umpteen times! My way is clear: I shall now comb the Bible, both Old and New Testaments, reading every second page and I shall seek out all references to two and four. Perhaps I should start with "The Book of Numbers"? I'm certain that a pattern will emerge as I go along. Once the picture is clear I shall draft my new creed and, as I'm already sharing these insights with you, you'll be the first to know.

You don't believe me, do you? Ah me! What it is to have a reputation for light-hearted badinage and meretricious persiflage (I got that from a Victorian novel). Yet why should I not have new insights to contribute? There was recently an established traveller/author on Spanish television propounding all sorts of theories of one sort or another. I sat through one programme that he devoted to a place in South America where there are carvings depicting winged beings. They did look as if they might be winged, but the trouble with formalized shapes is that they do involve the viewer in a degree of interpretation. Could it have been a pair of sacks over their shoulders rather than wings? In any case, his conclusion had to do with the distinct possibility that there had been people/beings who had mastered flight.

It certainly made me think. I thought about Western religious art. We have been depicting saints, angels and demons for centuries. Will someone in some remote future, eager for a new theory, suggest that we had creatures that went around with luminous Spanish omelettes miraculously affixed to the back of their heads? And that we had others who flew; and still others with red tails, horns and cloven hoofs? And, on a lighter level, will all our family outdoor snaps be taken as proof that, as we are inevitably facing the light, we were sun worshippers one and all?

And pondering this, I remembered a book I once read where some theory or other was being aired about the Aztecs - or was it the Incas? Once more we were treated to an interpretation of the carvings found in some exotic location. What the gentleman presenting his photos of the ruins had failed to take note of, and give its proper value to, was a small figure in one of the friezes: there he squatted in his limited glory, wearing a large cloth cap. It was clear evidence that the Aztecs/Incas came from Bradford. OK, I'm willing to concede a point; after all, one cannot pinpoint a geographical spot with perfect certainty after so many hundreds of years - it could, perhaps, have been Salford.

Who recalls the book, "Chariot of the Gods"? Wasn't it persuasive with its talk about beings from outer space? There was a great deal in the book that intrigued me and what was really disappointing was the failure of the author to provide all the necessary footnotes so that one could verify the fascinating information given.

Oh, but we do love to be informed of strange events and we *are* credulous. I have read a number of accounts of the mystery surrounding The Bermuda Triangle, but only one of them quoted the specific sources used to compile what amounted to a factual dossier. One thing it did was challenge other accounts of events. Let me give you an example: account A had said that a particular sailing ship had set out on a fine spring morning when the sea was calm and weather conditions perfect and had then disappeared. The dossier accepted these facts, but it added that, while that was true at 7.00 am, there were gale warnings that promised rough seas and high winds by evening. What a difference that makes to the story. It's the same with supposed cases of spontaneous human combustion. We read, with a frisson of pleasurable horror, of the man who sat down to read the evening paper and suddenly burst into flame…and the flames were of such intensity that no one could approach him. And when it was all over, there was nothing left - not even ash - except for his slippers and his monocle. That's the real clincher, isn't it? There's real mystery for you.

I'm not being a dyed-in-the-wool sceptic. I am happy enough to accept all sorts of things on the Hamlet principle than there are more things in heaven and earth than are dreamt of in our philosophy. I'm willing to be convinced, but I need more than the wonderful or the bizarre per se to persuade me, however much fun it is to entertain these freak events.

That's it, you see; we love to be amazed. We want a totally new idea or a totally new slant on old material. I imagine that is one reason why the novel "The da Vinci Code" is reaching such phenomenal sales worldwide. Yet the idea of Jesus being married to Mary Magdalene was first suggested long ago and, more recently, in France in the early fifties. Frankly, what difference does it make to the teachings of Jesus whether he was married, single or a widower? With regard to Leonardo da Vinci's painting of The Last Supper, one must remember that he was painting the picture for his patrons. This made him work within parameters - he couldn't, as a Monty Python sketch showed, include two giraffes and a hippo. He who pays the painter calls the image. And in those days, women had already been pushed to the sidelines and beyond in church affairs. I'm sure that there were women with Christ at that Jewish meal, but they are never shown in Christian paintings. Once again, the presence or not of a woman at the Last Supper hardly seems that important.

If I object to anything, it would be to speculation that masquerades as scholarship. And it is so obvious that the past is the perfect hunting ground for even the wildest and woolliest theories. You only have to look at all the ideas about who Jack the Ripper could have been; at all the theories about what lay behind John Kennedy's assassination; at all the interpretations of the personalities of various historical figures, to know that, with speculation, it's always open season.

27th October, 2004.

LARGER THAN LIFE

I once read that poetry preceded prose in written form. I do know that early bills of lading have been found in archaeological digs and those were in prose: you can't imagine an early ship chandler knocking his brains out to give form in verse to the list of goods being loaded - "By the beard of Tammuz and the veil of Mother Goddess Innin - I just cannot find a good rhyme for pilchards; I'll never get the job done on time and my clay tablet's drying rigid. Why couldn't I be working on something easy like wheat?"

But poetry came first when you went beyond the shopping list. How come? After all, it's prose narratives we indulge in every day. When we talk of what happened at the butcher's, what Mrs Blank told us about her husband's ulcer or what we're planning to cook on Sunday, we are involved in telling stories in prose. Why was prose a poor second? Even though nowadays all sorts of early prose narratives are being given recognition, prose didn't seem to really get under way in the English-speaking world till the eighteenth century when Samuel Richardson's "Pamela" launched what we consider the modern novel. There had been plays galore before then and poetry aplenty, but prose was mainly the medium for drafting laws, writing your letters, compiling historical chronicles and factual texts and, naturally, making out bills of lading.

There may be a hundred reasons for this precedence of poetry over prose, but I can think of two. The first is eminently practical: given a catchy rhythm and a spot of rhyme or alliteration, you can memorise something you've heard and enjoyed. It's a lot harder to memorise, verbatim, a page of the instructions telling you how to install your washing machine. That lacks a certain je ne sais quoi, wouldn't you say? The second reason is harder to pin down because, for me, it's a gut feeling about there being something about poetry that has magic of a sort. And poetry proper is about quality of thought/feeling/language; it is about a depth of searching in what it is to be human - and more than what I can only express in very pedestrian terms.

And, no, this is not an article about poetry, whatever gave you that idea? This is about something which, like poetry, reverberates in our being and is just as hard to pin down. I'm referring to myth. The myth is mightier than the truth; it is mightier than reality and it reaches the parts that other narratives don't reach. The figures of myth endure across the centuries and possibly even across cultures. I use the word "possibly" because cultures are so rich and so varied that there is no way one can be categorical. I hereby declare my ignorance, but I also state that, because of the nature of myths, it is likely that they are both intelligible and acceptable to others.

"What on earth is this woman wittering on about?" - I hear you cry. (Or "twittering on about" as the computer suggests)

Fear not. I will make all things clear. Moby Dick and Captain Ahab. Tarzan. Doctor Frankenstein. Dracula and Peter Pan. Doctor Jekyll and Mr. Hyde. Even Coleridge's Ancient Mariner and his albatross. If you consider these dispassionately, you can say that, among these, only Melville's "Moby Dick" is generally considered great literature – it's admittedly strange, but one of the most extraordinary novels of the last century. However, you cannot say the same about Mary Shelley or Bram Stoker's work. And when you boil it all down, you realize that there has only been one film made about the obsessive

Captain Ahab pursuing his whale, while films about the obsessive Doctor Frankenstein creating his creature have been legion - even though Mary Shelley might turn in her grave at the way her story has been abused in many representations.

The Creature was beautiful when Frankenstein assembled it and it was only the doctor's revulsion at what he had done that first made it seem hideous; and then it truly became so as, with time, the tissues began to deteriorate. And the Creature wanted love; it sought the love of its creator and when this was denied, it demanded a mate. And when that was also denied, it sought revenge. You'd be hard put to say which of the two is the hero of the tale. And in that Creature there wasn't a nut or bolt in sight to hold its head together so we can forget the rectangular-headed monstrosity of Hollywood's creation.

It's been the same with Bram Stoker's creation: Dracula has been filmed endlessly in a variety of versions that have sold the original short. They made every victim of the vampire Count turn into a vampire at the first bite. In the novel it is only as a result of a lengthy process involving a number of visits by the Count that the victim is eventually corrupted. And when the Count is destroyed, with a stake through his heart if I recall the plot correctly, there is a moment when his face changes expression and he becomes just a mortal shedding an intolerable burden. His eyes express gratitude to his executioners for the mercy that they have granted him in destroying him. Now, isn't that something?

And in the Hollywood versions with all those glamorous victims in low-cut negligees, there was always a moment guaranteed to break the spell for me. There was Dracula with his two pointed fangs, one on either side of his mouth, bending over his victim as she grew helpless with a mixture of fear and sexual rapture. And when he drew back, his mouth foully stained with her blood, she had two puncture wounds about two centimetres away from each other. So, what had happened? Had he plunged one fang in, withdrawn it, and then plunged the other one in as close to where the first had been as possible? Or had he suddenly developed retractable canines and sprouted sharpened buck teeth like Bugs Bunny?

The Gothic tale of Jekyll and Hyde has also been made and remade, but the films have remained reasonably true to the text. The Angst of the worthy Doctor Jekyll has always been given full play, but his alter ego, the criminally inclined Mr.Hyde, has rarely been presented as the physically meagre figure of the book. Instead he has tended to appear monstrous. Still, you can't have everything.

What all these characters have in common would seem to be that they give physical form to our fears and desires. It can be fear of our own evil or fear of things that have no name, like the fears of childhood that made sleep impossible and created nightmares out of shadows. The desires would be those on the side of darkness; desires that may cause us to yearn and, once more, to fear. You could call it the struggle between good and evil, but I prefer to see it as the struggle within ourselves. As far as a character like Peter Pan is concerned, he seems to give us license to play, to acknowledge the anarchic child within us who should not be forgotten. What of Tarzan? Like Mowgli, he has what we probably never had. They both display an empathy with and power over the natural world that we recognize as literally wonderful - something to cause wonder and awe.

I said Myths were more powerful than truth. If you want a great work of literature that reflects on the complexity of humanity, you turn to "King Lear", "War and Peace", "Middlemarch" or "Don Quixote". They are works of a stature rarely reached by writers. But they don't enshrine myths, though they may generate the odd one. Great literature is one thing; myths are something else.

15th October, 2004.

THE SPACE BETWEEN.

I have just finished watching a masterly Japanese film directed in 1953 by Mizoguchi. The title would be something like "Tales of a Pale August Moon". In August and September it was the custom to sit in your house, slide open the panelled walls, and contemplate the moon while music was played or tales were told. It's like Shakespeare's "The Winter's Tale": in his case it was the sort of story to be told by firelight with the snow on the ground outside and the family snug within and ready for a narrative of strange events, of wonders or ghosts and, even, of miracles. The film has that hypnotic quality I've noticed in other - few, I admit - Japanese films I've seen.

One element in those films is the gradual pace at which the story unfolds; another element is the way a great deal is left unsaid or seems unresolved till the film ends and you feel, on mulling it over, that everything needful was there. They are films that linger in the mind. I do like the lack of definition. As could be said about films of the thirties - they convince you of passion without having recourse to sex or nudity; they persuade you of terrible violence without having to show bloodshed; they present you with an ethical framework without moralizing.

Subtlety, that's what's needed. And creative thinking. And a need to present something for others to consider without your tedious explanations. And, oh dear! that is precisely what I'm doing, isn't it? You must forgive me if at this point I take issue with my computer. It always "corrects" me when I use a mark of exclamation or a question mark in the middle of a sentence and follow it with a lower case letter. No one has told it that both these punctuation marks, though they may generally function as full stops, may also legitimately function as commas. Thank you for your forbearance, I just had to share that gripe with someone.

So what is this Space Between? Perhaps it's best to give a few examples. Sasha Guitry, French actor and dramatist, said about listening to Mozart's music: "The silence that follows is still Mozart." See what I mean? You read that and you find yourself agreeing to something you can't really explain, but which makes sense. And there's a line of verse somewhere that says: "Cuando escucho tu risa se alegran los limoneros" - "When I hear your laughter, the lemon trees rejoice/ it gladdens the lemon trees." If you want to be a rotten pragmatist you can easily start nit picking.
1. How can my hearing your laughter affect a third party?
2. If the third party is a batch of lemon trees then who are you trying to kid?
3. What's so special about your laughter, anyway?
4. I've never seen a lemon tree rejoicing.

That'll teach people to write senseless twaddle, won't it? And you can sit there with your poetic imagination dying over the years from emotional malnutrition.

I am not anti-pragmatic. If the plumbing in the bathroom is shot to hell, I want a pragmatic plumber. I do not want someone to look at the pipes, turn to me with eyes filled with an otherworldly light and say, "Water is anarchy, water is life: containment is anathema," and then walk out and leave me with soggy socks, waterlogged feet and rising damp. As I say, I appreciate the pragmatic approach; it is essential to the good regulation of many situations.

What is also essential is the need for the poetic rather than literal approach to many other kinds of things in life. I once heard an excellent radio programme on the influence of Yiddish on the English language in America. That was many years ago and I forget the detail of it, but what impressed me was the way that the turns of phrase suggested far more than they said. There was a whole emotional world being tapped and manipulated. In answer to a critical remark you can say something like, "You want I should kill myself?" This leaves the listener feeling the burden of a terrible guilt. It's the same with the statement much exploited in jokes, "I'm only your mother." There she is - the loving unappreciated woman, the victim of an uncaring child's indifference. What a way to get the upper hand with just a four-word phrase!

I've mentioned jokes and poetry and I find that both these mediums are the ultimate in allowing the space between words to speak powerfully. We've all had the experience of trying to explain a joke: it kills it stone dead. I remember at a New Year gathering that a very kind and friendly German failed to get the point of jokes in English and in Spanish. We'd translate them; we'd explain them. He'd listen very earnestly to the German rendering and then, the explanation over, would nod with relief: he'd got the plot at last, and would say solemnly, "Ah, so!" The same happens when you try to paraphrase poetry. You come up with something like, "This person is playing around with the idea that you could put up with all the crap that life throws at you or you might consider suicide, but you are probably afraid of the risk that's involved because you haven't a clue what comes after you're dead." How banal that sounds. As you've probably

guessed, I'm talking about Hamlet's soliloquy that starts with that puzzling opening line:
"To be or not to be - that is the question."

Frankly, I'm not sure what that line means exactly. And I am glad that I don't know. You should not be able to paraphrase a piece of poetry because if you could put it into your own words and feel perfectly satisfied with the result, then it wouldn't have been poetry in the first place. It would be prose you were dealing with.

This is one reason why I dislike seeing poetry on English Language exam papers. I want to see poetry used, explored, felt, discussed and - particularly - enjoyed in schools, but I think it matters too much to be put on exam papers as an exercise in comprehension. Good prose would serve that purpose admirably. The poet Adrian Mitchell said he hoped his poems would never be taught in schools for exam purposes. Tough luck, Adrian.

The space between words, the something unspoken, matter enormously when you are looking, not for quantifiable information, but for feelings, concepts and intuitions about what it means to be human. You need space for them to reach out to you. Don't give me certainties and cut and dried answers. Don't tell me you know beyond shadow of doubt. To dwell in unknowing gives all those around you their own space too.

The shadows of doubt cast a comforting shade. And, as in Mizoguchi's film, it is in this zone of our understanding that dreams, myths, magic and miracles come to life. And we don't want a life empty of those.

6th August, 2004.

LOVE, SEX AND GETTING ON.

TO LOVE AND TO CHERISH.

Marital combat is an art. It requires dedication and a technique that you may take years to perfect. It is not easy. There are, however, certain factors which with patience you can learn to employ. There is no short cut to success and you may find yourself side-tracked into unsatisfactory petty arguments. Do not despair; you too will eventually learn how to engage in full-blooded battles.

The first point to bear in mind is that a good quarrel, like curry, cannot be hurried and, like a soufflé, must be tackled at the moment it reaches its peak. You must therefore cultivate patience. Patience is knowing when to be waspish and when to bide your time. A quick retort can ruin the most promising situation. It is not anger, but carefully hoarded resentment that will be your mainstay.

You will need to study the peculiarities of your family to ascertain how quarrels can best be fostered. As a rule, the seeds of a quarrel are best sown in the mornings. This is a time of strain and urgency as you all race against the clock. There is no time to rationalize feelings of annoyance. You are powerless to control the state of the weather; you are unable to escape the forthcoming dental appointment; and you can only direct an impotent curse at the alarm that failed to ring. The only course of action open to you is to vent your spleen on your spouse.

You realize you would be foolish to blame her/him for the contretemps. You will not speak unreasonably. You can, however, act unreasonably. If you're subtle about it, you won't even notice what you are doing. There will be some matter of no importance that will suddenly cry out for an exasperated sigh or a look of martyred patience. Under no circumstance should you openly criticize: you merely set yourself to act as an irritant. The innocent and unsuspecting partner will eventually be goaded into action. "What have I done?" comes the angry or wounded cry.

"Nothing, darling." Stress the "darling".

By exercising this annoying variety of righteous self-control and varying the pattern just outlined, you will end up with an irritable partner who will feel disturbed into guilt because she/he won't know what her/his rising anger is about. You will have established yourself to your satisfaction as the offended party and can consequently indulge in feelings of superiority as you step onto the moral high ground. From this satisfying position you can begin to gather coals of fire to set on the "offending" head.

Resentment can now fall on assiduously cultivated ground. This resentment has one principle purpose: it must set in motion a sort of arithmetic progression where succeeding irritants will grow in importance by carefully regulated leaps. Restraint and a fine sense of judgment are essential to prevent your patience from snapping too soon because you will be in need later on of all the emotional ammunition you can lay your hands on.

A poor memory is also necessary at this stage. Once a state of war is established you must forget the initial cause of your annoyance...you don't want to appear foolish, even to yourself. Besides, the unconscious or subconscious strategist gains more than the deliberate one and can act with the untroubled conscience of innocence: if you can deceive yourself, there is no need to feel a single twinge of guilt. You are on the side of the angels and they are ranked, three deep, behind you.

It takes two to make a quarrel. If you weaken and try to make cowardly amends or make an abortive attempt to patch things up, you will be frustrated by your partner who will now be busy turning the tables. For example, men are very good at looking for something they lost weeks ago. How else can they ensure that the search will be a fruitless one? Your loved one will remark, probably to the skirting board, that he distinctly remembers having left the screwdriver in the kitchen. You will hasten to cram the offending metaphorical cap on your head: it's a conditioned reflex, you can't stop yourself. There you are, excusing and damning yourself within seconds: you never touched the wretched thing and what can he expect if he leaves things on your only working surface? And, while you're at it, accuse him of criminal carelessness in the past. It is fascinating to see how many different approaches can be tackled in the same breath.

While you are busy counting the trees in the emotional wood he has provided, he will retreat into silence. Men do this very well. It will serve to increase your volubility. Your voice will grow more shrill and you will hate him for it. He is now in possession of the high moral ground and will take the chance to leave the house - and the door will bang behind him.

This introduces a very necessary element of uncertainty and suspense. Was it banged in sorrow, in anger, in the rush to get to work or was there a draught? *You* have the whole day to brood on it and *he* is now free to consider your many shortcomings. At this juncture, as neither of you has the right of reply, you can accumulate any number of complaints. You can re-live the morning's events. With a modicum of self-deceit you can see how reasonable you were and how infuriatingly and predictably illogical was your partner. Throw in a little emotion and, by evening, you can be a shuddering mass of self pity or a tight-lipped tower of self-righteous rectitude: either will do.

First one home from work prepares a succulent dish for supper, get the kids' tea and tidies up. If it's the man, then the woman can redo everything just to show him how it's really done. He will feel like a useless domestic appendage. If it's the woman, then the husband can point out how she could make life easier if she were better organized. She will feel like a brainless slattern. To re-establish the full flavour of the day's resentments, do some muttering between clenched teeth.

Once the decks are cleared of children, select a carefully timed incident to let your thin-lipped anger snap. It is up to one of you to be fiercely emotional and for the other to provide brutal frankness. It is the gladiator's net and lance meeting the lion's physical prowess. Give the battle all you've got. Throw every one of the day's thoughts and accusations at your partner. Rule out physical violence only.

It is at some point in the ensuing confrontation that you will feel a certain dissatisfaction creeping in as you hurl ever more ridiculous accusations at each other. This is the soufflé point at which you must resurrect your conscience, your memory, and your sense of humour. It will be a strangely natural process where you apportion and accept blame rationally.

The golden rule for the successful quarrel is in its closing stages. Dispose of all your ammunition and avoid emotional litter for the future. No one likes to picnic surrounded by the scraps of a previous outing. Imaginative touches for the different stages will occur to you with experience, but you should bear in mind that, if you are aiming at a work of art, your quarrel, like a tragedy, should be cathartic.

12th July, 2002.

THE SIX SEXES.

Yes, yes; I know I've mentioned sex…six sexes….but would you please control yourself? Show a tad of restraint, at least! This is not a sensationalist column. For all I know, there may be more than six sexes. I'm not an authority on the matter. There are male and female; there are hermaphrodites; there are women trapped in men's bodies and men trapped in women's bodies; there are female and male homosexuals, and there are also other conditions that I have little information on.

Someone once commented that the "average" human had 1.97 legs, 1.95 arms, 1.92 eyes and so on and so forth. You can get his point: if you get the average by throwing in a large sample of the population, you are bound to get some of those without the full complement of parts of their anatomy. In our society, there is no blame or shame attached to one born with a cleft palate or a clubfoot or the lack of pigmentation that makes an albino. We expect folk to be tall or short, to be blond or brunette and to have noses of varying sizes. All contribute to the average, just as you and I do.

There have been primitive societies where the birth of twins, seen as the devil's work, meant that those babies had to die. In other societies, those people we would label schizophrenics or sufferers from some mental disorder of some sort, would be treated with the caution and respect befitting special beings possessed by the spirits.

Swings and roundabouts, isn't it? What you are told about yourself depends on the schema of life that has evolved in your society. In our society we are very tolerant of many things. But sexual "deviations"...well, that's different, isn't it?

How many times have we heard homosexuality called "un vicio" - a vice? or been told that it's a perversion? Such attitudes spring from the belief that people become homosexuals out of choice and because they have opted for a "twisted" path rather than for the "honourable" way of being "straight".

If you consider this dispassionately, you note that it presupposes a masochistic streak: a deliberate desire to make one's own life difficult in a society that has marginalized and victimized homosexuals. We have. Which is why I was delighted to read about a Plains' Indian tribe in North America that reserved a very practical role for its male homosexuals: they could become wives. Within a polygamous society, they would be the second or third wives. This happened when the other wives were hard pushed to do all the work their lives involved either because of ill health or because there were too many children. The homosexual would take on the harder work. His role was not sexual: it was economic and social and he would be a valued addition to the family. What a sensible solution these "savages" had come up with - and they were indeed considered savages by our European ancestors.

I have found little on lesbianism. Perhaps that is because it seems to have been more discreet, less evident. Why, good Queen Victoria refused to believe that such a thing could exist, which accounts for the fact that when legislation on homosexuality was enacted, it referred only to men.

The ramifications of sexuality are many and complex and, thank goodness, are now being studied: where we can't be tolerant, we may at least find facts to make us see the whys and wherefores of sexuality. Then we may understand where we have formerly condemned.

And information is something we all enjoy possessing. I once had to teach human biology to girls. When we came to the section on reproduction, I was hard pressed to give them all the facts they wanted: why twins? why Siamese twins? why are some identical and others not? How could you get conception in the fallopian tube? What was a hermaphrodite and why? How did sperm get formed? And so many other questions.

And when it came to showing them an excellent French documentary on childbirth, I had the boys - who took the other sciences - coming to ask if they too could see the film. I showed it on a number of occasions in different schools over the years and I never had any snide remarks or misbehaviour. I did, however, have students who stayed back to ask questions they were embarrassed to ask in public. What they all wanted was knowledge.

In the process, I found out all sorts of fascinating facts. There was one TV programme about a Hispanic family somewhere in the West Indies. The mother gave birth to girls only. When some of those girls reached puberty, their voices deepened, they began to grow hair on their chest and their genitals began to change so that the clitoris became a penis and the testes appeared.

The family, living in a somewhat isolated community, had accepted this bizarre situation. So did the rest of the village. So did the young men themselves who could talk casually about it. "Cuando yo era niña" - When I was a girl - said one very masculine lad - his arm around his girlfriend's shoulder and his contented mother looking on. Scientists had heard of and studied the case. It was all quite simple: the mother's body failed to produce testosterone as required during pregnancy, but the "girls" were born with all the genetic information needed to make good that omission when they reached puberty.

And there was an article about two cases that illustrated the power of socialization. One was a woman in Scotland who failed to have children. The doctor's diagnosis was unusual: she had no womb or ovaries. What she did have, tucked away inside, were testes. She was, in fact, technically a man in whom the penis had failed to develop and who had breasts like a woman. There was a simple physical solution: "she" could have hormones to finish the process that had never fully worked its way through. The lady declined. She was fine as she was in her society and had no desire at all to be a male. The opposite was the case with a young African...was he a Zulu? I forget such details. His problem was that he suddenly began to develop breasts at the age of eighteen or so. A doctor examines him and discovers - yes, you've guessed correctly - that the young warrior has a vagina, uterus and ovaries. The solution is offered. A course of hormones should sort it out. The young man had no hesitation in deciding: he'd have a course of testosterone, thank you very much. Who'd be a woman in that society if he could be a man. Anyway, he'd always been male, hadn't he?

But what of those people who begin to feel trapped in the wrong body? It seems to become obvious to them from a very early age, from the time when they are aware of themselves as individuals. This can mean that at the age of as little as four the matter is already there in the child's mind.

I've seen TV programmes where such people have spoken about their experiences. All have ended up either doing a stint in a psychiatric unit or seeing a psychiatrist over a period of time as a result of a clinical depression brought on by their condition. Many had belonged to families who'd tried to beat "sense" into them. All of them had felt totally at sea as individuals and all of them had felt trapped in a body that did not belong to them. The rarer cases are those who are physically women, but who, nevertheless, know themselves to be men. Imagine that. You are a man and you look at your body, if you can bear to, and see that you have breasts and that your male genitals are not there. What a nightmare scenario! More frequently it is a case of a person who is physically a male but knows she is a woman. Once more there is that despair over, and rejection of, a body that denies you your real identity.

In neither of these cases is there clear physical evidence to explain their dilemma. What must most certainly be the case is that we may discover one day that we are dealing with a maverick chromosome or gene or enzyme or hormone. It also seems a neurological problem in that it is the thinking and feeling part of the person that is involved: will it be discovered to be some malfunction in the frontal lobes of the brain that control personality? Will it be a variety of all these factors? We may eventually come by the information, but it won't necessarily change such people's perception of themselves as female or male.

Life is so hard for some, isn't it? Which is one reason for writing this article. After nine years of teaching in an all-boys' school, I grew a little weary of hearing snide remarks about homosexuals. They tended to ignore lesbianism and centred on male homosexuality. There was a common fear that they would be approached by any and every gay in the community. My standard response was simple:

"Do you really think you are that irresistible?" And I would always add: "You don't fancy every girl you meet and every girl doesn't fancy you, isn't that so? Well, homosexuals are just as selective."

And even more depressing was the having to make them understand that paedophilia was most definitely not homosexuality. But the keynote was fear. Perhaps it wasn't to be wondered at in a community where the law, till very recently, lumped together bestiality with sexual relations between consenting homosexual adults.

Tolerance is not easy in the area of sexual relationships because we belong to a culture that, for many years, put far more emphasis on narrow sexual morality than on political and social morality. Thank goodness that things are changing.

30th May, 2003.

UNFINISHED BUSINESS.

Walking my dogs in the country recently I was conscious of how my large, half-Alsatian bitch is aging rapidly. She is nearly fourteen which, in human years, puts her somewhere around eighty. She is arthritic, has gone blind in one eye, is easily short of breath and needs a winch to get her in the car. "She probably only has a year or two left," I thought, and felt as if someone had snatched my heart and squeezed it hard.

She can no longer get up on my lap as she used to when I sat in my armchair - threatening both of us with gangrene of the extremities as she curled up awkwardly and squashed us both into the limited space available. So now I sit on the floor beside her every evening at some point to treat her, and me, to quality stroking time. When she dies I hope there will be no regrets to keep me awake at nights.

I say this because she is a dog. No, if I had meant "She is *only* a dog," I would have said precisely that. What I mean is that she will leave no unfinished business behind her for me to suffer angst over as I try to unravel the past. She has loved me unquestioningly, rejoiced mightily whenever I came home - whether after the absence of an hour or a week - and she has created no subtle conflicts. She has certainly never sulked nor has she pursed her muzzle in disapproval at some inanity of mine. In fact, once she stopped her youthful evils like chewing the armchairs, digging up my geraniums and chasing goats, it has all been smooth sailing. There should be no unfinished business.

It's different with humans as a rule. Perhaps that is the reason for the injunction not to speak ill of the dead, no matter if the individual in question was every kind of buzzard. It may also be a form of self-defence: you hold a lot against someone; that person dies; you are thus left helpless - you cannot challenge or take revenge. Rather than go around feeling powerless, you block it out of your mind and speak no ill. You go into denial and emotional retreat. But things are usually much more subtle than that because we can use finely honed weapons against each other that make for more than impotent anger; they create tangled and even unidentified resentments and wounds. How many times do we find ourselves going back over conversations and seething helplessly at having lost the argument or been made to look ridiculous or having been bested in some way. The difficulty about such encounters is that it's not so much what is said as how it's said that makes the crucial difference. I once read a woman's account of how she separated her two children before they came to blows. It appeared that they had been playing "Mummy and Daddy" and had fallen out. The mother listened to their account of how it escalated and who had started it till one of them came out in tearful defence with - "It's all her fault; she called me 'Darling' first!"

Even a simple "Good morning!" can be loaded with anything from goodwill to venom to mania. And, as speech is such a swift and sophisticated medium, there is no time to analyse the sources of potential tension or conflict that are arising. And, anyway, we're probably much more interested in giving tit for tat than in the truth of the situation. Basically, we are really good at picking up the vibes and are thus quick to respond in a way that makes the emotional temperature rise swiftly. And there are wounds we receive, particularly in childhood, that we may not even be consciously aware of; and they are likely to sit there, unresolved and getting seemingly fainter with the passage of time, till, because we can't see them, we expect them to have healed.

Comes bereavement and there is liable to be unfinished business every time.

You'd expect this to be most powerful with our nearest and dearest - child, partner or parent. With your children you can still feel there is time to set the record straight; with your partner…well, the divorce courts are bearing sad testimony to the fact that many couples can't sort out what they have created, or restore what they have destroyed. What about parents?

That is often a different ball game. There are, one knows, appalling parents whose death should come as a relief, and who are probably the ones who leave behind the most burdensome legacy of suffering, injustice and feelings of outrage and impotence. The average parent is something else. With such parents there is a long-standing relationship that has gone through many different phases. Each of us goes from total dependence on the parents through rebelliousness and rejection of them in adolescence and even, perhaps, into a sort of patronising superiority in middle age. They, in their turn, can go from having been the lords of the universe, with total control over their children, to a final state of being totally dependent on them. You traverse an emotional minefield in each other's company. At the end of the journey it would be surprising if your emotional luggage allowed you to sail through the "Nothing to Declare" exit.

Remember also the intensity with which we respond to situations in childhood, and if you can't call any to mind, then watch a child crying as if its heart will break, probably over something that seems trivial to an adult. It is passion we feel as children, violent emotion that shakes our very being, and when we are adults we rarely feel that degree of violence in our mundane world. Childhood can be an age of powerful emotional turmoil, but it is an age when we have yet to acquire adequate socio-emotional skills with which to handle the turmoil.

This idea was captured superbly in a Snoopy cartoon many years ago: one of the boys in the gang - was it Linus? - is on his way to play baseball when he sees a girl approaching. He stops, and hearts bloom over his head. He gawps at her helplessly while the hearts get larger. She draws level with him and the hearts threaten to engulf him. She stops and he takes action: he hits her over the head with his baseball bat.

Love it!

To be emotionally inarticulate is often the quagmire that lies between children and parents. We all drag with us a lifetime of the wrong words spoken, words left unspoken, feelings bruised, misunderstandings, yearnings, inadequate and frustrated attempts to reach each other. How could it be otherwise? I speak as a child and as a parent with matters to rejoice over and to regret in each role. There is a poem somewhere that opens, if my memory serves me right, with the words,
"My parents died a dozen years ago
And I have laid them to their rest today."
I think it went on to speak of how, once the burden of guilt and resentment was purged, it became possible to recapture the joys and to mourn for the depth of love unexpressed.

And there are so many situations, so many variations of the theme. No wonder people feel the need for bereavement counselling. Perhaps a step forward is to get some of that work done beforehand. I think of many people who were important to me and who have died without my having told them how much I owed them and how grateful I was for their influence in my life. As a result, I have started doing it, by mail. That sounds odd, doesn't it? But I have found that compliments that are heartfelt are hard to deliver face to face and equally hard to accept. Perhaps it is the British cultural heritage that causes this with its stiff upper lip and its fear of emoting in public.

When I finish typing this I shall go downstairs, sit on the mat and stroke Chica into a contented stupor...hers and mine. It's not surprising that some psychiatric centres encourage patients to keep pets. Nor is it surprising that having pets brings with it a degree of emotional wellbeing or stability. It's harder with people. Still, I'm working on it. I know I have emotional blunders to apologise for, thanks to give and spleen to be expunged by giving them acknowledgement or voice whether rational or irritable. I expect certain things will remain unresolved. I don't imagine I'll achieve synthesis, but I hope there's a point where contradictions can be held in some sort of balance so that one can cut down on the unfinished business that can make mourning so hard. And now I will stop because the mat and Chica await me.

11th October, 2002.

Chica died less than a year later: much mourned, and still much missed.

UNREASONABLE – MOI?

It happens to all of us at some stage. We've just had a heated argument with someone and we part company, more in anger than in sorrow. We then go over the whole fracas in our minds. The amazing thing is that we were so reasonable. Let's call a spade a spade - we were provoked, weren't we? and that So-and-So was utterly illogical, emotional, positively childish and beyond reason. And we were so obviously right. Honestly, some people are the limit. No wonder we raised our voice a little at some point - merely to make ourselves heard.

We then spend a period of angry reflection during which we go over every word we said, improving on it all and producing the polished invective, the barbed allusion, the quick riposte that failed to rise to our lips in the heat of the moment. That'll teach them! By the time we have done with recasting the argument, our newly created memory of the incident bears little relationship to what actually happened.

And if we could look at it objectively, we could imagine that precisely the same process has probably been going on with the other party. Yet common sense indicates that we can't both be so utterly in the right.

Someone said that no man is a hero to his valet. Perhaps we could all do with an imaginary valet to be summoned mentally at such times to steer us towards honesty? Unfortunately, once we've reworked the argument to our satisfaction, we can honestly believe that it is an accurate reflection of what happened.

This was first brought home to me one day when I witnessed an altercation between two people I was very fond of. Later, they both demanded my sympathy and, what was worse, my complicity, my collusion, in the fiction each had created to replace the reality of the falling-out between them.

Neither was put out by the fact that I had been an eye - and ear - witness to events, and that I was capable of judging how each had been at fault in some way. Each had become convinced that her own version of the quarrel was an accurate reflection of events. And it became a question of "She who is not with me is against me." As a result, as I could not give my unconditional support and approval to either, I managed to offend both. Two heated arguments followed and I went home feeling both angry and smug and began to recall every word of the heated arguments they'd had with me, conjuring up the things I might have said, recalling how reasonable I had been, remembering how illogical and emotional they had become…

All too often there are disagreements that have little to do with right or wrong. If we take the vexed question of the tube of toothpaste things might become clearer. Aha! Do I see you blush and cringe? Are you one of those middle-of-the-tube squeezers? Fear not. I come not to bring you harassment, but peace of mind. Read on.

I have combed through the Bible, both Old and New Testaments, and nowhere do I find condemnation or even any mention of this phenomenon. Nothing at all like: "And the word went forth that they must not squeeze the toothpaste tube in the centre, for those who did thus were to be cast into outer darkness where they would henceforth gnash their uncleansed teeth in vain." OK - you have a point, but I'm sure you'll agree that people, toothpaste or no toothpaste, must have picked stubborn little bits of food out from between their teeth; and even on this score the Bible is silent. There's none of your "They shall not use twigs from the olive tree or the pine, neither shall they sharpen the branch of the cypress, but, at the setting of the sun, the thorn of the gorse bush shall they use and that alone." What I attempt to do is assure you of the innocuous nature of your habit. It only becomes a problem if your family or partner squeezes the tube from the bottom. They may consider it a virtue, but, referring once more to Holy Writ, there is nothing to say that "They who squeeze the tube from the bottom shall inherit the Kingdom." In fact, the Scriptures are singularly uninterested in the whole issue of teeth.

How can one solve the great Toothpaste Controversy - which was cited years ago in America as one of the major factors that had led a particular couple to the divorce court? There they were, locked in combat...and that is the crux of the matter. It is necessary to disengage, and then look coolly at the situation before any blood is shed. So it might have occurred to them that for a modest outlay they could invest in a second tube of toothpaste and they could even have signed a conjugal agreement permitting each partner to use her/his tube in whatever manner each saw fit - squeezed with their teeth, worn on a chain round the neck or kept in the fridge. Whatever turns you on - don't worry; be happy!

Differences often boil down to nothing more than a matter of style with no rights or wrongs. We all need training in How-to-get-what-you-want-without-losing-your-sanity/partner/family. So many confrontations are simply a question of different priorities: I like an early morning lie-in and you are up with the lark. Does that make me lazy and you virtuous? I went late to bed, as it happens, and left the vegetables ready for lunch; and you went to bed early and said you'd prepare the roast in the morning. Sounds like an excellent co-operative effort. We probably all need basic groundwork in developing a variety of skills that would make us more flexible. Think of all the social styles available from the aggressive to the direct to the persuasive.

And talking of different styles, I blush to remember clashes I had with students when I moved the conversation into lunatic mode. Actually it was vitriolic monologue, not conversation, when my patience snapped and I'd rabbit on, firing rhetorical questions at the miscreant:

"You think I'm stupid, don't you? What do you expect me to do, eh? Do you really think you'll get away with it? I'm sick and tired of all the silly excuses you give me. Do you honestly expect me to believe them? Do you take me for a fool? Tell me that!"

And, having gone round in a circle, I'd start off again and woe betide the student who took me at my word and tried to answer those endless questions. At such times I spoke with the voice of unreason and despair. I was much wiser when I lowered the heat and spoke dismissively, "No work again? Shame. I'll have to send a letter home to your parents. A pity," or when I was amused, "You daft old thing. Fancy expecting me to swallow that old excuse again. See me after class."

Frankly, I wish I'd had some remedial training in assertiveness. It took me a while to see the difference between aggression and assertion. To assert is merely to state. You say that you like this or that, that you consider something rash or sensible, that you have certain preferences and that there are things you disapprove of. And you choose words that are not value-laden. Such words carry a minimal emotional charge. Take a simple example: words like "slender" and "skinny" carry positive or negative values; a word like "thin" is neutral. In asserting, you aren't confronting anyone: you are only stating your own position. You aren't being critical of someone else.

I also wish I had been taught to handle people who use the indirect approach so that others are forever trying to guess what they want. You know what I mean. They may remark that some plug hasn't worked for a week. They can sound aggrieved or look mildly accusing. They seem constitutionally incapable of saying, "Could you fix that plug for me, please?" If I'd known how to deal with that approach, I wouldn't have driven my husband round the bend by employing it for years.

What of negotiation, conciliation, compromise and all those strategies that may have somehow acquired a bad name? It's common sense not to back people into a corner. Such a confrontational approach makes them go from defensive to aggressive. And when you start by delivering an ultimatum, you have allowed yourself no room for manoeuvre and are stuck with your own inflexibility.

Perhaps the two most important strategies are the positive and the cool-headed. With the first you find something praiseworthy as a lead-in to negotiation and you don't demonize the person you're dealing with. It involves a way of looking at life, like the glass that the pessimist sees as half empty and the optimist sees as half full. With the second, you need to evaluate what you are facing, where you want to go and how the other person may be persuaded to accept it. You need to abandon the habit of negative criticism that too many of us were brought up on. Why, even the commandments are negative. It's "Thou shalt not" as the order of the day. I wish Moses had hung around for a bit longer for a few more "Thou shalts" or, better still, for a few "How about if thou dost...?" because that doesn't use the imperative to order you around. It strikes the happy middle road that invites your co-operation. And it obviates your having to justify yourself, which is too often where arguments arise; and apologies are sometimes so hard to give; and it's really tough to admit to having been a pig-headed fool.

11th April, 2003.

WORLDS APART AND WORLDS TOGETHER.

I've recently been to England and have, yet again, been fascinated by the racial and cultural diversity among the population. Up in Leeds, down in Bedford and back in Brighton it was Sikhs, Christians, Hebrews, Hindus, Muslims and Afro-Caribbean...partly the legacy of an empire on which the sun never set. And there were Italians, Chinese, Poles, Spanish, French, Tai, Portuguese and a growing number of East Europeans. What an amazing melting pot. Some spoke with a Yorkshire accent while others sounded like Peter Sellers at "The Party". Some spoke Estuary English - the successor of the old London accent - and others had trouble stringing a full English sentence together. For all of them England was, or was becoming, home.

It brought to my mind a young Italian lad I taught many years ago. Newly arrived in Brighton, poor Carmine struggled to learn the language and to fit in socially. A year later he was insisting that we call him Kevin and he had become an avid supporter of Brighton and Hove Albion FC. I suspect that if I met him now, he'd be a dyed-in-the-wool Brightonian, proud of his Italian roots and calling himself Carmine once more. The process of adjustment in a cross-cultural situation takes various paths and takes time. And what of an elderly Italian lady in our parish? Anyone approaching her with the ritual, "How are you?" would be treated to a comprehensive account of the state of her health - with fine attention to detail. The listener might grow catatonic, but she/he had asked after all! Now an Englishwoman asked the same question, in spite of suffering from foot and mouth and other ailments untold, would have gasped a simple, "I'm fine, thank you; and how are you?" before keeling over.

Each style has its limitations. In the first case you are in danger of frightening people off; in the second case you might scare your interlocutors witless by expiring at their feet. Wouldn't a halfway house provide a better third option? It would allow for a couple of things to happen:
    1.) the person asked could say a little of the truth and share a
        burden;
    2.) the person asking would be informed and involved in some
        measure.
So help could be sought and given. Every culture has much to offer, and the stiff upper lip, which can be magnificent, is not the only alternative available.

I was told once that one of the problems that plagued British negotiations with the Arab world was the question of personal space: an Englishman does not want people to stand too close - three feet is OK and four feet is just fine. Four yards may be overdoing things a bit, but he can cope with that. By contrast the Arab will get down to doing business at a distance of two feet; and nose to nose will see things going swimmingly. So what happens? The Englishman keeps his distance and makes the Arab feel rejected; the Arab closes in, making the Englishman feel threatened. The result is a slow chase round the room with each striving to establish and maintain the desired distance - with no chance of any agreement being reached.

Cross-cultural fertilization probably begins at a very basic level. It may well start off with the stomach. What do the English eat on a Friday night? It's as likely as not an Indian or Chinese takeaway, or Italian pizza. Yes, of course it could be fish and chips, but recent research into the eating habits of the nation seems to indicate that it is dishes like spaghetti Bolognese that lead the field. Someone should do a serious study of the political, diplomatic and civilizing effects of foreign food on the life of a country.

Gone are the days when my father spoke of how onions were anathema to many an Englishman serving in Gibraltar, and as for garlic...the consumption of it could turn you into a pariah shunned by all true Brits who, even at a distance of three feet, could be laid flat by garlic halitosis. And another thing that has changed radically over the years has been the acceptability of cross-cultural marriages. On my recent holiday, one of the things that gladdened my heart was the sight of couples of different races that I saw everywhere. Years ago, the film "Look Who's Coming to Dinner" created quite an impact. For the younger generation, let me explain that at the centre of the film is the romance between a black American male and a white American female.

She is blonde, young and pretty. He is a somewhat older, handsome, well-established doctor. The film did break new ground though there was nothing beyond a chaste kiss on the cheek to indicate affection. You almost had the feeling that once they got married they would never indulge in anything as vulgar as sex. For me, however, the question it posed was - How could such a fabulous bloke fall for such a boring girl and why didn't he at least get in touch with me first?

But Hollywood had to tread carefully in an America where there was still segregation whether in fact or in law. In one episode of the original "Star Trek" there was to be a kiss between Uhura and Captain Kirk - but it never happened. It wasn't as if the actress, Nichelle Nichols, had objected on the grounds that she was allergic to William Shatner. Not at all. It was just considered too daring. And in the musical

"Showboat" there is a tragic love affair between a white man and a beautiful woman who passes as white, but has, in reality, black ancestors somewhere along the line. The actress chosen was a fine singer called Lena Horne, but though she was very light of skin, she was a "black" woman and the part consequently went to Ava Gardner. The racial prejudice which the plot was pointing to was, ironically, alive and well in the film industry.

Nevertheless, if the power of the stomach will bring about change, so will the power of sexual attraction. And similarly with the power of the intellect, the emotions and all natural faculties - till cultural barriers begin weaken and to give way.

What has happened in England over the last fifty years is now happening in Europe. We have an old continent where the birth rate is dropping. Spain has the lowest birth rate in Europe; France has a similar problem; and so have other countries where the standard of living rises, because it goes hand in hand with a drop in the size of families. Added to this are the improvements in medicine that ensure a longer lifespan. The result is a growing ageing population and a diminishing young labour force to generate the sort of wealth needed to keep that society solvent. France is instituting unpopular measures with regard to pensions - the state can no longer afford them. This is but one reason why Europe needs immigrants. To Spain are coming immigrants from Morocco, from South of the Sahara, from Eastern Europe and from South America. They are needed, but they are too often seen as interlopers. There are racist groups whose xenophobic attacks on immigrants make horrific reading, but they cannot turn the tide of what is happening.

And what is happening is that Europe is facing racial and cultural changes that will take time to work their way through the initially traumatic decades. It's ironic that conquest in the past was effected by armies and generals and kings bringing death and carnage. What we see today is conquest of a kind by the less privileged who have become necessary to the powerful.

Perhaps the most joyful change I have come across concerns a village in the north of Spain. It's the sort of small place where the young people had all left as soon as they could so that the average

age of the population is now over fifty-seven. The villagers decided to take action: they invited a young Columbian couple to settle there and provided them with accommodation, furniture and employment. A year later there were festivities in which the several hundred villagers celebrated the birth of the first child to be born there in twenty years. Wonderful, isn't it? There's hope for us all when people can act so creatively.

13th June, 2003.

OUR DAILY POLITICS.

OZYWHO?

Ozymandias, remember him? I wouldn't be surprised if you didn't because he never existed. He's a fictional character who thought he'd live forever in people's memories. In fact, he built a colossal statue of himself and challenged one and all to look on his work and tremble. The statue, as statues tend to do, eventually fell down, broke and crumbled till all that was left was the plinth with two very large feet...looking, I have no doubt, pretty ridiculous among the desert sands. If Ozymandias had existed, he'd be an entry in my dictionary between the Ozark Mountains in North America and ozokerite - a type of wax. And, while I was at it, I looked up "Hitler" and noted that he was placed between "hitherto" and "hit list". And his entry was shorter than the ones for that simple word - "hole".

What's the point I'm making? I suppose it's that we don't live for ever and that even the greatest powers on earth eventually come to naught. There's no gainsaying that people are immensely powerful during and even after their lives - for a time. This was the case with such kings as Zoser, Lugalaggisi, the Hyksos - a whole dynasty, and Shalmaneser. So too with mighty conquerors like Tiglath-pileser, Menes the Fighter, Sargon who defeated King Lugalaggisi...see previous sentence...who had himself defeated the Lagash Empire in his day. And I regret to say that the Akkadian dynasty that Sargon founded gradually declined till even the city of Agade was no more. I'm sorry to pain you, but so it was.

Of course you missed it all on satellite TV news, but then, I'm talking three to four thousand years before our calendar started. I'm talking Assyria, Egypt and Mesopotamia.

We could profitably take Lugalzaggisi as a starting point if we want to pontificate about the transitory nature of power. Nevertheless, I'd rather come closer to home and have a look at Macbeth. Shakespeare reinvented history just as he reinvented the fairy from a powerful and anarchic little pest into a tiny thing that might sleep under a toadstool. Duncan was, it is true, king of Scotland. How good was he at being King? I don't know. Along came Macbeth and murdered him. That's true too.

It was around the time when Siward - Shakespeare's good and honest Siward who fights to destroy Macbeth and loses his young son to Macbeth's bloody sword - was murdering Eardwulf to become sole ruler of Northumbria. Macbeth wasn't around for too long. In 1054 he was defeated at Dunsinane by the combined forces of Malcolm and Siward. Please note - "defeated" not, definitely not, killed in battle. We know this because he died in 1057 when he was murdered by Malcolm. I did say "murdered" and I'm sticking to it.

Macbeth was dead, so who succeeded him as King of Scotland? Let me tell you that it was his stepson Lulach. (What had Lady Macbeth been up to, when and with whom?) Poor Malcolm - all his hard work for nothing. At this point he appears to have lost his rag and he slays Lulach the following year...so says my history book. He spent the next thirty years plus doing things like invading Northumbria (against his ally Siward?) and was actually killed in 1093 while invading England. He just didn't know when to stop, did he? And Donald Bane, his brother, finally got a crack at being king...for three years. And if Shakespeare hadn't written his Scottish play, we would never have heard of them any more than we have heard of Gruffydd in Wales who managed to defeat the English at some point. It just goes to show that if today's news is tomorrow's history, then tomorrow's history will eventually become a total blank for most of the world.

"The evil that men do lives after them,
The good is oft interred with their bones."
So says Mark Antony in two lines fed to him by Shakespeare. I wish I could disagree with the first line as I do with the second. Mark Antony was just being clever when faced with a crowd that looked decidedly ugly and threatening. The fact of the matter is that evil lingers on for a longer or shorter period. The good news is that even that comes to an end as a major force, and better still is the news that any evil man's lifespan is limited. (You have noticed that I did not speak of "evil woman". There's a simple reason. Women have very, very rarely held great power as rulers so the chances of

one of them being a monster of iniquity at that level are proportionately limited - though I've heard of a couple.)

What has interested me in checking out these characters in history is that their motivation can only be guessed at. You can understand Malcolm wanting to avenge his father's death, but I have a sneaking suspicion that he just wanted the throne. In fact, he seems to have wanted that throne and any other he could lay his hands on. May I be forgiven if I am guilty of calumny, but history is littered with similar stories of murder, treason, betrayal and wars all carried out to satisfy one man's desire for power. And talking of motivation, why exactly are we supposed to be going to war with Iraq? It does not seem to be because of the widespread and well-established violation of human rights in Iraq carried out by Sadam Hussein's government against its own people. It's not because of the plight of the Kurds. It's not to help a population that cannot survive without the food provided by foreign aid and by charitable organizations (and this in a country where money has been poured into armaments). The people of Iraq are indeed to be pitied.

Of course, I feel sure that there has been a creating and a hiding of weapons of all types of destruction. I recently heard an Iraqi scientist speak. He had been jailed for ten years for refusing to work on a research programme on germ warfare. He has since fled the country and can thus speak freely. Only a fool would think of Hussein as a man much and unjustifiably maligned. And it takes a very selective memory for the West to fail to recall that if Sadam Hussein has nuclear technology and chemical and bacteriological weapons in his armoury, it is thanks to what the west provided. Hussein had the money and Germany, France, Italy and Russia found in him a good customer. When Iran was the enemy under the Ayatollah Homeni, America also stepped in. Donald Rumsfeld met Hussein in 1983 and America also began to feed arms to Iraq that included live viruses. Anthrax was one of the items supplied. Commercial interests had joined with anti-Iranian policy.

By the time the genocide of the Kurds was under way, it was French mirage aircraft and German technological know-how with toxic gasses that made possible the destruction of 5000 civilian Kurds in one attack.

So far so good…or bad. I don't trust the man; I pity the people; and I still don't know why we are supposed to go to war. America said it would, jumping the gun and perhaps expecting the unqualified support of the world as it seemed to have had with Afghanistan. It now has to put its money where its mouth is. It could have taken quite a different hard line. Hell! The situation with the agreed disarming of Iraq has been dragged out for so long that some form of strong-arm tactics could have been initiated long ago to oust Hussein, to buy the gratitude of a victimised population, to do something other than launch a full-scale war *again*. Originally, given the debts incurred by Hussein, his credit was extended and the west might have done *something*, no matter how good a customer he had been, yet it was only his invasion of Kuwait that spoilt the honeymoon. He was attacking a source of oil for the west. Now that was most definitely not on and we had the Gulf War.

So when you boil it down, the west now demands the destruction of the arms of one sort or another that it sold Iraq in the first place. So much of it was done secretly, sailing close to or driven by the winds of illegality that no one knows exactly what was sold. O irony of ironies! Maybe this is one reason why Bush's sanctimonious tone makes me feel physically unwell.

Actually, I hadn't mean to write about this. Let me admit right away that I am thoroughly confused by it all to the point that I have even given up following the news assiduously. I respect the people who, wanting to stop the war, have offered themselves as human shields. They have shown the courage of their convictions. I am also filled with a kind of relief to see how there have been massive demonstrations world-wide against the war. This feels new. Governments and kings have never asked anyone's permission to start a war and people have ended up following where they were led. As Paul Valéry said, "Politics is the art of preventing people from taking part in affairs which properly concern them." At least ordinary people are taking part now by making powerful political statements through these actions.

And I still don't know what my position is. I feel ignorant about the Politics of the situation. The politics of ordinary people I trust as a statement of what they feel. The Politics of America I find extremely suspect, their "logic" seems irrational, their motivation is suspect and their leader…..well, is there anyone reading this who truly admires President Bush for his ethical acumen? This man who, as Governor of California, approved more executions in the electric chair than any of his predecessors? Then I look at what I know of Sadam Hussein and I feel that the solution - if only we could effectively isolate the two of them on a desert island - would be to leave them to it, alone.

My difficulty is that I distrust those at the top without feeling that a blanket anti-war policy is the full answer. The expression "peace at any price" is as frightening as "war for any reason". Strategies are needed that deal in options, that offer hope of solutions and which don't see confrontation as the only alternative.

And, coming back to where I started, these men who hold the future of nations, perhaps of the world, in their hands will all be dead within the next sixty years. Amazing, isn't it? You play ducks and drakes with the life of a nation when, in the life of the world, you are only an unpleasant hiccup, but as Kissinger said, "Power is *the* aphrodisiac." If only world leaders could have humility injected intravenously, we'd all be better off.

28th February, 2003.

IS IT CRICKET?

If it's cricket, it's fair and honourable; if it isn't, then it's suspect. And what happens when you are playing cricket and all around you are playing rugby or wrestling in mud or indulging in a spot of hooliganistic support of a football team? What chance have you got against the more physical games or the violent hordes? This isn't too far from the rule of law - same dilemma.

I've been brooding about this, I have; and the events following the war against Iraq have helped me to crystallise my ideas. When Saddam Hussein was eventually captured, the world press and institutions of law and order bent over backwards in their calls for a just and fair trial. You might be forgiven for thinking that we live in a strange world that tolerates outrages against human rights and genocide for years (against the Kurds, in this case) and then does its damnedest to protect the rights of the man who - to put it mildly - hasn't shown any respect for the rights of those thousands.

The same happened with Milosevic whose trial, now into its fourth year, has been suspended because of his poor health. He has been offered all the safeguards available against unjust treatment. He is medically supervised and has whatever support he requires to conduct his own defence. He is, after all, a lawyer by training. And where, we ask, are the voices of his victims to be heard? Does it make sense?

And you inevitably also think about those 600 men kept in Guantánamo Bay: the small fry captured in the process of the supposed war against terrorism. Who has bent over backwards to protect their rights? Haven't they, rather, been treated as if they had forfeited all rights by their actions or - worse still - their *suspected* actions? The American administration argued that Guantánamo Bay lay outside the jurisdiction of the US courts. The inmates had thus no access to the legal system and were denied the basic right to a lawyer. It has taken two years and much pressure to get the US Supreme Court to rule against the administration and allow detainees the right to appear before an American judge.

And, as I write this, I have beside me a newspaper photo of a captive in solitary confinement. His cell is a free-standing cage - with bars instead of walls - that would appear to measure about four feet by nine, with a height of about nine feet. The photo was taken in Abu Ghraib prison where, I imagine, the temperatures reach wicked heights and very cold lows. Allied to this are the court-martials of American servicemen and women with regard to the interrogations they helped to carry out at that prison, interrogations that involved sexual humiliation and physical assaults. And, once more, we are talking small fry, as such prisoners probably had limited information to offer. What happened to the interrogations of yesteryear detailed in the book, "Spy Catcher", written by an English officer? He was highly intelligent and employed a mixture of his training and his instinctive understanding of men to unmask spies attempting to enter Britain during World War II under the guise of asylum seekers. He used his brain and his gut instinct and he achieved results.

And now, President Bush resides in the White House and has a host of cohorts to redesign his public image and work on a damage-limitation exercise for the leader who reserved the right to suspend the Geneva Convention on treatment of detainees at any time. While this goes on, there are the men and women who allegedly carried out the interrogations/torture who are being tried. The techniques used by them involved hooding, keeping prisoners naked, use of dogs... all approved by the authorities. Who of those "authorities" is being tried?

Cheek by jowl with such items of news comes a reference to the images shown on television of a terrified South Korean civilian in Iraq, weeping and crying out that he didn't want to die, as a hooded Iraqi kidnapper threatening to behead him. And on the same page is a report of 35 people killed and 140 injured by a car bomb in Iraq.

I am not pleading the innocence or guilt of either side in the issue. What I am concerned with is the questions that arise when you subscribe to the rule of law. If you believe in it, then you find yourself hamstrung from the start. You have to obey certain rules, while absolute dictators and terrorists can ignore them. Terrorists have the advantage of crossing borders easily, while the forces of law and order of one country cannot pursue and capture them on some other government's territory. They can use torture; you can't. It's the age-old problem of the bully and his victim; of those who play by the rules and those who cheat. It's just not cricket.

"Give them a taste of their own medicine,"..."They've forfeited the right to be treated in a civilized manner,"... "Why should they be given the benefits of the law when they are trying to destroy it?" I'm sure I've heard plenty of remarks like this uttered, and may have felt a degree of sympathy with them too. So what is it that keeps me clinging to the idea that people like the detainees at Guantánamo and leaders like Hussein are entitled to the benefit of a legal trial and to safeguards of their rights?

And the short answer is that on the other side lies chaos and that you become a lynching society at your peril. I mean that literally. If the rule of law is abandoned then you have no legal point of reference to which you can appeal should the time come for *you* to do so.

Nelson Mandela forgave his oppressors because he had lost everything to them for 27 years. Sounds ridiculous? His reasoning was clear: they had imprisoned him, deprived him of his family, destroyed his marriage and abused him physically and mentally. The only things he had been able to keep from them were his mind and his heart. If he had, on his release, sought the revenge of doing to them what they had done to him, he would have lost both to his oppressors. He said, "I had to let it go." To do otherwise was to become like them.

The rule of law has many limitations and can be used and abused, but it is what we have built up over centuries. It may need change, updating and amending, but it must surely not be ignored. The choice is between upholding it or returning to the law of the jungle. If we all have basic rights and freedoms, then we try those who break the law for flouting those rights. And there is a punishment to be meted out to them under the very laws they have chosen to break. We cannot afford to break the rules ourselves in the search for justice.

23rd July, 2004.

STOP THAT JOKE!

Once, slavery was the order of the day in the western world and no one turned a hair at the thought of buying and selling human beings. Those who objected to it were the cranks. In time, the cranks won the day and nowadays we would no more consider tolerating slavery in our community than we would consider killing everyone over the age of sixty. (Some of us have a vested interest here.)

Our perceptions do change with time, and one of the sources of change is the world of the arts. There was Dionysus and his Maenads in Ancient Greece: they were connected with the theatre and with orgiastic excess. You didn't tangle with them lightly. Those Greeks had cottoned on to something that linked the theatre with license, anarchy and revolution. This insight was also there with the Elizabethans, who lumped thieves, vagabonds and players - actors - in the same category in law. Shakespeare's theatre world spent a good deal of its time getting round restrictions imposed by the

City...that's why they ended up on the South Bank of the river, which was outside the jurisdiction of the worthy London legislators.

The same still happens with every totalitarian regime. They will aim to muzzle the arts. They also know that an image is worth a thousand words so they will dictate what can be considered art. Hitler did it and the satirical art of Germany - the raw, vital and viciously critical Expressionism - gave way to pictures of heroic Siegfried (as in Wagner) look-alikes. In Russia, Stalinism resulted, artistically, in celebrating the working class on enormous canvases depicting muscle-bound figures...a bit like Siegfried, now that I think of it...who stood proud and gazed with the eyes of love on their tractors in the middle of the Steppes.

One can honestly say, about such pictures, that they are awfully big.

A person with some powerful conviction about workers may produce a masterpiece that features workers, but you cannot dictate an ideology to the arts and expect the result to be great art. Dictators know that art is dangerous and will slap censorship on it before you can write a rhyming couplet about them. Poets and dramatists are among the first to be targeted. They are all ranked, along with journalists, as threats and enemies to the System. That is why there will come into being the underground theatre, underground papers and underground publications. The arts are about life, about human nature, about society, about abuse, about what is real or true and what isn't. It is about ugliness as well as beauty. Whatever it is, art is not safe. It is not anodyne and comfortable. In "The Lion, the Witch and the Wardrobe", the godlike Aslan is defined in the words "He's good, but he's not safe." I find that a very satisfying statement about a creator. I don't feel that real creation can be something safe. It would be a contradiction in terms.

Which brings me back to the title of this article. Like the arts, the joke can be a powerfully creative tool. Every repressive regime will spawn criticism, irony and satire. The wonderful thing about jokes in such situations is that they vanish into the air. You hear them, you laugh, you have indulged in a communal act of defiance - however small - and there is no evidence left to convict you. You can then proceed to tell someone else the joke and thus spread the gospel of resistance. It gives you some sense of freedom, even if spurious; and it keeps the critical spirit of revolution alive.

And talking of freedom, a young man we know went on a cultural tour to - I think it was - Czechoslovakia some years before the fall of communism. His student company was presenting "King Lear" one night and the cast were both flattered and irritated to be interrupted by enthusiastic applause at what they considered random points during the play. It was only after the performance, at a reception, that one of the cast, in conversation with a member of the audience, found out what it had all been about:

"We clapped when you spoke the word, 'Freedom'."

Imagine it. There had been no planned demonstration, no orchestration of response, but someone must have started clapping and the rest had joined in. I find it both moving and exciting to think that people will retain their sense of personal freedom even after years of brainwashing.

And jokes do a fine service too. The best jokes about and against priests that I have heard, came from priests. It's been the same with Jews. The best jokes concerning Franco came from Spain. Each best knows her or his own. And jokes keep alive the spirit of revolt, of mockery, of a refusal to be conned and to take as gospel that which is only someone's very fallible construct. We may kowtow and give lip service, but somewhere inside us is the worm of revolt. And, once we have given it house-room, the worm turns, sooner or later.

It's a heartening thought. I think jokes teach us a healthy disrespect for supposed ideologies. Furthermore, they work at an emotional level in which we apprehend truths that specific words would not convey. Like music, jokes go straight to our being. However, it may not be the ideologies we have to beware of, but the trivia that bombards us daily on the small screen. "Big Brother" is one example. I saw a little of it: the filming itself was tedious and gave no evidence of the skills a camera man worth his salt takes pride in. The content was pedestrian enough. Like home movies, it seemed adequate for friends of the family – no more.

Then there is the trivia that is aimed at the lowest common denominator. When I say "common" I mean it in the sense of "vulgar" and when I say "lowest" I mean it in the sense of "least in value". I am speaking of the sort of TV programmes that have proliferated of late. The recent "Hotel Glamour" is a classic of the type I have in mind.

I watched in disbelief when I first tuned in, just to see what the fuss and advance publicity had been about. The word "glamour" has overtones of Hollywood at its height when the stars were women and men who seemed the epitome of elegance, beauty, charm and intelligence. What "Hotel Glamour" provided was an exaltation of the unrefined meeting the crude in confrontational mode. Exhibitionism and lack of restraint featured high in the show. Glamour? Not in a month of Sundays!

"It's what people want," says one school of thought, if thought it can be called. What a dishonest way of justifying the peddling of entertainment trash. People are able to watch mindlessly, that's true, as I know from personal experience. They are also quick to respond to what is better, what is good, what is excellent. Equally, they are capable, apparently, of accepting political twaddle that they are helpless to resist, but they are quick enough to respond to better political terms that may come along. And until that happens, it's up to the subversives and the tellers of jokes to keep the flag of Dionysus flying.

22nd August, 2003.

FOLK IN UNIFORM.

In "Pride and Prejudice" the younger, very silly sisters of the Bennet household go wild when a regiment is stationed near their quiet village. Their mother, every bit as silly as her daughters, claims to have been very fond of a "red coat" in her day. She doesn't talk of soldiers, officers or gentlemen, only of the uniform itself, and she comments on how "Colonel Foster looked very becoming…in his regimentals."

You don't have to be as silly as Mrs Bennet to have felt the appeal of a uniform.

Many years ago there were two Italian training ships that called annually at Gibraltar. They were the "Montecucoli" and the "Amerigo Vespucci". The first was a modern ship and excited little interest in itself; the second was a sailing ship the likes of which we had seen in many a film of pirates and sea battles; and the sight of its bellying sails was a picturesque and romantic vision. And out of these training ships came the young cadets in uniform to fill the streets of the town and stir the girls into a mood of rose-tinted dreams, flirtation and desperation: every girl hoped to get an invitation to the party held on board each year. Logistically it could only be very few who could get the coveted invitations. The rest were left desolated. And desperation also possessed the souls of the local lads who saw themselves ignored by the girls, cast in the shade by these uniformed Italians, and pitch-forked into a contest they could never hope to win. It didn't last long. The ships moved on; the girls felt bereft; the boys felt relieved but resentful as they licked their wounds; and the cadets sailed on to another Mediterranean port where they would again wreak havoc on the hearts of the adolescent population and, doubtless, would consolidate an inflated and barely justified opinion of their own charms. They were just ordinary lads, but in those uniforms they became "such stuff as dreams are made on" and the girls fell.

Me? I was only interested in the actual ship itself and the working of the sails, wasn't I? Of course I was. How could I possibly have fallen for those white and blue uniforms, the cadets' charming broken English, the dark liquid eyes that they had learnt to use to devastating effect and their practiced line in flirtation?

The whole business of uniforms is an interesting social phenomenon. I have yet to meet a Gibraltarian male of a certain age who, at the mention of the GDF - (the Gibraltar Defence Force in which, years ago, they all served a short stint of a few months as the local version of National Service) - doesn't begin to salivate heavily as he launches into an account of that time. From what one gathers, they didn't sleep for six months, being far too busy playing nocturnal pranks on each other that ranged from the sublimely lunatic to the near sadistic.

I have little doubt that the uniform had much to do with it: it was the great leveller as eighteen-year-olds from all social backgrounds were pitch-forked together, all wearing berets they disliked, clodhoppers on their feet and - in summer - a uniform whose tunic always managed to look like crumpled cardboard.

All those youths were suddenly torn from the bosom of their loving families who spoiled them rotten when they were *finally* allowed home after the first week's "internment" in barracks. The mothers and grandmothers mourned as if the lads had been sent to some war zone. The lads themselves were having a ball as a general rule: it was the first time many of them had left home, had been on their own, were making their own choices and weren't being held accountable by their tyrannically loving womenfolk for every breath they took. In their case, the uniform had entitled them to membership of a group that suffered military disciple during the day and indulged in personal and group anarchy at night. And taking this idea a step further, it was not uncommon some years ago to hear men who had been in the army and would refer to the war years, 1939 – 1945, as the best years of their lives. They were not certifiable; they were stating a truth.

I'm sure the reasons are complex. Someone described a soldier's life in wartime as 90% boredom and 10% panic. The panic would go with a surge of adrenalin; the boredom would bring with it no attendant fears of mortgage payments, fears of unemployment or sleepless nights as children cried. It was a life that guaranteed one sort of freedom from certain types of care. It also bestowed on you the membership of a large all-male club and conferred a 007 status on you that you'd never be entitled to again. You were a man with a gun and you were meant to use it. In extreme cases, some men never did adjust to civilian life. I know of Vietnam veterans, some belonging to an elite unit trained to kill soldiers and civilians swiftly, efficiently and without compunction, who have taken to living away from civilization, far even from remote logging camps in the mountains because they know they are not safe to be with - one of them nearly killed his own mother when she came quietly up to him and placed a hand on his shoulder. I have certainly met an English ex-army man who couldn't bear to sleep at night in case he dreamt. What atrocities he had committed when in uniform he wouldn't tell you, and it's too late to ask: he drank himself to death.

A uniform, in some way, denies you your personal identity. In its place it confers a group identity that responds to an established set of mores and rules. There was a fascinating example of this, years ago, in London when a great production was under rehearsal of a cycle of Greek Tragedies. The cast were provided with masks and rehearsals began so that they could get used to wearing and handling the dramatic but rather cumbersome headgear. Within days it became clear that there was a serious problem. The cast were all experienced professionals; the main characters were responding well enough to the director's instructions, but the chorus were behaving extremely oddly. They had become anarchic, refused to co-operate and were generally being a real pain in the butt. There was a showdown. Masks were removed and a serious discussion ensued during which the members of the chorus were rational and co-operative. It was only when they put the masks on and acted as a group that they emerged as a bloody-minded unit that refused to accept the director's stage discipline. The actors themselves had found the whole experience unnerving.

There are so many kinds of uniform, aren't there? Whether you are working for the London Underground, belong to a religious group, join the armed forces or follow the latest fashion with the slavish devotion that your friends also display, you could be said to be in uniform. Uniforms certainly have their charms, but they create a corporate identity that can sap your individuality. They need not do so, of course, but they can. It took the Nuremburg Trials to discredit for ever the defence - "just following orders". And it also highlighted the extreme dangers of surrendering your conscience to group control - whatever that group happens to be.

8th October, 2004.

A BUNCH OF TWIGS.

Who was it told his son to snap a twig in half, which the son easily did? Then he asked him to snap a bunch of them; and he failed. The lesson to be learnt was that there is strength in numbers. And wasn't it a policy of the British in India to divide and rule? Shakespeare knew the courage that comes from being part of a group. At best, as when Henry V welds his army together with the rousing speech about St Crispin's Day, it leads to deeds of valour undertaken for a cause at the cost of one's own life - and a lot of bloodshed too, of course. At worst, it creates a mob that rampages mindlessly as it does after Mark Antony's funeral oration on Caesar's death. It is not "friends, Romans, countrymen" who go marauding round the city; it is a wild rabble with license to do as they please. They find Cinna, a supposed conspirator involved in Caesar's death, and are preparing to kill him when he cries out that they've got the wrong man - he's just good old Cinna the poet, not the politician - and one of the mob cries out, "It is no matter...tear him for his bad verse!" Damn it! what's the use of being a suddenly powerful mob if you're going to be baulked of prey by something as unimportant as reason?

So, if strength in numbers can be power for good, near good, or ill, isn't it heartening to see an awful lot of the positive around? I refer to velvet, rose and pink and orange, and I'm not talking fashion but people-power. Georgia saw the Rose Revolution. The Ukraine has had its Orange Revolution and it's taken three election processes following fast each on the other, but the people who took to the streets in bitter winter weather and stayed there for days on end determined to see justice done, have defeated election-rigging and everything else a regime based on the old Russian communist model could do. Yuschenko is now president and has a difficult time ahead, but his election has given a new impetus to and established the meaning of democracy. Not everyone voted for him, naturally, but it is no longer a case of the tail wagging the dog.

Kyrgyzstan, another former Soviet republic, has gone for pink. Isn't that charming? No need to go for strident colours when you're looking for the good of the people. But be not deceived. A core of protesters had clear political aims: so would you have had when a president has rigged 69 out of 75 votes for his daughter, his son and his allies in a forthcoming election. However, there were a lot of people who joined in for the "fun" of it and there were others who could truly say, "I'm only here for the beer," or was it vodka? Now, I'm sorry if this distresses you, as it does me, but what was for some a politically conscious desire for democracy was for others a chance to end up looting and destroying. Since then, the two new potential presidential candidates have formed some sort of, probably uneasy, truce and the country can try to settle down again.

Serbia also witnessed a demonstration of people power, and so did the Lebanon with its Velvet Revolution that has severely weakened, even if it hasn't totally eliminated, the Syrian hold on the country. After their civil war, the Lebanon invited Syrians to help establish peace. They were to stay for two years. Twenty-eight years later they were still there - what's a score years among friends? And it has been said that the eight and a half million people - and it takes courage to do what they did - who voted in the elections in Iraq despite threats and intimidation, are having a knock-on effect in the Middle East, this from Algazira Television which is violently anti-American.

Isn't it all quite extraordinary? A mass of people uniting can exert enormous pressure. Gandhi realised it and marshalled a goodly number of India's millions to oust the British, without the need for an armed insurrection. Sadly, the bloodbath came later after the insensitive and rushed Partition of the country. In Chechnya an armed struggle has left the country in a lamentable state. The use of force, in some cases, achieves a great deal less than passive resistance and public demonstrations.

And even more heartening is the fact that it needs only one individual to set a process in motion. In Northern Ireland, the recent Macarthy murder has driven what may be the final nail into the coffin of IRA political credibility. The murdered man's sisters are impressively lucid in their explanations and their demands for justice. The IRA has been seen as housing violent men who use their status in the organization to murder with impunity. It has also shown how the IRA, once it realised how the case was developing against it, was willing to murder these murderers: thus compounding the lawlessness of their individual members with the organization's contempt for the rule of law, for trial by jury and for those processes that aim to safeguard the freedom of the individual. What may have begun as a politically motivated organization has degenerated into a form of Thugs Anonymous.

In the USA, it took a tired black woman, too tired to move to the end of the bus where there was only standing room for non-whites, to spark off the Civil Rights demonstrations under Martin Luther King and other leaders. Within the last few weeks, Dorothy Stang may have done a similar service in Brazil. She was an elderly American, a Sister of Notre Dame, who was working in the Amazon with rural communities, teaching them to develop sustainable farming methods. She also gave evidence in Brasilia against logging companies whom she named. They were, and are, invading state areas, creating a deforestation crisis and using hired gunmen to intimidate and eliminate peasant farmers. Gunmen shot her six times as she walked to a meeting of poor farmers.

There are so many ways to change the world we live in, if we care to do so. The changes can be small or great, but they all matter. They can be immediate or long-term and both are needed. Such is the case with the Aga Khan University of Central Asia. There are branches in Kazahstan, Tajikistan, Kyrgyzstan, UK, Karachi and Allah knows where else. The stress is on Muslim civilizations in all their richness and variety of language, history and culture. They have led the way in the medical training of women, higher education generally of women and the liberalising influence of an education that is not exclusively linked to technical and pragmatic ends. The theory is that students who think and develop their own critical faculties will be far better engineers or doctors than those who see their work only as involving academic expertise. When one hears so much of Muslim fundamentalism - and Christian fundamentalism, for that matter - it is heartening to hear of such educational reform.

It acknowledges that it is not always the answers that matter most: we need to know how to ask questions. And equally heartening is the initiative in Botswana, where about a third of young people are HIV positive. They've held a beauty contest - "Miss HIV Positive, Stigma Free" - in which candidates were judged on "beauty of courage". Their message was that frankness is essential because unless things are out in the open you cannot fight them.

Reading about all these changes has cheered me up. Gibraltar has its own People Power and has had its individual forces for good. I know that if I start listing them, I shall sin by omission, but I'd like to mention one case: it only took one battered wife who changed things first for herself and, later, for others, to bring things out into the open and to give the issue a high profile it had never had locally.

There's not just strength in numbers and in heroic figures; there is a serious potential for good and for change in us ordinary folk.

18th April, 2005.

INDIAN DIARY

PASSAGE TO DELHI.

Three years ago when my friend, Popri, suggested that I go with her to India, I laughed a careless laugh. Silly idea! We were both due to celebrate our sixtieth birthday at the time and my daughters, over from UK for the occasion, also urged me to go. I laughed again. No. I couldn't really afford it. It just wasn't on. There was no way I was going to go.

I had bought the airline ticket, had had all the right jabs and had spent hours pouring over maps and books before I made any sort of decision. In truth, to be absolutely accurate, I never decided that I *would* go.

And when I went for three weeks I promised a friend I'd write an article about India. What colossal ignorance! What arrogance! An article? It was like Ernie Wise writing those dramatic "masterpieces" that took him all of sixteen minutes; or like thinking - "Hey! I've got a free morning; I think I'll scale Mount Blanc up whichever face is the tough one." How can one possibly do justice to a country like India? It is enough to look at the records it holds to get an idea of its complexity: it holds the record for standing still - seventeen years; it can lay claim to the longest-running court case which began in 1205 (when King John ruled over England and Robin Hood was supposedly prancing around Sherwood in green tights) and which was eventually settled in 1966 in favour of a descendant of the original claimant - a mere 761 years of bureaucratic hassle. And India also has the wettest place in the world, Cherrapunji, which once logged an unbelievable 26.46 metres in one year. If we care to look at religious gatherings, it holds that record too. India is one of the world's major industrial powers yet has massive problems of poverty the likes of which have long disappeared from Europe. Oh, yes, I would write an article, comprehensive of course, about India. I had blithely planned the impossible in my innocence. What I did do was keep a diary that gives a truer picture of what I saw and felt than would any article written retrospectively. So here begineth my diary:

- on the plane to Frankfurt I finish reading "City of Joy" about the slums of Calcutta. It should be de rigueur reading for any visitor to India, harrowing and inspiring. My younger daughter, Susy, who has twice been to India, feels it will prepare me for the culture shock and the poverty I will encounter. At Frankfurt airport - an inauspicious start as I wait for twenty minutes in rising panic for the flight to Mumbai to come up on the board. It doesn't. In fact, it can't because there is no such flight. I finally remember that I'm supposed to be flying to Delhi. We less-than-seasoned travellers can make such small slips.

I find the right place to be and hand my ticket to a charming young trainee who tells me the flight is fully booked and I'm to wait on standby. What? Does she know how long I've had my ticket? I feel my face contort and fill up with ridges like a constipated prune. I fume my way up to gate A 55 and stand, seething, while I wait for a security check. Why is everyone around me nattering away in German when they must know I can't understand a word? How on earth am I going to contact Popri who has gone on ahead and has promised to meet my flight in Delhi? When can I kill the travel agent? How do I sue the airline? the German Chancellor? the EEC?

Then a wonderfully unflappable older woman takes my ticket, reduces my rising hysteria to manageable proportions and explains the weight problem that is causing the situation and sends me off to have a coffee. I settle for a beer while I consider what she has said: I know that we passengers have a hefty forty-kilo allowance and there are an awful lot of us for a very large plane. The size of the plane will add an enormous amount of additional weight of fuel for a long-haul flight: will we actually get airborne or will we have to taxi all the way to India?

Once in the plane I enter an emotional decompression chamber. I have left Europe and India means nothing to me yet apart from maps and schedules.

Delhi: for me it becomes a city where black kites over-fly the streets against a milky, misty sky and where I watch life on the street from our hotel window: the young man on the terrace opposite doing the laundry, possibly for our hotel; the crowds shifting and changing below; the heaving, rushing traffic. The streets in Old Delhi need resurfacing, the pavements are broken, a drain has surfaced somewhere, but it is all teeming with life and activity. The whole place sizzles with many worlds: social, commercial, official; worlds affluent, normal and poverty-stricken; housewives, stall holders and beggars. Wonderful smells drift in the air from the food stalls, there is the sound of Indian music coming from the shops, the scent of burning joss sticks, and all around are voices calling out in Hindi and myself none the wiser. The traffic is like wave after wave rolling towards you. Taxis, battered lorries, private cars, bicycles, cycle and motor rickshaws all seem to aim for the same spot once the traffic lights change. They hurl themselves forward and they make it - don't ask me how. I discover the uses that the hooter can be put to. You use it as an alternative to gears and brakes and to alert, to warn, to ask for space, to thank, to tell off and to apologise. The air is further filled with a cacophony of sounds from rickshaw bells to shouts and the pollution is so bad that you can almost touch it in the air. I am to learn in time that no one is issued with a driving license unless she/he can produce documentary proof of insanity. However, I see no sign of road rage and not once in the city streets do I see an accident though there seem to be umpteen near-misses and hairbreadth escapes.

The average local bank is dark and grubby and smells of many bodies and musty legers, and lazy electric fans stir the air overhead. They cannot change our travellers' cheques and we are helpfully directed elsewhere. We go past tiny shops where the paint is flaking and the goods spill out of the doors: the smaller the shop, the grander the name - The International X, The Global Y, The Cosmic Z. The pavement is not for walking on; it is for setting out your goods if you are a hawker or a man with a small food stall, and you sit on it if you are a beggar. Pavements are for squatting on while you wait, for standing and chatting on, for lingering and staring into space, and it is the road itself where traffic and pedestrians operate to their mutual confusion.

We've changed some travellers' cheques and it's lunch in a large modern restaurant cum cafeteria where the turnover of customers is high and most of the dishes are traditional. What an abstemious people are Hindus and Moslems. Beer? Beer? Nai! Nai! I am offered something called "fruit beer" which I decide to pass on. I'll stick with fresh limes and soda. At the hotel I hear Popri refer to me as the Mem Sahib and feel I should do something in keeping with such a form of address - like go find a tiger-hunt? And the receptionist said I looked like Mrs Gandhi. Moi?

My first day leaves me trying to make sense of everything I have seen, and failing. But we now have our rupees, a rented car and driver, have got our bearings and have even finished planning our next ten days' travel when we will tour Rajasthan. My three weeks begin to look woefully inadequate. We return to the hotel where the air conditioning has three settings: Arctic, Polar and Freezer. The ceiling fan has only two settings...the lazy drift and hurricane mode. We settle for Arctic and I stand at the window watching the street again. Stray dogs, tolerated everywhere, are dossing down in doorways; the terrace across the street is empty of life and I look at that opalescent morning sky that has not changed throughout the day. That haze is the face of pollution. It is late when I finish writing up my diary...and so to bed!

18th October, 2002.

DELHI OLD AND NEW.

Delhi has been built, rebuilt, conquered and lost so many times that my brief excursion into its history leaves me bewildered. I hold on to one simple fact: Delhi is that part of the city rich in layers of history; New Delhi came with the British occupation. We drive out of our old neighbourhood towards New Delhi, to where there are wonderfully extensive parks with wooded areas and the ubiquitous informal cricket match in full swing. The streets become roads and the roads become mighty avenues leading to the impressive government buildings originally designed by Lutyens to convey the grandeur of the British Empire and to house its administration. The buildings are indeed magnificent and the whole place seems dead by comparison with our humble end of the old city. However, modern-day political India has taken over these bastions of imperialism and houses its ministries here; and the India of the ordinary and the poor people has taken over the avenues where the cows lie down placidly on the tarmac and chew thoughtfully on a bit of cud watching the traffic that zips around and past them; and the families living on the verges and along the hard shoulder in tiny shanty hamlets have festooned the railings of the central reservation of the avenues with their washing that hangs limp to dry in the humid and exhaust-laden air. One in the eye for imperial aspirations!

Popri has read that there's an open-air all-India craft fair somewhere in New Delhi and we head for it in our rented car with Shekar, our excellent driver. The fair is huge, varied, exotic, cheap and exciting. It takes us two days to do something like justice to it and we indulge in an orgy of shopping – gifts for friends, things for ourselves and many more items that it seems criminal to leave un-bought. Do I actually need eight strands of jade in green and blue and red? Must I have four ropes of pearls and five pashmina stoles? What of the half dozen papier-mâché boxes and notebooks assorted of recycled and charmingly textured paper? I buy for neighbours, family, friends. I rack my brains to think whom I can buy for and it occurs to me that I could resell some of these splendid bargains to help defray the cost of the trip. Yes, of course I can. Reassured by the thought I plunge once more into the shopping spree of a lifetime till I am foot sore and punch drunk…or should it be purse drunk?

An evening dining out in a restaurant overlooking the old city - the air calm, the darkness warm and the city a myriad pin-points of light below us. There is a floorshow that is very much an attraction for tourists where jobbing dancers go through their routines with greater or lesser expertise. I am in a mood to enjoy it all. Popri has discovered that our driver, on duty all day and still waiting below for us in the car, is given nothing extra for meals and has to wait till he returns home at night in order to have something to eat. On about twenty six pounds a month he can just live decently, but there is no leeway for extras of any sort. We start to subsidise him every day.

Today I have seen the Bengal Lancers: there they were, the genuine McCoy, the life-size flesh and blood originals that I knew from childhood from my brother's box of handsome lead soldiers. The sight of the Lancers made me incoherent with excitement as I fumbled with my camera while they drew further and further away. I have seen urban elephants lifting heavy feet as they walked ponderously down a side street. And I have seen lepers. They approached the car when we were stopped at traffic lights, holding out begging bowls gripped between what had once been hands and are now shiny stumps, all fingers gone. They expect you to give, if you give at all, a couple of rupees - one and a half pence - and I am ashamed of my wealth and I feel guilty because they expect so little. And I have spent so much today. To hell with the going rate. Give more and, I have been told, I will be mobbed by the children begging, those professional beggars who demand with a persistence that becomes aggressive. These "villains" may be all of six years old, carrying an infant on their hip and out begging by eight in the morning. My grandson is two and living in England. I look at these children and see him. There but for the grace of fate go my family and I. Two rupees? You must be kidding.

Over the next couple of days I am dazzled by magnificent buildings, enchanted by tiny squirrels with striped backs, impressed by the culture and amazing achievements of the past. I am soon suffering from input overload in terms of information. We have visited the observatory that is Jantar Mantar with its lovely salmon pink buildings. Our guide is a courteous old gentleman, an archaeologist, who asks for seventy five rupees to show us round and instruct us, but we decide, acting on the advice given to us by our travel agent, that it is too much. "Nai, nai," we say firmly as we walk away. Then we look at each other: one pound and twelve pence is too much? We go back and manage to beat him up to a hundred rupees and spend a delightful time wandering around the buildings and gardens.

Then it's time to go to Connaught Place to find the American Express offices. The office walls are covered with improving maxims and elevated thoughts and I rejoice to read, among them all, one that says, "Love your enemies - and drive them crazy."

We go to the Red Fort with a guide. It is a fascinating place. There is little left of the fabulous wealth plundered by succeeding waves of invaders: the golden throne with its one hundred kilos of gold, rubies and diamonds; the massive silver doors; the solid gold handrails. The repeated rape of Delhi by Iran, by Britain, by whoever came...wealth beyond belief...facts and figures that dazzle and eventually exhaust my capacity to absorb or be amazed by them.

And while the Mogul kings lived in such luxury, what went on in the lives of ordinary people? And still you can buy semi-precious stones more cheaply than you can buy cheap costume jewellery in Europe - aquamarine, turquoise, rose quartz, topaz, garnet, jade, cultured pearls: you name it.

I am also overwhelmed by sights I can barely cope with. My capacity to respond emotionally is taxed to breaking point. I walk out with three hundred pounds in my well-concealed money belt and I see a man cross the road with his begging bowl. He rocks his body from one side to another as he pulls himself onto and along the pavement. His legs are cut off at mid-thigh. I feel the weight of having been born lucky. There are families whose home is the pavement, there are people walking barefoot. I hear a dog crying as it stands out of reach in the dry moat of the Red Fortress. It has only three legs and there is a huge running sore down one flank. It is the last straw that breaks the camel's back and I find myself weeping helplessly for all the misery and poverty I have witnessed in three days. I can't control it and it eventually works itself out leaving me so shaken that I find it impossible to eat when we get back to the hotel. The image of the dog is to haunt me and haunts me still.

Today our calmest of drivers loses his composure. He parks in a massive car park and, when we return, the car is land-locked and we end up waiting over an hour in the fierce early-afternoon heat. An old gentleman goes past and pats Shekar's arm muttering a few words to him. I know no Hindi, but I can interpret this: "There, there, don't get your dhoti in a twist." It is only days later that I wonder if Shekar was fearful that we might complain about his "lapse" in having left the car unattended.

Next day my stomach begins to rebel despite the fact that I drink only bottled water and only eat cooked food. The golden rule is that you eat it only if it can be peeled or has been cooked - and I have followed it religiously, even using bottled water when I brush my teeth. I keep re-reading my "Lonely Planet" comprehensive guide to travel in India, trying to remember everything it says from pneumonic plague to hijdas to havelis. I become aware that I am constantly in a position where I would be grossly over-charged if I didn't haggle. I've also decided that the proceeds of whatever I sell on my return home will be divided down the middle, with half of it going to some Indian charity.

Question: does a belief in reincarnation stifle development both personal and social? Does it lead to the easy dismissal of those who suffer because they are assumed to have led bad lives in a previous existence and have thus only themselves to blame for their present plight? Do those who suffer become passive in their acceptance of a guilt they have actually done nothing to merit? Does a belief in reincarnation, like a belief in heaven, make life more bearable?

I go to bed enriched, miserable, exhausted, euphoric and overwhelmed. The colour of these days has been saris in the most glorious shades and patterns, and so too with the turbans. The sound have been the metallic blare of music, the complex rising and falling of voices in song, the dog crying, the sound of Hindi all around me. The sights have been legion. I am to learn over a year later that I have been seduced by India in a way I shall never forget.

25th October, 2002.

FROM MATHURA ONWARDS.

We leave Delhi like many an earlier invader, loaded with the treasures we have taken from her: Delhi feels definitely female, for all its military past. The traffic is dense, but we travel in air-conditioned comfort in our rented car - out of the city, through suburban sprawl and then past hovel, shack and shantytown sprawl for mile upon mile. It's all buzzing with life and activity. This ribbon "development" becomes sparser and our roadscape eventually changes dramatically. Now there are camel carts; sleek black cows looking like polished adamant; women of graceful carriage who bear huge loads balanced on their heads. Tiny black and cream pigs root around rubbish heaps and micro donkeys with mega loads raise delicate hooves as they move aside on the road...I shall take one home with me when we leave. Our car, which has been running on gas, has to switch to petrol and the ride becomes bumpier - ah! there's nothing like gas for a smooth ride; and it's environmentally friendlier.

We're off to find Krishna's birthplace in Mathura and then plan to arrive in Agra in time to devote a couple of leisurely hours to the Taj Mahal. Shekar has never been to Mathura and relies on our instructions. We rely on our maps and try to sound authoritative. In other words - a prayer to Krishna would not come amiss as none of us really knows where she/he is going, particularly when we hit the tertiary roads.

We are now in metal country and brightly painted rickshaws are decorated with much aluminium in the way of sparkling studs and gleaming strips. We are arriving at our destination at last. Men doze on their string-sprung beds in the shade of trees by the roadside, fruit stalls splash the pavements with bright colours and men curl up for a mid-morning siesta by their stalls. Around them swirls the usual vibrant current of life and movement, from the odd hawker to the barrow boys to the women shopping or selling.

We arrive at the shrine with its garishly painted entrance and our bags are searched by six humourless women in military uniforms. They are clearly under strict orders not to smile, ever. Inside the enclosure there is a strong military presence with well-armed soldiers walking or lounging about. There is a smell of urine. If Delhi suffered from invaders then Mathura has fared no better, having been subjected to ever more fanatical and bloodthirsty invaders over one thousand three hundred years till it was torched in 1757. Now it is a bone of contention between Moslems and Hindus with back-to-back temples and mosques - just waiting for some fanatic to take action. Little wonder that a military presence is considered necessary.

We remove our shoes to enter the temple. Below it lies what we have come to see - a small windowless cell. Our Brahman guide tells us the story of Krishna's birth. It is a variant of the Oedipus tale: a child will be born who will destroy the king. The unfortunate parents-to-be are put in a dungeon and every child born to them is killed, but, somehow, the child Krishna survives. Murals now decorate the dungeon walls and attendants at a stone altar pour water in your hands for you to drink and anoint your head. A dozen pilgrims squat on the ground in a kind of absent, prayerful waiting.

We leave the cell and recover our shoes. A monkey with a splendid rose and cream-coloured bottom walks along a wall and an old bitch with hanging dugs and mangy coat wags her tail feebly at a temple attendant: all are apparently acceptable within the sacred precincts. As we leave, we pass the souvenir shops…everything garish and tasteless…Fatima and Lourdes.

En route once more and we are driving through Suffolk - flat fields, flat distances and a tree-lined road. Cowpat cakes are drying in the sun. The best laid plans of Popri and Mary keep going up the spout and we end up having lunch at four, our schedule already shot to pieces. Cycle rickshaws pass by with their varied loads: one carries heavy slabs of marble, another transports a fat armchair, another takes two women with all their shopping. How long can men do such back-breaking work? They are all lean and seem old yet ageless, but their eyes look weary.

It is not far now to Agra and we urge Shekar to get us to the Taj Mahal on time, but we are soon into urban traffic which includes an elephant and a large bull that decides to mount a cow in the middle of the road. By the time we arrive at the hotel it is six and the Taj Mahal, four kilometres away, closes at six thirty. Foiled again! Never mind, we'll just have to adjust tomorrow's rather crammed timetable.

Up with the lark the next day. What can one say about the Taj Mahal that hasn't been better said by poets and singers? It is elegance and restraint made tangible. It is light and grace and perfect proportions. While fortresses, built to last, have been destroyed, this monument continues in its perfection with its gardens and sweeping terraces that overlook the river. You want to know what it's like? I suggest that you give it more time than we did, choose a day that is fine and when the night will provide a full moon - and see it twice.

Our guide takes us to a craft shop. Every guide gets a small commission if he steers you in the direction of a particular shop. We leave and once our lack of interest is patent prices can drop by as much as three hundred per cent. Cars are not allowed near the Taj Mahal so we board a cycle rickshaw to return to where Shekar awaits. Our rickshaw driver is determined to take us to yet another shop,

"Very good, no buy, just look: I take you," and I have virtually to shout at him before he desists. I can't blame him, he's trying to make a living and we are "rich" tourists, but I'm thoroughly frustrated as he ignores our instructions. We pay him over the modest sum he charges for the ride and he suddenly starts to demand more. This rickshaw driver will not die of hard work, he will be throttled by some exasperated tourist.

We have discovered that "nai" is interpreted as "yes" unless repeated mindlessly and endlessly. It is also advisable to ignore people, to look away, to give them no chance to hook you in, to act as if they don't exist: I hate this and dislike myself for doing it, but end up doing it in self-defence. We are fair game to them. The foreigner holiday-season is very short and all touts, be they six or sixty, must needs make the most of it. I understand and can even sympathise with them as they try to rook me, but to them I am only a potential source of income, not a person, and to me they become a trial. Fortunately, I am saved from further bitter reflections by the hawker, a young lad, from whom I buy my postcards. He introduces himself, to my delight, as John Smart and engages us in an Italo-Hispanic conversation with an Anglicised basis. He is witty and sharp and deserves better than what life offers him - but, then, so do they all.

We are ready to drive on to Fatehpur-Sikri, a wonderful city that was only inhabited for fourteen years. The Mogul emperor, Akbar, may his silken socks still be serving him well in Paradise, had the best of liberal ideas - like marrying three wives of different religions and developing his own designer religion out of their combined faiths, but he wasn't that hot on some aspects of basic engineering. The beautiful city was ready, a large man-made lake was in place, the city was occupied, and within fourteen years the water supply had dried up. It is now a perfectly preserved ghost town. Ironically, it is the descendants of the artisan families who carved the tremendously intricate marble screens, and the descendants of the holy man buried in the city who have outlived the Mogul line of conquerors. "Isn't it refreshing," I think, "that holiness does not preclude marriage and progeny?" As for all the information we are fed generally as we visit temple or fortress or city, I choose to believe everything our guides tell us though I am discovering that some guides invent what they don't know. Who cares? I'm never going to remember it all anyway and what are a few facts here and there?

We leave for the Keoladeo National Ornithological Park. En route it's water buffaloes replacing the ubiquitous cows. The tiny donkeys are now sporting striped legs in blue, red and yellow and their manes are dyed a flaming magenta. I really do want to take one home. A stop for lunch. I continue to misread menus - chilled camel juice? I consider the hideous possibilities. And, to my horror, fried monkey nuts! (A lesser involvement with the fauna of the country would have helped me here.)

Only an hour can be spared for the park. We ride a rickshaw and the guide cycles alongside. "Not enough time," he says as he reels off a list of all the birds we might see had we planned better: thirty kinds of warblers, eight types of heron, snake birds, black backed this, green tailed that, polka spotted the other. We are impressed, but after fifteen minutes we feel we just want to see at least one of the wretched things. And suddenly they begin to appear. Wonderful! Wonderful! Purple storks, painted storks, kingfishers, all sorts and sizes of deer, rhesus monkeys with rose madder bottoms and a massive sluggish lizard by the side of the road. And more and more birds. The Park deserves a full day's visit, but we have to leave - we're well behind our schedule. As we draw away I pride myself on spotting a flat-footed speckled hoojah perched nearby.

It grows towards dusk. More and more camels on the road and the occasional kamikaze peacock that darts across trailing its mighty tail. We grow weary; then darkness falls and it becomes the stuff of nightmares. Drivers tear along with no lights on or with blazing headlights that they refuse to dip. We are blinded by them and, to compound the problems of visibility, mosquitoes and tiny flies smash into the windscreen and smear themselves across it. On the road - mopeds, bicycles and camel carts, none of them with operational reflectors, loom out of the darkness with horrifying suddenness. At one spine-chilling point we find ourselves facing two cars that are tearing towards us on the narrow road, leaving us nowhere to go. One is a criminal optimist attempting to overtake the other who is a son of a ...camel...and won't let him. We are transfixed with horror and I think, "This is how it happens to you. Within the next minute I shall be dead or horribly maimed." The first car overtakes and zooms past us with only inches to spare. The experience leaves us horribly shaken.

By the time we enter Jaipur we are in a state of nervous exhaustion, so tense that we can't even feel relief as we crawl through the traffic congestion of this busy city. Our travel agent gave us incorrect directions and helpful citizens obligingly do their best to direct us even when they are no wiser than we are. It takes an hour to find the hotel.

Never, never, never again, we promise ourselves as we sink into our beds, will we travel the night roads in India.

1st November, 2002.

JAIPUR.

Shakespeare had something to say about "things ill-begun" that only get worse; and so it seems to be for us in Jaipur. Our nightmare night ride is followed by sickness, loss of a contact lens, a shower that leaks, a change of room to one with a *toilet* that leaks, and the gradual revelation of the full ineptness of our travel agent. He sends us incomplete faxes, has given us illegible train tickets, has failed to book one fare and has managed to book us on a flight from Udaipur to Mumbai on the day *after* we should have left the city. When we sit down and manage to disentangle the mess he's made and the way he is never there when we phone, we think: "We'll look back on this one day ...and weep!"

Jaipur is a beautiful city laid out with a geometric order that is a great help to the traffic - which can tear around with more than its usual gay abandon. Jaipur, The Pink City, the capital of Rajasthan. Pink is the colour of welcome and was adopted to mark the visit of the then-Prince of Wales (the Edward VIII who never was) in the thirties...so we were told. But for some reason, Jaipur does not choose to welcome us. We spend a dreary first day filled with disappointments with Popri feeling rotten and probably running a temperature. We go shopping and the places that promised much in the line of folk crafts are dusty and dingy and running out of stock. The street where we look for semi-precious stones seems to deal mainly in gold. It is a malodorous lane packed with small shops where armed guards stand in the doorways in their paramilitary gear.

We arrange for a guide for the next day: a most courteous gentleman assures us that the guide will await us *at the tourist office*, we must not forget that, at 8.45; that is to say, we will meet him at 8.30 - so we must be sure to be there at 8.00 on the dot. He hopes we have grasped that. We leave him, bemused, amused and exasperated given that he has treated us poor women as if we are incapable of organizing anything without a firm male hand to guide us.

We get back to our hotel - A "Palace" as they all seem to be called. It is a fine private house that has been turned into a hotel. The family, an aristocratic-looking lot, occupy the first floor, but the place is beginning to look a bit run down. Popri crawls into bed and I sit out in the courtyard. The house is too sombre and dark with its remains of past splendours: family photos taken on tiger hunts or polo playing or driving early Daimlers. A delightful little library with the glassed-in bookcases is given over to mould and silverfish and all the rooms are invaded by a Celtic twilight.

Outside the encircling walls is a different world with rubbish piled on the side of the street where small hogs, dogs and lean cows root around; next to them a child squats and defecates; a very, very old woman washes herself in the water that drizzles out of a pipe; two men urinate against a wall. Pools of filthy water fill the ruts in the street. I can see why Susy's letters from India were oddly equivocal. I am to find out for myself the same ambivalent responses. Like her, I will fail to find synthesis and, like her, I will look back with longing and nostalgia on it all, because this is not a holiday - it is a thousand experiences.

Today I see a hijda. As we wait to cross a busy street, I notice a young woman on the other side wearing a full skirt, bodice top, shawl, much heavy jewellery and even heavier makeup. The traffic chokes itself to a stand and when she crosses it is with a man's stride and I realize that the lad is about seventeen and close-shaven under the makeup.

Next morning we get to the tourist office after a frustrating mystery tour of Jaipur. Our guide had been told, by our courteous gentleman, to be sure to meet us at the *hotel* and he has been cycling around for an hour in our wake. We finally converge on the same spot and drive to nearby Amber with its magnificent fortress-palace. There are extensive perimeter walls that ride the surrounding hills above a lake. The location is perfect in defensive terms and we approach the actual fort in the perfect way - riding on an elephant.

Inside the fortress are wonders galore and a pack of monkeys roaming the courtyard. There is the pavilion with ceiling covered in silver disks that make everything seem to glitter. We are shown a ramp built specially for the maharani's rickshaw: she was incapable of walking given the opulence of her clothing and the climate where temperatures could reach over 40°. We later see one of her outfits at the city museum: forty-seven yards of stiff brocade for a skirt, eight and a half kilos of gold and precious stones to decorate a dress. How ironic that a display of power should render you helpless - like the Chinese empress with the hideously long, curling fingernails which made it impossible for her to carry out the simplest task, like scratching an itchy nose. The maharani, apparently, would await the return of the maharaja who might have been out and about or could have put in a hard day's work in the hall of audiences. She would wait above the entrance to the main building, discreetly sitting behind a screened window, watching for the precise moment of his entry so that she could shower him with rose petals: how's that for a deeply meaningful existence?

What we are impressed by are the ingenious devices once designed to cool the air, like the use of scented water running down grass curtains and along channels where pierced marble screens let breezes through.

We leave and move to the next stop on our tour, a carpet factory - not that we plan to buy anything there. An hour later we move out to the nearby heritage restaurant after arranging to have the carpets we've bought shipped to Gibraltar and to England. I know, I know; but how could we resist those glowing colours? At the restaurant I fall in love with the single musician with his luxuriant whiskers, twinkling eyes and turban. We visit the tiny turban museum by the restaurant. Get a turban and you don't need an identity card. Twisted, knotted, folded, draped; in dozens of colours and shapes, they place you geographically, socially, in terms of caste and employment.

Next stop: Jantar Mantar, an extraordinary observatory with what look like immense and immensely elegant sculptures designed by Henry Moore. They are, in fact, sophisticated constructions that will measure the position of stars, will calculate eclipses, handle azimuths (exactly!) and do all these and more with amazing precision. Sadly, as we walk round this impressive open-air observatory I begin to turn into a zombie. Heatstroke? I shall tell you here and now that if you must ride an elephant in searing heat, then you should remember to wear a hat. I break into a cold sweat and end up sitting outside the next-door museum, dousing myself with water to stop from passing out.

Fortunately I do manage a short spell in the museum. It is full of interest from tiny, graceful paper pictures cut out with...wait for it...sharpened fingernails, to early copies of works by Aristotle and scholarly astronomical works from around the world. There is a portrait of the present maharaja's father as a young man; I stand and gaze enraptured. After so many pictures of Mogul emperors and maharajas with florid faces and curling lips, there is this amazingly handsome young maharaja who could serve as a model of all that is beautiful in a man. As I walk around, I recover somewhat, but we are soon blotto with facts and our guide falls tactfully silent as we drift around and, like late summer butterflies, just alight on the occasional item that catches our eye or imagination.

We have had a full day so it is back to the hotel where the special dinner up on the terrace and the succeeding floorshow are lost on me as I crash out. Despite everything, this day has helped to redeem Jaipur in our jaundiced eyes.

Before I fall asleep I acknowledge some pangs of homesickness: I am homesick for faces, places and sounds. We are, indeed, creatures of habit. I have once felt like this before, in Morocco. I believe it is the language difference that does it. Where I can understand or be understood, I feel at ease. Here, I am travelling in a kind of isolation as words, voices, street cries and conversations convey nothing at all to me. I am the outsider. I shrug the thought aside. I certainly didn't travel this far to be in England or Spain or Portugal!

Shekar is waiting for us early next morning, looking newly pressed. How does he manage with one tiny suitcase? We suspect that he sleeps in the car, in fact, is required to do so by his employers. Well, at least he will be saving the money we give him for his accommodation. We set off on the next leg of our journey. Beyond Jaipur the fields are splashed here and there with the magenta, orange and yellow of saris. After two and a half hours we arrive at Ajmer and have to fix our deficient travel arrangements at the railway station. Delays and hassle. Men push in front of us as we queue up. "We're only women," says Popri glaring at them. If looks could kill we'd be knee-deep in bodies. Eventually we can set off for Pushkar. It has been highly recommended by our travel agent (so what?) and by our guide to India.

"Ha," we think cynically.

8th November, 2002.

PUSHKAR.

We were wrong. Pushkar is a joy. Pushkar - blessed little town set round a small lake surrounded by temples. Our hotel - Palace, of course - is whitewashed and unpretentious. I find it delightful with the long veranda running outside the rooms where you can sit over a leisurely breakfast and watch the morning light spreading over the lake. Jasmine scents the air and parakeets fly noisily around the trees in the small garden below where tiny squirrels dart round your feet when you sit down there in the shade with your lime soda and your detective story. The room is simple and pleasant; the mattresses - as ever - are rock hard and surprisingly comfortable for all that.

This is the perfect town to relax in after our hectic schedule. We potter around, walk a bit, go to see a temple and decide against it because the street and steps are dirty and we'd rather keep our shoes on. We need to sort things out with our travel agent and are brought to realize that there is no way we are going to make it to Jaisalmer, the fort in the desert that we have heard much about, *and* manage to get down to Mumbai in time for Diwali. He has totally ruined our carefully laid plans and we sit and seethe in the garden till the peace and quiet of the place work their mundane magic. We decide to cut our losses. Jaisalmer is out. "We'll make it next time," says Popri with a sly grin. Is she planning our next trip to India or are we talking reincarnation?

Pushkar really is a tonic. There are beggars, but not that many; there are camels parked just round the corner; cows stop to lick the remains of some poster off a wall with every sign of relish; hippies who arrived years ago are still here watching the world go by and, when evening falls, we sit in the garden and listen to the chanting from the temples across the lake as pinpoints of light begin to stab the darkness.

We are reluctant to leave, but needs must. We have a night train to catch at Ajmer so we spend the day packing, doing a bit of shopping and sorting things out. I step out to collect a coolie outfit I've had made by a local tailor, a twenty-four-hour job, and am approached by a raggedly dressed young man.

"Please, you give ten rupees," he says firmly and explains in fractured English that he has been a labourer lifting heavy weights. Then he touches his testicles and startles me by using the word "bloody" idiomatically. I get the point he's making. His employers got the profits and he got the bloody hernia. It's been a tale worth more than ten rupees.

I've been remembering that when I arrived in Delhi I shied away from the salesmanship I found in shops. It was always a case of "You just come in and look, not buy." Then, given half a chance, they would have you sitting down drinking - "Pepsi? Tea?" - while they unwrapped, unfolded, displayed not one but a myriad shawls or swathes of material or saris which piled up on the carpeted floor like wave after brightly coloured wave. The British strain in my makeup would feel that I was being forced to buy because, if only out of courtesy, I should reward so much effort. I resented it, damn it! Now I know better. It is their job to sell and they are consummate salesmen. It is your job to resist or to select or reject. All it takes is a clear idea of what you want and a will of iron! Mind you, we did learn a good deal en route about the different types of pashmina and why some are more highly prized than others. I also learned about one trader's wife who made the best tea in Delhi which I was cornered into drinking: with the cinnamon, cardamom, sugar and milk it was not what I wanted and I prayed that the cow had been inoculated or pasteurised or well boiled before they had milked it. However, his gratification at my praise - for it was a fine drink - was a reward in itself as I sat with him and his friend under an awning and away from the blistering heat outside. Come to think of it, it is a most civilized way to shop once you adjust your ideas and stop rushing around, because you are pampered as you sit with your Pepsi and have the goods brought to you from the inner recesses of the shop. They have so much stock that only a fraction is on display so it's a system that works for both of you. We've met it here in Pushkar and I succumbed to it guiltily one day when I wanted to rest my weary feet. I took up the offer of chair and drink though I had no intention of buying and didn't buy...and no hard feelings at the end of it.

I'm incubating a cold and I sneeze away my last hours in Pushkar in the garden. Terrified of driving at night, we end up in Ajmer with hours and hours to kill. We eat well at a hotel and linger in the lobby as long as seems compatible with the coffees we order. We then join Shekar and doze in the car. He refuses to leave us till he has seen us on to the train and this despite the fact that he has a night drive back to Delhi ahead of him. We shift our luggage on to the platform. A young couple are asleep on the ground with a child, all lying on a dirty sheet. This is their "home". I feel distressed and realize that there is another child. As I stand up, I notice that there is also a baby clinging to the mother. I feel utterly helpless. Our train is snorting its way towards the platform and they wake. I snatch a five-hundred rupee note from my bag and thrust it in the woman's hand. They stare at me and I don't know how to apologise, so I bow awkwardly. I shall give three quarters of whatever I make from my sale to some Indian charity.

We're in the train and Shekar asks Popri for her blessing. What a lovely man he is. Popri is clearly moved. He has been the best bit of luck we've had - honest, unflappable and concerned for us. We are sharing a compartment with a married couple who are already abed.

The train pulls out of the station and we climb into our bunk beds. Good night.

22nd November, 2002.

UDAIPUR.

9.00 a.m. We are nearing Udaipur. I have slept well, only registering vaguely the departure of the married couple at some point in the night. Popri is up and has taken out the croissants we bought in Pushkar at the German bakery - I kid you not. We pull into Udaipur ahead of schedule. The ubiquitous cows, pigs and dogs root around outside the station. I have been told that they all have owners, but they stray here and there, always tolerated and not even shooed off when they seem to get in the way. Our new rented car awaits. Once out of the suburban sprawl, I get an impression of a relatively open and unpolluted city.

It is, in fact, a small city of well less than half a million souls. It has a fantastic history - truly the stuff of fantasy - and, with its constant water supply, has parks and gardens to delight you and, of course, the tranquil waters of Lake Pichola with its two summer palaces built on two islands. Imagine changing from your summer to your winter palace as if it were from a frock to an overcoat. Money may not buy happiness, thank goodness, but there is something to be said for it, is there not?

Our hotel, the Rampartap Palace, is built just by the shore of the lake and we have a room with a view. Our "palace" is a modern haveli, a modest mansion. The manager, Deepac, is a charming and very helpful young man; well, he's probably around forty, but I'm getting to the point where even judges are beginning to look too young for the job. We decide not to go on any tour this morning. We get out of our tired clothes, hand in a large bundle of laundry and, clean and showered, we order coffee and sit down to plan our stay. We read, check maps and town plans and consider. With a list of priorities at the ready we feel empowered once more and in control. After our moratorium at Pushkar we're prepared for a spot of culture or whatever we find. This place makes me feel human.

The car at 3.00. It is scorchingly hot outside. We manage to book a coach tour for next day, take films to be developed, buy films, help a man from Navarre who is having trouble making himself understood, and I buy two detective stories to keep me going. We pass a number of old havelis with their wall paintings that still celebrate the resistance of the great Mewar leader against the might of the Moguls whom he resisted for over twenty years. These paintings depict an elephant with Mogul rider on one side of the entrance, facing a Mewar on a stallion on the other side. The dynasty still survives after over a thousand years, long after the Moguls burnt themselves out; and I find it heart-warming that, not only is that long-dead leader - Maharana Pratap - still a presence in the city, but that his horse, Chetac, that saved him from death at the cost of its own life, is still commemorated with him. It is indicative of this dynasty that they were not Maharajas - great rulers - but Maharanas - great warriors - and the tradition of death before dishonour applied to women and children too. When faced with a no-win situation, it was time for "juahar" and they immolated themselves while the men donned saffron robes and went out to meet certain death against overwhelming odds.

Suddenly we are about to pass a haveli with a larger-than-average courtyard and six men sitting in a circle with two dogs and discarded cups of tea. They motion us in when I hold up my camera in enquiry. They even move their Land Rover so that it will not spoil our photos. We are invited in and they introduce themselves: "My brother-in-law Major..." I miss the name; they offer us tea, talk to us and even invite us to their country estate. Even their dogs are friendly. Popri and I develop an attack of British reticence and, after chatting for a short time, we say we must move on and bow ourselves out politely. Why, oh, why? We have no pressing engagements. We should have stayed and drunk tea and perhaps even visited their estate at some point. Damn the British stiff upper lip. We've wasted a chance to get to know people in a way normally denied to tourists. I said this place made me feel human. Oh, it does, it does; and it is to offer us so much in the next few days.

One day takes us to a beautiful garden with a variety of fountains that reproduce the sound of rains from drizzle through to downpour to make the hottest months seem, somehow, cooler. Another day sees us on a tour of temples way out in the country. We climb hills and I expect to get to Gaucín at any moment. Why have all temples got steps with such high treads leading up to them? Have legs grown shorter over the centuries? The best thing about Rajasthan is that nearly all the temples are very much in use and history seems alive here. Our first temple dates back to the fifth century; it is a cluster of tiny chapels complete with some erotic sculptures. Isn't it an interesting comment on human nature that what is glorified in one culture may be labelled soft porn in another? We see other temples and end up in one where we mingle not with tourists, but with the faithful who have come to pray and to leave garlands. Our driver stands guard by the car so, as I'm feeling a bit worse for the heat, I leave my heavy bag in the rented car. "Look after that," I say very clearly to our driver, "passports in there." Not to speak of the travellers' cheques we'll need to cash later. "Yes, yes, you not worry. Bag safe." We cross his path some minutes later inside the temple where he has gone for a spot of "puja" - prayer. I just hope his prayers do the trick for the bag too; I'd hate to find the car has been broken into.

Another day we see the miniature painters at work, squatting on the ground with their paints beside them as they produce the loveliest of paintings in the most unpropitious of studios; we visit the beautiful City Palace and Museum where once the Maharanas distributed their weight in silver and gold to the people. The deep pink building is magnificent and so are its mosaics, paintings, the mirror work, and everything about it. I warm to these Mewars who have managed to move into the later twentieth century with social works, hotel enterprises and financial acumen. There was one who was the only Indian prince who refused to attend a mass audience held in honour of Edward, Prince of Wales. Bully for him, we think. If I say little about this palace it is because there is far too much to describe and talk about. I really feel you should see it for yourself because I know I cannot do it justice.

We also go to a delightful puppet museum. It's a bit run down but it is full of fascinating items and photos. Udaipur is definitely the place for puppet theatre. You don't need to understand the language: the mime and the actions of these little wooden figures convey it all from the coquettish flirt twitching her seductive hips to the stunned young buck who suddenly sees her transformed into a fellow as the puppet is upended and appears as a mustachioed bloke. Then there is a craft village to be visited. At one of the houses that dot the compound (reproductions of regional dwellings) a four-man band with dancer strikes up a lively measure as we approach: our guide waves a refusing hand and the music stops as suddenly as if it had been switched off.

We do some shopping - material, miniatures, puppets. We are treated to a simple floorshow at the hotel where the dancer, a girl of about thirteen, moves with a wonderful sense of rhythm. A toddler leaves her mother to join in the dancing; the mother joins her and pulls me in; Popri ends up with us too. Earlier, Deepac, who calls us "Aunties" with respectful affection, had joined us on the upper terrace in the cool evening and had spent time talking to us as if he didn't have a business to run. Need you ask me if I like Udaipur?

One of the highlights of our stay is to be dinner at the Lake Palace Hotel on Jagniwas Island. We take a motor launch out and move through the dark, velvety water till we disembark near where they used to feed the crocodiles once upon a time. There is a floorshow, drinks and a wonderful spread of food in a delightful dining room with a view over the lake. I see fresh salads and the sort of dishes I've been, literally, hungering for. Sadly, oh, so sadly, it is my day for Udaipur's revenge and I abandon Popri to the culinary delights while I am vilely ill in the toilets. Later I sit out in one of the very pretty courtyards with its floodlit pools graced by water lilies, and nurse a lime and soda while I wait for my innards, which are in orbit somewhere, to return to their usual place.

There is still so much to be seen in and around Udaipur, but our stay comes to an end and we have to catch our flight to Mumbai. We must leave this beautiful city: I can even forgive it that last disastrous meal that never was! I think if I were a composer I should want to produce something inspired by this Venice of the East (a totally inadequate, misleading and presumptuous name given to it by some European.) What a pity that Mozart never visited here. Tomorrow it will be farewell to Udaipur.

29th November , 2002.

MUMBAI.

Before leaving Udaipur we chat to a German couple staying at the hotel. We tell them of our hideous night drive to Jaipur. The man laughs at our fears; he sees it as a risk you take if you come out east. "At least we came here by train and we're *flying* to Mumbai," we say and he tells us cheerfully that the figures for flying are just as bad, 100°/o higher than the worst of any other country in the world. Gee, thanks! It's good to know that just when you're about to set off on a twenty-five km. drive to the airport - which was worrying us anyway - before catching a flight, which is certainly worrying us now.

Thanks to Popri's sterling work yesterday, our tickets were changed and our seats are booked. As we go through a security check I begin to worry. The guard looks closely at the contents of my capacious handbag and starts sifting through the photos. He holds them up and asks where I took them. "That's Pushkar, that's Udaipur...pardon? Oh, the Rampartap Hotel," he nods knowingly. It's been simple curiosity!

We leave on time. The plane is small and half-empty so we're allowed to choose our seats. Dinner is served and before I have time to worry about the size of the plane and its distance from the ground we're landing in Mumbai ahead of schedule. We're going to stay with a cousin of Popri's and there is a car waiting to whisk us off. We drive through a prosperous city, down wide roads and then into quieter side streets with well-appointed houses and large trees. Kaloo is waiting for us and gives us the warmest of welcomes. She is younger than we are, but does a wonderful job mothering us. She wants to cook all the special dishes that she remembers as being Popri's favourites, and as the family return from work, I am introduced to them. The conversation is conducted in a mixture of Hindi and English and I am content to sit back and pick up the gist of some of the conversation only: with this Hindglish being spoken, I feel that I should confer on the family the status of honorary Gibraltarians, Llanitos: now I know how we Llanitos sound to others as we speak our particular brand of Spanglish.

Anjou, the daughter, drives us down to Chowpatty Beach. It is like an eastern Brighton with all the tawdry ephemera of the fairground: stalls, rides, food, ice creams and horse rides. We're at the popular end of the once-exclusive Marine Drive and we walk and talk till tiredness takes its toll and we return to the house where we hear the first bangers being let off in preparation for Diwali. I really like the sound of this festival whose presiding deities are Ganesh, the elephant god, and Lakshmi, Vishnu's consort. One guarantees you luck and the other guarantees your finances. A most refreshingly honest festival!

Next day Popri goes off to sort out things of her own and I stay home sorting out purchases, finances and diary. I sit outside in the covered terrace till the heat drives me indoors: the humidity is so high that my glasses are forever sliding down my nose and my clothes cling damply to me. Outside in the main streets the pollution is the worst I've experienced so far. I cover my mouth and nose with a scarf, men on motorbikes wear masks. I know that laws have been enacted to reduce or eliminate toxic exhaust fumes. The only problem is the fact that the filter required is too expensive for the average motorist. Heigh-ho!

In Mumbai I learn more about those Hindu families who fled Pakistan on partition. Popri remembers the trains arriving at stations with a cargo of corpses and the lucky ones who had survived the carnage caused when they had passed through stations in Pakistan where the trains were fired on as they went by. Such people left their homes, businesses and even families as they fled in the clothes they stood up in. As Deepac said in Udaipur, "I admire them. They arrived with nothing and worked very, very hard and now they run successful businesses all over India."

Kaloo gets nicer by the hour. She is a lovely person who worries about everyone's welfare from her husband's health to the man who sweeps their drive to the maids assorted to the driver whose brother was recently killed and who now has to support two families.

Popri and I get together to plan our remaining days, but she has so much to do and so many people to see that it's hard to organise anything. She has arranged a three-hour restoration job for us: facial, manicure, pedicure and all. Apart from that we will be visiting family for Diwali, we have a lunch appointment with a friend of Popri's, and there's a visit to a cousin I met over forty years ago…and I need to see Popri's excellent travel agent here in Mumbai to book myself on a flight to Kerala where I will spend two days on my own. Outside the house the bangers make the night hideously noisy as we sit on the terrace and try to introduce a note of order into what will be the busy chaos of the next ten days. Mumbai, I gradually realise, has little in common with Rajasthan. It is a secular and commercial city that hums and buzzes with activity. There is no time here for the leisurely shopping over a cup of cinnamon tea. This is all modern and what was an ordinary shop in the north is only to be found here in some trendy craft arcade or commercial centre. What does retain the small-town character is your neighbourhood market where you can get anything from your fruit and veg. and meat, to material, to jewellery. You will find a bespoke tailor too and get repairs done and goodness knows what else.

We have lunch with friend Kumla at the CCI - the Cricket Club of India. It is a magnificent place redolent of the Raj with its large dining room, spacious lounges, reading areas and, outside, a veranda from which to watch any match in progress. I actually get fish to eat which is a real treat. We've been so far inland in Rajasthan that it was not a safe bet, though I saw seagulls in Delhi. Well, I thought I did and Popri's withering, "Mary, we're about six hundred kilometres inland," was something I could dismiss, coming as it did from the childhood friend who, faced with a world map, had said that the North Pole was "Upstairs".

We walk for hours to get some last-minute shopping done. It's easier than sitting interminably in taxis that crawl along slowly, trapped in the huge press of cars that is Mumbai traffic. I read Indian magazines. They are written in English but necessarily use so many Hindi words that I am flummoxed. It sounds wonderfully exotic: "Our model wears a flame-coloured chapatti with sabzi embroidery. Her dhal is of cotton with details picked out in dahin. The whole ensemble is complemented with a banyan worn at a slight angle on the head." I thoroughly enjoy it. Articles, letters to the editor and short stories are very informative on matters like the caste system, belief in or rejection of reincarnation, working women and many other topical issues - including attitudes to sex.

Despite its museums and some fine monuments, there is little to see in this city that can compare with the wonders of the north, but here I am learning other things about India and its people, and this living en famille is an experience not to be missed.

One day I take myself off to Elephanta Island. I take the local train, go to the women's carriage and travel in relative comfort while the other carriages are so crowded that they appear to contain an assortment of random limbs, heads and trunks all crammed in any old how. I get myself on to the ferry and we cross the bay. The sun shines and the water fills with diamonds. The temples on the island with their huge sculptures are a shadow of what they must have been before being vandalised, courtesy of the Portuguese - so I'm told. I potter around, avoid the ubiquitous monkeys as I eat my sandwiches, and have a cold beer up in the restaurant with its view of the bay and the city. Back to the ferry, where a very old man wearing only a dhoti hands me solicitously on to the gangplank. This is private enterprise: he has created a job for himself and you would need to be a dyed-in-the-wool boor not to tip him handsomely for this utterly unnecessary service he offers you.

The beggars are back with a vengeance. One day some children run after the car and, when we stop briefly, they press their faces to the windows and hammer on them with their hands: well, wouldn't you? There are also amateur beggars. These are people who are too old to work and they beg with a degree of awkwardness. They are embarrassingly grateful for what they receive. I know that I will give everything I make from my sale to Indian charities. How odd that I have had to learn generosity by stages.

There are faces and people I have seen that I know will haunt my mind, like the man selling peacock-feather fans at the traffic lights, his eyes blank and his face devoid of hope, and I too slow to buy a fan before my taxi moved on. Popri has a busy day helping a motor rickshaw driver: as he was driving her round he went the wrong way somewhere and he's been fined by the police - and his license is not up to date. The sums of money involved would seem very reasonable to us, but to him it spells ruin. Popri pays for both the fine and the license and he wants to drive her everywhere for nothing: it is blessed to receive at least a little from such a man because it restores his self-esteem, but he has a sick wife and a living to earn.

Diwali. The day is made alarming by the bangers being set off every few minutes, and the night is to prove even louder as Mumbai seems to explode. The smell of cordite thickens the air. I have dressed for the festival in a borrowed salwar kameez. We visit family in their office for prayers. There's a priest, who is the son of a priest, and a full ritual; later there are further prayers and offerings on a minor scale at Kaloo's. Everyone has been so kind. I'm included in the giving of gifts, in visits, in anything that comes up. There is no fuss; I'm just absorbed into the family's life.

My airline ticket to Kerala comes through. Susy has recommended it, Popri has loved it and I am looking forward to something totally different to everything I've seen so far.

6th December, 2002.

KERALA.

When I said I was going down to Kerala, a friend of the family said jovially, "Ah, you are going to the capital, to Kochi. So many palm trees! Many, many palm trees!" He then repeated it and I had smiled, but as soon as I stepped out of the plane I found myself gawping and thinking, "So many palm trees! Many, many palm trees!" How right he had been.

This southern state is so different from the India I have seen. The language is Malayam with English thrown in to some extent; there is a visible Christian presence; there is a more equitable distribution of wealth than elsewhere and a higher literacy rate. As the rented car takes me towards the capital, I enjoy the sight of villas set back in large gardens. There are also the small thatched houses of the poor - clean houses with some space around them. This is not the hideous poverty of the Mumbai slums where the colour of poverty is grey, grey, grey in those shanty towns huge and squalid with their thread-like streets that act as open sewers.

Here it is space, wonderful space, that I am aware of - a high blue sky, verdant fields and near-empty roads that give way to suburbs. We pass St George's High School which sports a large painting of the saint – a maharana with a splendid turban - demolishing a very eastern-looking dragon. I spot the Catholic Syrian Bank and a host of other names that are evidence of the eclectic nature of this state. There are old Portuguese houses to gladden the eye and I will later see, in the backwaters, huge and spindly Chinese structures that hold and operate fishing nets. Tonight I plan to visit a sixteenth century synagogue that was built by the Jewish community that could trace its roots back to the Diaspora. And the synagogue is decorated with charming blue and white tiles supplied by the Dutch of Kochi.

I get the driver to stop at a bank. Like the neighbourhood banks in Delhi it smells of ledgers and dust. The administrative manager goes by the name of K.P.Baby. He is helpful, but things move slowly here and, after all, cashing travellers' cheques is not their usual trade. I put my signature to blank forms - I must be insane! And Baby and I chat till the forms are filled in, a letter is carefully written by hand and my money is produced. "Goodbye Madam." Outside, the traffic has become slow and heavy in the streets. Is it the rush hour? There is certainly a lot of hooting going on. By the time I reach my hotel it is late. So little time to do so much! I am forced to opt for a practicable schedule. Today, what's left of it, I will visit the synagogue and then attend a performance at one of the Kathakali centres. While I wait for a taxi with, I insist "an English-speaking driver", I book a twenty-four-hour tour of the backwaters.

The young woman at reception wears a flame-red sari, moves with the grace of a ballet dancer and has a long plait of satin-smooth black hair. I am filled with envy. Soon the taxi is at the door and the driver beams at me: "I am Anthony." We speed off into the hooting mass of traffic with Anthony weaving and swerving in and out. Is it a second rush hour? It is soon brought to bear on me that I have been given the one taxi in Kochi driven by a lunatic with a streak of terminal optimism. He picks up speed and turns round to face me: "I am a Christian," he says, happy to be conferring such welcome news. Great! Terrific! When we crash we'll make it to the Pearly Gates together, hand in hand and carrying our heads under our arms.

Fortunately the dense traffic gives him few chances to exercise his Kamikaze skills and we arrive safely at what we would call the "Juderia" - the old Jewish quarter - where narrow streets of great character lead up to the synagogue. It is familiar, this lovely building, as if someone had transported it from Europe. I look about me, stroll around and then just sit enjoying the peace and quiet. I want to spend far longer here than I can afford and Anthony is champing at the bit by the time I emerge. Why do I never realise that it can take far longer than I expect to get from A to B - whatever my map may seem to indicate?

We drive back towards the city, across a bridge that spans a stretch of water. I ask Anthony about the theatre we are going to and he explains (I think) that the lovely lilac flowers below us are choking the waterways. "Where do you come from?" I enquire and he tells me that we should get to the theatre on time. Our conversation has a mystical edge to it as we go beyond the limitations of daily speech. He has a rough time understanding what I say and I can barely make out his replies to questions I haven't asked. Nevertheless, he gets me to the Kochi Cultural Centre with four minutes to spare.

The small theatre is empty as the audience is ushered upstairs where we watch the actors applying their elaborate make-up. They squat on the floor and, by the light of an overhead bulb, they use their fingers and bits of twigs and water to create wonderful masks. The hero/god can be recognized by his green face which has been built up with card that somehow adheres to cheeks and jaw-line. The demon scowls ferociously into his hand mirror to check the efficaciousness of his handiwork - a blue and black face onto which white paint has been delicately dribbled. The female interest has long finished his simple human makeup and waits around for the others to be ready.

Back in the auditorium the musicians strike up. One sings and plays the drums, the other plays the cymbals. The drumming grows louder and louder till it seems to be bursting inside you. It is like a series of breakers, each reaching its climax before dying off to be succeeded by the next.

Then come a short lecture and a demonstration of the basic expressions, the extraordinary rolling of the eyes, and the gestures and movements of this spectacular form of dance drama - religious in origin. It takes years to train to be a Kathakali performer. We haven't time for the 6 to 8 hours that you'd be treated to in the temples at festival time, but our performance lasts an action-filled ninety minutes.

A female demon suddenly leaps on stage with a frenzied shriek. "She" prances and postures, rolls her eyes and glares and stares. It is true comedy and I begin to giggle. The Canadians sitting in front of me turn and frown: this is Culture! It is indeed and the highly disciplined movements allow for tremendous flexibility. Tenderness, ferocity, humour, tragedy and vulgarity are all possible. At the end I clap till my hands ache and can only regret that I haven't the time for more, or for the massage from a member of the company that is also on offer in the hall across the street.

Fish for supper. What else in this zone of islands, peninsulas and waterways? I shower and leave everything packed for an early start. Outside, the "rush hour" is over by ten and the insistent hooting has stopped. I fall asleep immediately.

A forty-minute drive takes me to my river boat. There is a crew of four. Laid end to end they are just about the length of the boat: there's a cook, a captain, a guide and an odd-job man. There's a small bedroom, a covered area fore and aft - which latter houses the kitchen. From the moment I step in I am entirely at my ease. I sit on one of the bamboo armchairs and drink in the sub-tropical vegetation. A little boy on the bank watches me. "Hello," he smiles widely and we engage in a laboured conversation that is full of goodwill. Then we cast off and drift gently away from the palm-fringed river bank.

My guide points out the rich birdlife which includes a short-tailed drongo - honestly! He waves his hand toward a shore in the distance and tells me that this is the setting for that wonderful novel, "The God of Small Things", which I read a few years ago. Over the next eighteen hours I find that this area is blessed indeed. The river provides fish and shrimps and cockles. The cockles are cooked for food, the shells are ground and become calcium tablets. The palm trees provide coconuts to be eaten, to be made into ornaments or rope or matting, or the outer fibre can be used to create anti-mosquito devices. The riverbed is dredged for building sand and there are wild pineapple trees the leaves of which are woven for mats. Fermented coconut milk provides you with toddy - an alcoholic drink - and the river mud is rich in fertilizer. There is a simple process for combining the lumps of surface coal strewn about together with the cockle shells to produce lime and water-purifying tablets. The inhabitants have enough for their needs and enough to sell in the city. Their houses are modest, but brick built. Along the shore there's a line of children returning from school - smart and playful.

The fishermen wave as we pass, so do those diving to bring up baskets of sand from the riverbed. Boys wave from the bank. This seems a truly contented population. In this area, the squalor and despair of Delhi and Mumbai shine by their absence.

The day is broken up with visits to small enterprises - women making rope with the aid of an old bicycle wheel that acts as a spinning wheel; a lime works; a coconut-drying plant. It is also punctuated with food. For over a fortnight my digestive juices have had little to work on apart from the lining of my stomach so I insist - "No chilli," the cook looks at me in disbelief: have his ears failed him? "No chilli?" He is horrified.

The lovely water hyacinths beautify the waters while threatening the river. A sail, another sail, a boat filled with produce being rowed to market. Then comes a foul sound. It is a motorboat speeding past and I curse. This may be the shape of things to come, but I resent the intrusion of technology. We anchor for supper away from the shores and small islands - ahead of me there is nothing but water. I drink fresh coconut juice and munch on lovely fresh coconut and watch the colours around me grow almost imperceptibly paler. Then we turn back.

Throughout the day I have been content to listen to Raina, my guide; to hear the dull slapping sound of women beating their washing rhythmically on the shore; to wave to all and sundry till I've felt like the Queen. I've even resented mildly the stops we've made to visit those tiny enterprises. We anchor for the night. Colours disappear as dusk thickens into darkness. The banks show points of light. I want it all to happen again - no speed, no going anywhere. I have been truly happy here. That's not such a common experience, is it? We look forward to happiness and we recall it, but how often do we recognize it when it's there?

When I leave the boat the next morning I want to weep. Instead I take photos and bid the crew farewell. Yes, you really must go to Kerala and see for yourself. It's a place for emotional cleansing and is easy to find - only about 200 kilometres from heaven.

Then it's back to Mumbai for a couple of days - packing, things to be collected, leave-taking, and a plane to catch. Thank you Kaloo and family! Thank you India! Thank you, thank you!

13th December, 2002.

THIS WORLD OF OURS.

AN EYE FOR AN EYE AND A LIFE FOR A...WHAT?

I am a hypocrite when it comes to eating meat or, perhaps, I'm an inconsistent hypocrite. I am a carnivore at heart, but I begin to find it harder and harder to eat certain types of meat. Talk of spring lamb and I see one frisking in a meadow on uncertain legs, a life of happy grazing ahead of it. How could I possibly eat one of them? And suckling pig? The idea now seems barbaric...it's just a baby, for Pete's sake! "Kid" affects me similarly. If you've held a little kid in your arms and delighted in its gawkiness and funny bleating voice you'd know what I mean. And there are creatures like rabbit, pheasant and partridge where you can identify every small dismembered piece of the little bodies when they are served up. I end up mentally reconstructing them so I can't eat them either.

That leaves me with pigs and cows. A slab of beef or a piece of pork on a plate, you'll admit, gives no indication of the shape of the animal in its entirety. Yet I know how intelligent pigs are supposed to be and it should feel like eating a distant relative, which is certainly how I'd feel about dolphins. Now, cows are probably charming creatures. You may guess from the cautious tone of that sentence that I am afraid of cows. To me, every cow is a fighting bull unless it hands me at least a statement from a notary public that testifies to its harmless provenance and, as I have had occasion to remark before, I expect any documentary proof to be pretty convincing. Be that as it may, I will very occasionally eat beef though I've never had the courage to face up to any cow I have ever met. And so on to venison. I occasionally eat it because I've been told that culling is essential to the health of the herd as a whole. Do I truly think of the gravity of what I'm doing? - I'm eating The Monarch of the Glen! Chicken and turkey, however, I often eat. I know, I know; I told you I was inconsistent and, for some reason or other, I don't see chickens and turkeys in quite the same light as pheasants - but I still manage to feel vaguely guilty about them. Fish is OK for the moment, but I daren't establish a relationship with a goldfish for fear that all will be lost.

No, this is not an article about turning vegetarian. The point I'm making is that, if I had to kill an animal in order to eat, I would soon be cultivating a taste for fruit and veg. With food, I am one of those who let others do the dirty work.

Which brings me to something which has been very much on my mind this week: the fate of the woman I have never met who, formerly unknown outside her limited circle, has become a newsworthy item worldwide. Amina, a divorcée, has had a child out of wedlock in Nigeria. According to a law passed a few years ago in her region, she can be put to death for this "crime". To be exact, she can be stoned to death. The case has been heard, she has been found guilty and she will be executed early in the year 2004 when the baby has been weaned. What of her partner in "crime"? What of the neighbour she has named as the putative father of the child? the man she said had promised to marry her? He has been declared innocent. You see, he had a watertight defence, didn't he? He declared that the woman had lied so he has been cleared of the charges against him.

Apart from the fact that a DNA test that could prove who lies and who doesn't will not be considered under Sharia law; apart from the sexual politics behind a law that discriminates so blatantly against women - what shocks us most about the case is the sentence. We find it all so appalling that last year when another woman had been similarly condemned, public opinion across the world was stirred: there were petitions, pressure groups, governments exerting whatever influence they had, and a team of lawyers who were able eventually, on appeal, to have the original sentence quashed. There will, doubtless, be an appeal in Amina's case and one prays for a similar outcome.

I said that the sentence was the nub of the matter, but that is not accurate. It is the form of execution that horrifies us. The stoning will be carried out by members of the community. Do they look on it as we look on jury service? They will be instructed on the size of stones they may use. They must not throw very small stones that would fail in their object or take too long to do the work, and they must not use very large stones that would kill her instantly. After all, she must pay her dues to society, mustn't she? Stones of a suitable size will be provided, one supposes; a circle or a line of people will be formed; a requisite distance will be set between them and the victim, or should I call her "the criminal"? Someone will cast the first stone and the stoning will begin. The woman will surely scream when she is hit - unless she is gagged; she will bleed and she may try to protect herself if she is not either tied to a stake or partially buried to stop her moving. Eventually she will be declared dead and throughout the process she will wear some kind of all-enveloping burkha that will, presumably, protect the sensibilities of those who are stoning her.

Who will be involved? Will it be the neighbours who gave her away to the authorities? Will it be both men and women? Will the man she named participate in the stoning? Will he be watching? Or will he be having a meal with friends or walking the town or sitting under the shade of a tree?

The whole scenario feels outrageous. The idea seems to be of ensuring the complicity of many in what could be considered a communal or community murder. There's a terrible logic about implicating so many in the killing of one woman. It is a way to establish that we must all subscribe actively to the law. No one can draw back and indulge in the freedom and luxury of conscience that comes from disagreeing with what we may consider unjust laws. I wonder if there isn't a penalty for anyone refusing to take part in the stoning?

We, on the other hand, have long abandoned the death penalty in many western countries. Gone are the days in England when the family might pack a picnic and make a day of it - watching the hanging, drawing and quartering of some political or religious rebel.

Is there still a death penalty for treason? Can you still be executed out of hand for desertion in times of war? Which states in the USA still employ the death penalty? In some states you can be gassed, in others you are given a lethal injection, in yet others there is still the electric chair. We have indeed come a long way from an execution as a spectacle for the population to enjoy. Instead it is left to a few officials to organise and carry out the death sentence, and it is seen by a very few people - like members of the family of the person being executed, or members of the family of whoever he/she has killed, and there may be journalists or the odd other. The general public is kept informed, but will never see images of the actual process where a person is in her/his death throes with mouth taped. We have anaesthetised death for the general public. What we don't see can't hurt us so we can sleep soundly in our beds because our hands are clean.

I remember a "Star Trek" episode in the original series where two nations on a distant plane have been at war for centuries without resolving the conflict. At some point they both realize what a futile waste of time, money and devastation of property is involved so they come to an agreement: they compute the number of casualties suffered annually and agree to destroy such a number themselves every year. Peace is not declared and the war continues, but it is a much cheaper and tidier business where randomly chosen citizens present themselves at an elimination centre for a painless death. They are proud of their solution. They have done away with the maiming, physical suffering and destruction of war.

Captain James Kirk, standing firm in his funny little boots, is outraged. I forget how he did it, but by the end of the episode this anodyne form of warfare has been well and truly challenged, and people have been brought to the realization that their "civilised" solution has blunted their sensibilities by hiding the ugly reality under a mantle of supposed enlightenment. A spot of the real sufferings attendant on war stirs them into reassessing their position and they end up opting for peace.

Perhaps the death penalty as we know it has become so remote that the horror of state violence is not even acknowledged. We ignore the irony of a system where we declare private murder a heinous crime and make it punishable, let's face it, by state-sanctioned killing. So I'm back at the point of letting someone else do our dirty work for us when it comes to killing. The injustice of Amina's situation, the prejudice against women that is enshrined in the law she has infringed, the manner in which people become accessories in stoning her to death all help to make clear the fact that the death penalty, in whatever form, would appal us if we had to participate in it actively in cold blood.

13ᵗʰ September, 2002.

After I had written this article there was an appeal against Amina's execution. The death sentence was upheld at first, but she was later released. However, I have recently seen a photo in a newspaper of a man tied to a stake, his head hooded. He was lying crumpled on the ground. Around him at some distance was a ring of men and one of them had come forward to do his duty - he had just plunged a dagger into the "criminal". It appeared to be a communal stabbing as opposed to a stoning. The paper reported that two of the crowd suffered heart attacks during the execution. Women are not the only victims of such a primitive legal system.

August 2006.

WHAT A LOAD OF BANANAS.

Surely the most expensive pound of bananas in history must be that sold by Steve Thoburn of Sunderland in 2001. To be perfectly honest with you, I should say that he was selling his bananas at 34p per pound, but the particular pound I refer to cost one hundred and ten thousand pounds and 34p. The extra £110,000 was the result of the court case that ensued when he served a particular customer.

Mr Thoburn was held to have broken the law. Yes, he was a properly licensed trader, like his father before him. No, nobody suffered a rare tropical disease from eating the fruit. No! of course this was not a case of organized crime: the idea! And they weren't filled with explosives if it comes to that. If you must know, it was a matter of 46.368 grams. That's about the weight of a small egg. Don't jump to conclusions: Mr Thoburn did not give short measure, nor did he overcharge, but 46.368 grams is 46.368 grams and we mustn't lose sight of the facts.

You will, no doubt, recall that I spoke of a pound of bananas. Well, there's the rub. We've gone metric, haven't we? - and pounds are an imperial measure. Mr Thoburn knew this, but, perhaps out of loyalty to family tradition, he sold his bananas by the pound as had his father before him. You may call him a supporter of lost causes and call his action Quixotic, rash, mad: the Council called it illegal.

There may be those who are shocked to the core that a trader could so behave in England's green and pleasant land. They may feel that the whole concept of a truly Common Market is under serious threat and may begin to totter in the face of such anarchic acts. Why, it might spread and people might try to subvert our uniformity by demanding the return of the foot, the yard and the mile. They might even try to opt for those gloriously confusing measures in the old "Shilling Arithmetic" like rods, poles and perches. Someone might even attempt to reintroduce the curve in the cucumber, just when the dead straight one is within our grasp.

Brussels has required and nearly achieved unity, uniformity and conformity in some areas. It has done its best to clone us; and along comes this wretched pound of bananas to undermine it all.

People who think thus can only be grateful for the steady vigilance of Sunderland Council in enforcing the 1985 Weights and Measures Act and the 1994 EU directive that took effect in Britain in the year 2000. And, in particular, they should thank whatever cosmic power they believe in for the work of the Trading Standards Office that unmasked Mr Thoburn, catching him "in flagrante delicto".

In a sort of under-cover scenario one assumes some officer risked...well, whatever one risks in such a case...and asked for a pound of bananas (a perfectly legal request) and was served a pound of bananas (an illegal act, please note). Then followed the court case that cost the Council £75,000 and for which Mr Thoburn's customers and sympathisers raised £35,000 to pay for his defence. It seems, but I am open to correction, that it is an offence to sell loose goods by the pound. Which leads me to suppose that had the bananas been liquidised, mashed or powdered and been suitably packaged there would have been no offence.

As matters stood, Mr Thoburn was found guilty and given a conditional six-month discharge. That had cost the ratepayers £75,000. It's hard to believe that there was no one in the Council with a sense of proportion, a sense of humour or a touch of "laissez faire".

Did the case have to end up in the law court? Was it not possible to turn a blind eye? Could persuasion have worked better or was it a case of Council and Trader red in tooth and claw?

I must admit to curiosity about the under-cover officer. Was he a long-suffering public servant sent off on a slightly idiotic and embarrassing job or was he zealous and out for blood? or was some higher official, the essence of terminal Bumbledon, full of messianic fervour in the cause of weights and measures metric? And what of Mr Thoburn? Was he helping people who were confused by the new measures or was he sticking by the pound in a crusading spirit?

It does occur to one that Steve Thoburn could have been let be. It reminds me vaguely of when the Catholic Church introduced Mass in the vernacular: it suited me fine, but suddenly you couldn't find a Latin Mass for love or money, and that mattered to folk who wanted their Mass as they had always known it. And it's like an exam board that changes the syllabus so that what was unacceptable yesterday becomes obligatory today.

Why is it that, whenever there's a directive, we develop the herd instinct and lose our sense of perspective, our critical faculties, all personal judgement and our common sense? We end up, instead, with a highly developed faculty for echoing stale words that we have received from the powers that be. It makes you wonder how close we are genetically to the lemming.

And if I look back on the whole banana issue, it becomes clear that my calculations have been inaccurate. It was not the pound, but the 46.368 grams that were *not* weighed and, consequently, *not* served and not paid for that cost £110,000. Yes, it was the un-weighed, unsold grams that were never bought nor paid for that cost so much. I feel there's a flaw somewhere in this, if only I could put my finger on it.

All in the cause of unity and uniformity. The great advantage of uniformity is that no one has to think; the great disadvantage is precisely that nobody has to think or need bother to think - just refer to your book of directives or rules or what-have-you and you need never bother again with the issue of personal responsibility.

And it's just occurred to me that there was a perfect solution to the whole confrontation: had customers asked for 953.632 grams - i.e. one pound - everything would have been legal!

10th August, 2002.

Steve Thoburn carried on with his cause, together with several other shop-keepers - the Metric Martyrs as they called themselves. He eventually appealed to the European Court of Human Rights. Very sad to report, he died on 14th March 2004 at the age of thirty-nine. He deserves our admiration for having challenged a bureaucracy that is too often faceless and needlessly powerful.

August, 2006.

ROMAN GAMES AND THE LIKE: 21st CENTURY STYLE.

Most of what I've read about the Roman Games in their massive amphitheatres has sunk without a trace. I know that they went in for spectacular effects at some stage, like flooding the whole arena in order to stage splendid sea battles in the middle of Rome. You might say that that was the Cecil B. de Mille period.

The people of Rome expected such entertainments and the rulers knew their value: it was a way of celebrating their own achievements in war and of buying the population. They couldn't buy votes because there wasn't universal franchise, but they could buy complacency or conformity. Gradually the games changed, but, as I said, I can't remember the details of it all. Nevertheless, there is one fact that stuck in my mind the way a fishbone can stick in your throat. It has to do with clowning about.

We know there had been fights to the death between gladiators...though they can't, surely, have always been standard practice. I mean, tried and tested gladiators didn't grow on trees and you didn't want them to be expendable after years of training. But the time came when, and I'm taking my history from Hollywood at this point, the crowd could bay for blood and the famous thumbs-up or -down sign came into being.

What's so strange about that? My grandmother used to tell me of bullfights in her youth when the crowd kept screaming "¡Caballos al toro!" - Horses to the bull! - And the management had, on one occasion, scoured the streets of La Linea for any old nag they could buy so that the crowd could enjoy the spectacle of horses having their bellies ripped open by the bull. Of course, you didn't run out of horses too quickly because you could always patch them up by packing them with sawdust to hold the blood, and strapping them with lengths of cloth to hold the animal together. There were further details which I won't go into.

I know that I once attended a bullfight in Madrid and found myself sitting next to an aged Harpy who didn't just shout; she stood up and screeched at the bullfighter who, in her opinion, wasn't getting near enough to the bull. She wanted blood. OK, so maybe her life was one monotonous treadmill and she wanted a few thrills. What I say is what I saw and heard - and was repelled by.

And what of this clowning I mentioned? That seems to have come after the end of Republican Rome and at the time of Rome's decline - the time of increasingly dictatorial and uncontrollable emperors and of the persecution of Christians. I'm sure others were also caught in the net for political or other reasons. These people were thrown to the lions.

It wasn't like Kirk Douglas, sword in hand, facing such beasts. To offer the audience real entertainment, the organizers would strap grinning masks on to the faces of those about to die. They would also secure huge sandals to their feet. Then these victims would be sent out to the arena to stumble about and fall over, always grinning hugely as they ran from the lions or were torn apart by them. A real comic turn. The horror of that has stayed in my mind. To kill in what might be called "honest combat" is one thing; to deny a person any dignity and to make a mockery of suffering is quite another. Like my old Harpy in Madrid, those Romans must have relished what they saw. And what they saw was not the people behind the masks.

So what has all this to do with the twenty-first century? Let me elucidate (lovely word, that) - I sat in my house last night and the bodies piled up around me. Many had been shot, some had been blown up in a massive explosion, a couple had been knifed and a number had been subjected to humiliating physical abuse. I was responsible in a way because I had been the one zapping. I know it wasn't for real; of course I do. But it was "entertainment".

Think of that. "Entertainment" is watching violence. And we watch it daily. And our children and grandchildren watch it daily.

I remember the argument years ago about the question of whether or not violence on screen and pornography could affect young people. It featured in some newspaper. I also remember the bottom line: there was no evidence to bear out the theory that young people were influenced by it all. Youngsters knew the difference between reality and fiction.

It was a time when sociology was "Social Science" and, in trying to gain respectability as a science, it adopted a scientific stance, namely - social phenomena had to be measured, data collected and hard facts recorded. A lot was learnt about how to study society in a disciplined and controlled manner, but in some areas it was a case of common sense going out of the window.

It now appears - forty years on - that watching violence and pornography influences young people. What a surprise! So now we know this because there has been research to prove what we all said long ago. And it's many times worse nowadays because there are so many video games where children can work out how and when to kill people on their screens: they are no longer passive viewers - they have become the instigators and controllers of violence.

I find myself returning to the question of testosterone in the young male of the species. The tendency to violence is there and I'm sure it played a vital part in the survival of the species long, long, very long ago. But we no longer have to fend off wild animals at the cave mouth and therein lies the problem…too much testosterone without a valuable function to serve.

I once taught drama to a group of twelve years olds - a mixed group - and there was a nucleus of the boys who seemed incapable of creating any improvisation that did not involve a fight, beating someone up and putting in the boot. I decided to wean them off it: "I want you to improvise a scene featuring a car, friends, a field and a daisy." That would teach them!

They improvised all right. Their story was about a group of lads out for a day in the country. They stop their car, pile out, and one of them spots the daisy.

"Look! A daisy!"

"I want it."

"No, I want it."

"I want it too."

"I saw it first so it's mine."

"Like hell it is!"

And all four of them went into a spontaneous punch up.

I eventually solved matters by insisting that they work in mixed groups.

Because boys have testosterone to cope with, I'm sure they are the ones who suffer from this new form of computer "entertainment". Do I really need to wait till someone spends tens or hundreds of thousands on research to show that X% of those buying the more violent video games are boys and only a mere Y% are girls?

What about pornography? I once worked in a small school where I got the Head's permission to do some work with a mixed class using a couple of pornographic magazines. The parents accepted it and there was not a single complaint. The girls spoke of how the magazines made them feel. They felt disgusted. The boys found themselves involved in dialogue with real females rather than fantasizing about sex objects. The magazines clearly projected the image of woman as a thing, as passively awaiting or encouraging instant sex. She was often depicted on the ground, on all fours like an animal. No wonder the girls expressed outrage and the boys, considering the reality of the girls they sat next to, said they couldn't reconcile them with the women in the magazines.

If our long discussion made clear the image of woman as possession or victim, it also made clear - and the boys began to realize - the fact that the male readers were made victims of a sex culture that denied them relationships, concentrated on unrealistic physical prowess, and created bizarre expectations of what sexuality was about. Sex was being peddled as performance and perversion.

How's this for the better alternative?... "Sex begins over breakfast." I don't know who said that, but it's true, isn't it? Sex is part of relating. The real danger of film and video violence is that it destroys sensibility. Your sensitivity to others, to their feelings and rights and personality, is undermined. In its place comes a brutal and blind egocentric cult of self-gratification. Does that provide a link with the events of ancient Rome?

It is appalling to think that what films propagate so often is the confrontational approach. Every difference is resolved with fists, guns or knives. And, cleverly, it is all also anaesthetised. People may be slaughtered in their dozens or hundreds in a film, but how much are you shown of true suffering, of slow and painful death, of the results of maiming and brain damage? Those things are not marketable products in a film meant for general release, so death is tidied up and the hero is invulnerable. How often have you remarked on how good a shot the hero is and how the baddies must be boss-eyed to shoot wide of the mark with such persistence?

I once felt that the best way to kill interest in a topic was probably to put it on the school curriculum. Now I find that is too narrow an opinion for me and I can't subscribe to it. So it is that I wonder how we can find space in overcrowded timetables to introduce children to certain serious matters outside the purely academic world.

Let's see. We know that wife battering is a fact of life and that there

are wife batterers in Gibraltar as in any town: shouldn't it be de rigueur in our schools for the matter to be aired? Can't we have girls prepared to note and deal with their own potential passivity and to recognise the profile of the man who beats his partner? Shouldn't boys be alerted to the way this crime works, why it happens, how they can be involved directly or via a friend?
Ditto child battering.
Ditto granny bashing.
Ditto shared parenting.
Ditto relationships.
Ditto the conflicting expectations that each sex has about marriage.
Ditto having children.
Ditto everything that is going to decide the quality of our lives.

Thank goodness, most of us in our society have tolerable to happy lives overall, however difficult life may be at times. It's just that the thought of the stress on aggression that is becoming commonplace in entertainment and the perversion or total elimination of sentiment in relationships all worry me.

25th April, 2003.

THE STRIDENT VOICE OF CONSUMERISM.

You hear it on television and radio and we've been so conditioned that, when we do object, it's to the length of time the adverts take before we are returned to the programme they so insensitively interrupted. Some companies commission the best in the market which produce advertisements that you can actually look forward to for the first few times they are screened. I remember the elaborate Cava adverts on Spanish TV that come out before Christmas. They reached the stage where you wondered if they were denuding themselves of profit in order to pay for their elaborate sets and star-studded cast - I mean...Michael and Kirk Douglas in underwater sequences (thanks to special effects) accompanied by a bevy of mermaids! It tells you a great deal about the world of advertising too: what on earth has Cava to do with mermaids? If you drank it under water it would rather dilute the product, don't you think? And I have a sneaking suspicion that the Douglas family can afford the best of French Champagne.

I cannot answer for Europe in general because we only get Spanish television. In Spain there are some adverts that are tastefully elegant and quiet; after all, if you're advertising perfume or a discreet and near-silent household gadget you don't want it all to explode onto the screen with loud voices and music. A similar thing happens if your advert is designed to appeal to the viewer's sense of humour: you let the situation work for itself, though I remember one set of adverts designed on the lines of a sitcom where they even incorporated that teeth-grating element, canned laughter.

I suppose the worst adverts at present are connected with cleaning, children's toys and special offers. Take the special offers - and take them far away if you can. They are made cheaply and, if they're telling you how to improve your face or figure, they usually feature young people with perfect bodies and luminous skins. They all wear rigid smiles. I think they're induced by the need to look as if it were the most normal thing in the world to stand in your bikini in front of a camera while a little contraption pinches away at your muscles and makes them jump and jitter around as if they were possessed. And the voice in the background - determined, cheerful, a shade too loud and hearty - makes you want to ram the little contraption in the speaker's mouth.

Children's toys also feature repellent voices. Toys for boys are backed by an excited strong male voice that delights in speed, explosions and general mayhem as it extols the phenomenally good time a boy can have with a toy that you know will pall after the first few hours. But I can almost forgive that voice when I think of the adverts for girls' toys.

The voice chosen for those inevitably sounds as if the speaker's vocal cords had been carefully scraped with a Stanley knife in order to give them that high-pitched sound which is assumed to be indicative of childish, girlish innocence. Such voices laugh and giggle with barely contained happiness as they extol the delights of all the fantastic things you can do with your doll. Such delights come in two modes. One is the Motherly in which you can change the doll's nappy, wipe its bottom, feed and burp it and - oh joy - push it around in a pram. Mode II is the Frivolous where your doll is an anorexic clone with silicon implants. She can be dressed, have her hair dyed, be festooned with jewellery, wear make-up and lead a hedonistic life with all the additional equipment you get her, from cars to boyfriend.

The cleaning adverts hit out at me personally and I resent that: I am not around twenty-three; I don't look fit and healthy and I'm not raring to get on with my cleaning. When I do get round to it, I don't smile and flash my capped teeth about, and my kitchen is not, like those in adverts, the size of Wembley Stadium. I take umbrage at these advertisements and can only be thankful that I, unlike those glorious young housewives they feature, have not taken to holding conversations with characters who pop up out of the packages or bottles to tell me how to clean my house. That's reassuring as it makes it clear that too much cleaning leads to hallucinations and, I'm sure of this, eventual insanity - which is a danger I'm working hard to avoid.

I think that what I most object to nowadays is the feeling of being constantly hassled, enticed and pushed around by those who advertise. I'm sick of having bumph pushed through my letterbox, tired of special offers and angry with myself for having become a faithful member of the consumer society. Yes, I confess to this shameful weakness. I may go out shopping for one thing that I need: let's say it's pepper-corns. I return with some exotic vegetable I've never seen before, a new type of duster guaranteed to leave surfaces clear of dust for six weeks and a broom with revolving head, chromium hubcaps and revolving aluminium stratified couplings to ensure that you sweep under the most awkward pieces of furniture and reach into the most inaccessible corners. Why? Because they had no pepper-corns and, once on a shopping expedition, I feel I have to buy something - anything.

Yet I'm tired of being told, instructed, cajoled, persuaded and generally conned into wanting what I don't want, don't need and haven't any time for. What I spend stupidly in the course of the year - and this is no joke, because I've actually kept a record over the last six months - could underwrite a well that ensures fresh water for some African village; or could feed a number of children for six months; or could provide medical supplies, buy books for schools or goodness knows what else. Does it surprise you to know that I'm developing a guilt complex?

The difficulty about having been brainwashed, being conditioned and then trying to swim against the tide of both crass and subtle advertising, is that I need to change my whole way of thinking. That's not easy. And a final cause of deep regret in this society is that valuable initiatives on TV to improve life, and important public campaigns to ensure road safety, healthy living, concern for the environment and care for the least fortunate within the community and beyond its boundaries, just don't have enough time or appeal.

The worst indictment I know of our values has come from Gleneagles. The amount of aid promised is deemed, by established charities and experts on the Third World, to be woefully inadequate. They feel that the millions pledged should be doubled. And a month ago I read of how the head of Barclay's Bank's investment banking division is in line for fifteen million pounds a year. We are talking of a single executive. Chicken feed! There's a US hedge fund manager - don't ask me what that is, but it spells dollars - who, within a year, has pocketed a billion dollars in fees. I can't really speak about the state of Denmark, but something is rotten somewhere, and I feel part of it.

Shall I apologise if I've distressed you? On reflection, I think not.

15th July, 2005.

SLUGS REALLY LIKE VERMICELLI.

We have slugs and snails in the patio. They are discreet and keep themselves to themselves; however, come the night, they will slide out and make their way round and into the kitchen. In the morning we find their silvery trails tracing routes across the kitchen floor where they have gone on their scavenging sorties. Outside, some of our plants look the worse for their ministrations. What to do?

I have no problem with the snails: I just collect them, put them in a box and drive them out to some reasonably verdant spot where I release them. But it's different with slugs. Country slugs are of the slim, jet-black variety. They look tougher and well adapted to heat and dust. My slugs can get fat and are blondes to a ...man? woman? bisexual? (I have not enquired into the matter; what they do in the privacy of the flowerbed is their own business.) The question is this: should I release them into a potentially hostile environment? And the second question is: how can I stop them spoiling my plants?

The answer came to me in a flash recently. It has led to my Feed a Slug and Save a Plant Campaign. So now I leave a smidgeon of the dog's leftovers outside the kitchen door at night. In the morning, the bowl is clean. Slugs appear to be partial to just about anything and have been doing sterling work on bits of vermicelli and they're actually waiting outside the door by eight in the evening - honest! One of them obviously has a watch.

Which leads me directly to this week's subject: crime and punishment. It is truly a direct route: the slugs' "crime" was the damage they did to my plants; the punishment could have been slug pellets, but why make the little perishers suffer unnecessarily? In human terms we have a similar, though immensely more complex, dilemma. Humans gather in groups - be they families, villages, tribes or nations. For the good order of these they evolve ideals, rules and prohibitions. There's always going to be someone who won't subscribe to or abide by these. That is where you get what could be called "crime", and that requires control, which often evolves as punishment. So far, so clear.

In the Wild West, a man in the middle of nowhere really needed a horse. If you stole his horse you might be condemning him to death. Hence "horse thief" became a term of abuse - you couldn't get much lower; and the penalty for that type of theft was probably death, with or without the benefit of a trial. In a small village in medieval England, theft of mangelwurzels might lead to time in the stocks where you became the object of the world's unwelcome attentions as, shackled and helpless, you could be pelted with rotten vegetables - and with worse, if livestock had gone past that spot. You became a laughing stock. I suppose it was a case of letting the punishment suit the crime. And it that vein, it is said that 650 years ago when the longbow, in the hands of English bowmen, was a weapon to be feared, the French if they captured English bowmen in battle, would cut off their middle and forefingers. And at Agincourt and Creçy, the defeated French armies were treated to the sight of triumphant English archers holding up their right hands, palm inwards, with their two crucial fingers raised in triumph. (And I don't care if it's apocryphal or not. As far as I'm concerned, it deserves to be true.)

There's an element of punishment as a deterrent in all those. Which raises the question of what punishment is or can be about. Should it be about retribution? revenge? restitution? reformation? Is its main purpose to protect society? Given the erratic and often illogical evolution of societies, punishment can involve all of these and can serve other and more sinister ends: collectivist societies, whether fascist or communist or monarchic or other, can use punishment as a weapon against the freedom of the individual. It becomes a weapon of control for the perpetuation of a system and not a method of fostering the safety of its members.

Theories come into it. A well-meaning Victorian, a social reformer of some sort, got involved in prison work and devised, according to his lights, the perfect system. He designed the actual building, one that would serve his concept of how to reform prisoners. I stand open to correction on the detail of this because I read about it over thirty years ago, but the basic idea was to give the prisoner every chance to turn to God and learn a better way of life. The cells offered superior accommodation: each prisoner had his own cell, sharing it with nobody. And the chapel was both imaginative and beautifully constructed. Every prisoner had his own small section, screened from the others by dividing panels. Each section had a full view of the altar. The whole chapel was beautifully panelled in wood. Within a couple of months or a year in this environment a prisoner would go barking mad. Why? It was because the system required the total isolation of each man so that he could the better meditate and find God. It was solitary confinement. Even the guards did not disturb his privacy by talking to him. The isolation made life in the prison a living emotional hell of loneliness. The experiment was not repeated and the newly created nervous wrecks were farmed out elsewhere.

Following a different ideal, a judge in Granada has earned a reputation for the creative sentencing of young criminals. In one case, a stunned adolescent was sentenced to serve on a literacy course till he could read and write. A year later, in a televised interview, one saw the benefits to the boy, and to a society he could now have more rewarding access to. Community Service has aimed, perhaps somewhat imperfectly, to do something similar. It has also been a matter of decongesting prisons that have been bursting at the seams. Too many people are in prison either awaiting trial or serving a sentence. In Spain there is a system of compassionate weekend release of prisoners. It hasn't always been intelligently administered and has sometimes turned into a weekend of criminal activity.

There was a period in history when there was apparently less need for reformers because the common villain got away with some short, swift form of punishment like being whipped, put in the stocks, ducked in the village pond or being branded. The ones who ended up in prison might be totally innocent of any crime. They would, however, be dukes or earls or some branch of whatever family might legitimately have a claim to the throne. I suppose it ensured that you met a nicer class of person in jail. Rival claimants to the crown and their relatives could end up in prison or on the scaffold, not necessarily for what they had done, but because of who they were and what they might do. Of such a group came Lady Jane Grey and Mary Queen of Scots, both threats to Elizabeth I and both executed.

Now we have the opposite in many ways. White-collar crime can lead you to open prisons and easier sentences; and blue-jeans crime can land you in the standard sort of jail. And as has been said by many - if you want to learn about crime, prison is the best possible training ground. That's a major issue. A prisoner costs the taxpayer a great deal of money. He or she is put in with others who may have greater criminal expertise. The result is all too often the establishing of a way of life, a life of crime, with prison as a regular part of it. The problem lies in that some crimes respond to the positive approach and some don't seem to. Perhaps it all needs rethinking.

A long way from slugs? Not at all. I'm not talking about feeding all law-breakers on vermicelli. Do I look like a woman with a vermicelli fixation? (Anyway, spaghetti would be more substantial.) It's the principle: what is the purpose of punishment and what do we hope to achieve with it? And what are the effective alternatives to the prison system?

27th August, 2004.

DISCOVERIES, THEORIES AND A TOUCH OF DOTTINESS.

HERE TODAY, GOON TOMORROW.

I wonder how many of you out there take care to avoid any miasma that may be floating around. What? Not one of you? Don't you realize how dangerous it is? Do you actually want to fall sick? Aren't you protecting your children from the pernicious effects of this well-known source of infections?

Of course you aren't; yet, recently enough, any reputable doctor would have lectured you about these toxic vapours. Now that we know about bacteria and viruses we know that the miasma was just one more theory to explain what was not known. Theories also sprang up during outbreaks of the bubonic plague, and with these theories went remedies. That "pocketful of posies" remembered in the nursery rhyme was as much use in fighting the plague as a carrot for igniting rocket fuel.

I am aware that I have been known to mount my hobbyhorse with regard to theories, but, perhaps, my being a teacher has made me ultra sensitive on the subject. A teacher's professional position is a peculiar one: doctors are regarded as authorities in their field; lawyers are not told by government or clients how they should deal with their cases; the local authority does not feel it knows how to fill cavities or extract teeth - that is left to dentists. With teachers, however, there is no similar assumption that the profession knows its business. Nowadays education seems to be a political battlefield; forty years ago it was an academic one. Both battlefields are mined with theories.

"You are wrong, Mary - you can't possibly separate the study of literature from the study of language!" rose the cry when I argued that children doing C.S.E. were doing twice the work for one certificate. It changed a few years later to two subjects and I was suddenly right. "We will introduce modules in every subject," said a headmaster who, when asked to enlighten us, was unable to define a module.

Grammar had to be taught, then grammar was not to be taught formally. Correct spelling was essential: spelling wasn't a priority. And think how many other changes we've seen in the educational system and in exams in the last fifteen years and you'll agree that it's reached the stage where every teaching certificate awarded should carry a government health warning. Ah! Theories! Theories! What's de rigueur one day is old hat the next. In a way, I have nothing against theories: au contraire, I think they are essential for exploring our world. My gripe is that theories, which are milestones on the road to knowledge, are treated as ultimate truths. It's awfully easy to fall in love with any theory you've developed, which is why academics and scientists will shed blood in defence of their ideas and have even been known to cook the books in their research.

Actually, the scientific road is littered with the most splendid theories, now discarded by any but the lunatic fringe - I gather that The Flat Earth Society may still have active members. And alchemy, the precursor of chemistry, occupied men for centuries as they tried to find a way of turning base metals into gold. Perhaps I should not have referred to "the lunatic fringe" because Sir Isaac Newton, who defined the law of gravity, invented the calculus and worked on optics and planetary motions, spent just as much time on alchemy as on these other ventures. And in this year when smoking is all set to be banned in pubs in England we should remember that, once upon a time, all sorts of beneficial effects were attributed to the smoking of tobacco such as cleansing, restoring and reviving some of the body's functions. And so it was, also, with radioactivity. It became fashionable to attribute health-giving properties to it and certain brands of toothpaste and laxative boasted a radioactive component - and such practice was legal till 1938.

Then there was luminiferous ether, a medium that permeated the universe. Newton believed in it; it was basic to nineteenth century physics and was defended as late as the beginning of the twentieth century - and it didn't exist. My favourite theory that has, sadly, bitten the dust, was that held by a Harvard astronomer in the twenties who explained the dark patches on the moon as being caused by swarms of migrating insects. And my favourite theorist is the German, Johann Becher, a perfectly reputable mineralogist, who believed that with work, the right materials and, probably, a bit of luck - he could make himself invisible...but dare I laugh after watching so many episodes of "Star Trek"? And even geniuses who made amazing discoveries failed to see things that would seem obvious to later scientists. The greatest astronomers believed in a static universe; now we know that it is constantly expanding.

Don't be deceived by all this apparent learning on my part. I was the woman who was given Stephen Hawkins' "The History of Time", as I think it was called, a science book for the layman, and I only understood the introduction that had been written by a fellow scientist. The text itself defeated me. So, I'll be honest with you: I'm reading Bill Bryson's "A Short History of Nearly Everything" - again. I manage to follow it for about ninety per cent of the time, which is a credit to him.

One thing that the book has done is to confirm me in my belief that every theory can advance the cause of knowledge either by being correct or by being incorrect. In the first case it offers a firm base for further study: in the second case it offers a wonderful row of intellectual coconuts for others to shy new ideas at, demolish and find a better idea. After all, you have to start somewhere, however mistaken your premise. Consider Archbishop James Usher who concluded in 1650 that the world was created at 12.00 midday on October 23rd in the year 4004 BC. He started something, didn't he? The great Charles Darwin worked out that the Weald in Kent, Surrey and Sussex was 306,662,400 years old. It was too much for folk to swallow. We now hold by a figure of billions. I can't say that we know how old the world is because I imagine there are new theories round the corner, new knowledge and discoveries that may change the picture again.

Which brings me back to where I began. A theory is no more than that. We can trust theories implicitly, which may bring us peace of mind and security, or we can treat them as a challenge, as something to be questioned and tested. The earth travel round the sun? Nonsense: man is the centre of the universe so the sun and every planetary body circles around us. Those who accepted this were safe; those who questioned it were in trouble with church and state. Theories become holy cows. And when new theories come along to replace them, there can be serious trouble. Every new idea that has pushed science further, if it challenged an existing and firmly held theory, has had a rocky passage. Vested financial interests have nothing on vested academic interests and the emotional charge generated by bruised academic egos.

Cynics may see the bandwagon potential of new ideas, but for the average lesser being it is a matter of developing a critical eye and a healthy disrespect for theories - what an educationalist called "Inbuilt crap detectors" - as far as possible.

17th December, 2004.

SERENDIPITY.

When you look at a pig, I don't suppose your first thoughts are: "Let's go pick some apples and then set fire to the house."

Roast pork and apple sauce are what I'm talking about, and about a story I first heard when I was in junior school - one of the tales written by Mary and Charles Lamb. The story was set in China, I think, in that apocryphal time of far away and long ago. People lived in primitive huts and they kept pigs. They ate their meat as they ate everything else - raw. Then one day a hut caught fire and the family pig died before they could rescue it. As they snatched the smoking carcass from the flames, they burnt their fingers and instinctively put them in their mouths to soothe the pain.

Anyone who likes crackling will realize, as did the owners of the pig, that there's a world of difference between raw and cooked pork. Because it just wasn't done to burn meat, they took the carcass away and feasted mightily and secretly on it. However, word leaked out. I expect they came back to the village looking greasy round the mouth and rounder about the waist. The next thing was that another hut burnt down complete with pig. So it went on till there was a danger that no house would last out the week. I expect that was when the elders took a hand in regulating matters and when someone pointed out that a costume-built fire would serve the same purpose and would give architecture a chance to develop.

Serendipity is about happy chance, about making fortunate discoveries by accident. I'm pretty sure that many a major discovery is the result of an initial bit of serendipity. What on earth led the Sumerians to make beer in around 3000 BC? To make beer you need some sort of vegetable matter and then you ferment it with the aid of yeast. Was it a careless housewife or farmer who'd left the ingredients lying around, too close to each other and for too long, and who discovered, rather late in the day, that the veg. was inedible? And was the discovery the result of a cautious tasting of what was there? I'm sure that the refining of the process took time, but the initial idea would hardly have come full-blown into someone's mind.

Penicillin became big news when I was a child and we all heard the story of its chance discovery. It was, we were told, one of a number of cultures being studied for something or other. Then someone chanced to notice that bacteria were getting short shrift on this particular Petri dish and, presto! Well, "presto" in the sense that the contents of the dish were investigated further and led to the identification and production of what we know as penicillin.

I expect the same thing happened with sand and it may well have happened in the desert as anywhere else. My dictionary informs me that glass is a solid consisting of metal silicates or similar compounds. My husband tried to give me a crash course in silicates and metals. He always forgets that I never studied any chemistry whatsoever. I did manage to narrow his information down to the matter in hand and he admitted that sand fits in with the silicates' profile. So, subject your sand to a lot of heat and it begins to change and becomes glass at some point. Did it happen round a camp fire or next to some metal smelting furnace or pottery kiln? The element of chance must surely have been present because sand doesn't look remotely like glass and, furthermore, you can't even imagine glass before it's been invented, any more than you can imagine something like trensonar molecules before you've read about them.

And what made someone decide to unravel a cocoon and find that the fibre could be spun and would produce what we now value as silk? Maybe it was some bored little children with nothing to do one fine day. Can't you just see them at it and mum coming up behind them.

"Chou-lin and Chin-chou! How many times have I told you not to mess about with mucky insects? Throw that rubbish away and wash your hands. It's time for lunch."

And the discovery had to wait another thousand years till someone became curious about the possibilities.

And carrier pigeons were, one imagines, not actually *trained* to return home over hundreds of miles. I mean, birds will return to nest or food supply, but how do you train that homing instinct? Do you hurl them into space strapped to a supersonic boomerang to ensure their return? Carrier pigeons have been in use for around 2500 years so it isn't long enough for man's intervention to have hastened the evolutionary process. The homing instinct must have been there and someone must have thought of using them for the purpose of communication.

Some happy discoveries are not so much the result of chance as, perhaps, of laziness or desperation or circumstances. A friend told us how he had landed off a ship somewhere on the West Coast of the USA and ordered breakfast at a quayside café. He wanted coffee, fruit juice and bacon and eggs.

"With or without?" said the waitress.

Apparently, you order your bacon and eggs with jam - or without if you're being awkward. Was that "discovery" the result of a rather bare larder? Back to the opening of this article. What put the idea of apple sauce and pork into someone's mind? Or gammon steak and pineapple, or gammon and peach? Why cranberry sauce with turkey?

As for the case of desperation, who but a very hungry person would consider snails as food? Now, I think snails are delicate and graceful and I enjoy watching them. I may remove them from my few flowerbeds, but only to relocate them in some fertile patch of countryside. I may watch them with pleasure, but I don't feel my salivary glands in full spate at the sight of them. The same applies to frogs' legs. I also like frogs and toads and lizards, but only extreme hunger and a lack of other sources of food would make me look upon any of them as a potential breakfast - with or without.

What was once the food of the poor and hungry is now for those who can afford it, as is the case with oysters and gin.

But whose idea was it to put together steak tartare? The thought of raw onion is great. Raw egg I have no objection to. Condiments are fine by me. But to mix them together to bind raw minced beef is a little, shall we say, unexpected. Remember the Rowan Atkinson sketch of Mr Bean ordering steak tartare, the cheapest thing on the menu, and then trying to dispose of it when he realised what it was?

It must have been a form of serendipity that led John Montague to make one of the great breakthroughs in fast food, way back in the 18th century. He was such a gamblerholic that he couldn't bear to leave the gaming tables even for a meal. He was the 4th Earl of Sandwich. Need I say more?

Don't you hate it when you fail to find the last couple of words in a crossword and have to wait till the following week for the answers? I certainly do. And I should hate to think of any reader going away and trying to find out about the exact nature of the "trensonar molecules" I mentioned earlier.

I'll come clean. The bit I was writing required something you had never heard about so I felt I had no option. There you have it: I made them up.

7th May, 2004.

THANK YOU, ELISHA OTIS.

Why do we have skyscrapers? What made such structures possible and practicable? I've carried out a survey, asking precisely those questions....yes, a modest survey... so I only asked six people: satisfied? As I was saying before your scepticism interrupted my train of thought: what made high-rise buildings a working proposition? Why skyscrapers? I got the following replies:
1. Use of reinforced concrete.
2. Use of steel girders.
3. That stuff – what's it called?
4. Big machines.

5. Cantilever construction – (don't ask me, I just took down what was said.)
6. How should I know?

The real answer is….because of Elisha Otis. He was the man who invented the first safety elevator - the lift. It makes sense, doesn't it? Imagine trying to walk up ninety flights of steps. Say you stood five feet six in your sock: you'd arrive at the penthouse measuring five foot three, having worn your legs down to the anklebone. A couple more trips down to get a packet of cornflakes, to take the dog for a walk or to retrieve the door key that you left at your friend's house, and you would have been reduced to little more than a wobbly head on a pair of raggedy shoulders.

I remember a holiday in Paris when a friend found an attic flat for us to stay in - free of charge! It was small, basic and simply furnished: all of which suited us fine. It was also on the sixth floor. My husband, furthermore, had found an excellent book that detailed interesting Paris Walks. It *is* surely the best way to see Paris. So we walked. We walked solidly for ten days and laboured up and down those stairs several times a day. Those who meet me now have no idea that I was once a willowy five foot eight.

I'm sure there are older people in old properties in Gibraltar who may enjoy grand views of the bay from their windows, but who, when they come home from the supermarket loaded with the week's shopping, would give their eye-teeth (whatever they may be) for a ground floor flat or a lift.

So there you have Otis, benefactor and inventor. I wonder if he invented anything else? Some inventors seem to go in for the Big Break and they become famous for one thing and one alone. When you think of Marconi, you think, not of pasta as I did as a child, but of radio-telegraphy; and Edison devised the first practical electric light - so did a man called J.W. Swan, as it happens, but he's somehow been forgotten, though he later worked with Edison to produce Ediswan electric lamps. And there was Herr Diesel - Rudolph to his friends - with his engine; and what of Count Ferdinand von Zeppelin and the airship?

It's pretty obvious that they all did more than just have one brilliant idea and then fold their arms and do nothing else. They must, at least, have spent some years revising and refining and coming up with new improvements or minor inventions en route. There is one prolific inventor, whose name is so little heard that I've forgotten it, who was responsible for any number of mundane inventions that have made life a great deal easier for all of us. One of the many things he came up with that concertina-like hood that stops you being blown about as you move from the airport corridor into the plane. This man could not stop inventing. Wherever he saw a problem, a source of discomfort, an inefficient piece of equipment, he set to and improved or invented as was needed. Thanks to him we enjoy a more comfortable lifestyle generally. He is just one of the unsung benefactors of society.

His style of operating was clearly logical: he came; he saw; he invented. I suppose he went around noting problems and then went home to sort them out, to experiment and to find solutions. That is one way of doing things: you deliberately sit down to work on a specific task. That involves using the left hemisphere of your brain. That's the logical one. Then there's the other way of making important discoveries which occurs when you are occupied thinking of what you are going to have for supper or you are watching a sunset or, even, when you may be picking your nose.

If we consider Newton's theory about the force of gravity, we get a mental picture of him sitting under a tree, with a falling apple headed right for his head. The left side of his brain probably registered the event as a warning to sit elsewhere in future, and it was probably the right side of his brain - the artistic, creative, intuitive one - that cottoned on to what gravity was about. It's like the wheel. The Aztecs developed an advanced civilization. Let's forget the nasty habit they had of indulging in human sacrifice and let's think of their ability to pronounce names like Quetzalcoatl and Huitzilopochtli, of their expertise with textiles and their amazingly complex and accurate work on calendars. Yet, despite such achievements, they had not discovered the wheel. Now the Sumerians were using wheeled vehicles at least four thousand years before that. As the Aztecs clearly had brains enough between them to overcome all sorts of architectural problems, and to do so to the admiration of our own age, why hadn't they come up with the wheel?

My own theory is that they weren't giving the right sides of their brains a chance. I don't suppose some early Sumerian actually sat down with a twig and a smooth expanse of sand and thought, "I should really invent something circular that rolls along." It's much more likely that he was watching his son rolling pebbles down a slope. The son was thirteen and should have been doing something useful like milking the donkey or watering the vegetable patch.

"For Jana's sake, get off your backside and do something useful," said dad.

And when the boy slouched off, dad began to roll the pebbles down the slope. And it was probably some time later, perhaps when he was picking his...teeth, that he realised the possibilities of circular objects that rolled along. And, talking of wheels, I love the bit in one of the "Carry On" films when Kenneth Connor as an Ancient Brit, invents the wheel and shows it off proudly to Jim Dale.

"I shall call it 'A WINDOW'," he says triumphantly as he fits it into the wall of his cave.

And outside the cave the carts are bumping and thumping along on square "wheels". That's probably because both sides of the brain were dormant at that point. All of which gives me a number of ideas on inventors and inventions that I should like to follow up. Too many, in fact. Perhaps I should give the left side of my brain a rest. That means abandoning logic, sequential thinking, deliberate intellectual activity and any attempt to write further for today.

1st August, 2003.

FANTASY, PURE FANTASY AND THEORIES.

Continued reading of Bill Bryson's "A Short History of Nearly Everything" has helped me further crystallise some ideas on the question of theories. The wonderful thing about theories is that anyone can develop them and feel dead right. The terrible thing about theories is that anyone can develop them and feel dead right.

The book itself is splendid. It is a book to be taken slowly and considered carefully and it is jam-packed with detail, information and the kind of facts that seem to come out of science fiction. Great stuff! Just imagine: a baseball thrown at 160 kilometres an hour will pick up .000000000002 grams of mass on its trajectory back to base...or whatever it's called in baseball. The weight of the earth is 5,9725 billion, trillion tonnes (- if you want your answer in kilos, then just multiply that by 1,000). And the earliest forms of life on earth probably arose about 3.85 billion years ago. Aren't you glad I've told you all this?

But this is by way of being a digression and there's a limit to how much of that sort of information we can actually take in and remember later. The book is also chock-a-block with theories once held firmly and now discarded, or now held firmly in opposition to other, different theories held equally firmly. Theorists can even disagree with their own theories. The great Einstein came up with the "cosmological constant" which he was later to call "the biggest blunder in my life". Science agreed with this judgement for, at the time, the universe was seen as fixed and eternal. Now that it is seen as constantly expanding, Einstein's idea is no longer seen as a blunder at all.

One thing that really delighted me was the fact that so many of the scientists of one sort or another who have been trail blazers appear to have been fruitcakes too; and that men who came up with amazing theories and insights into the universe could also hold other ideas that were ridiculous by anyone's standards.

If we cast a look at the past, we find that the road to knowledge is littered with the corpses of dead theories, some of which took a long time to die and whose death throes were prolonged by scientists who refused to take new ideas on board. The road is also littered with dead scientists who were way ahead of their time and whose ideas were ignored, rejected or actively attacked by the established authorities.

We all know that Galileo set the cat among the pigeons when he refined Copernicus's idea of a sun-centred universe. For claiming that the earth was not the hub of everything he was forced to recant by the church/inquisition and ended his days under house arrest. Yet he was right and they were wrong. Then you get someone like Franz Josef Gall who "discovered", "documented" and popularised phrenology - a theory now totally discredited, which theory explained how the personality and character of a person could be established and explored by analysing the shape of the skull's indentations, convexities et cetera: i.e. a lumps-and-dents-and-bumps study. He made a great living out of it and probably died a happy and wealthy man for all the nonsense he'd propagated.

That's the trouble with theories. How do you distinguish arrant nonsense from incomprehensible fact? So much depends on the age in which you live and the ideas generally current at the time that it is hard to be either wise or objective.

Does anyone remember that horrendous term, "refrigerator mother"? It was coined to account for autism in children. If the child was apparently incapable of relating to others it *must* be because its mother was unloving. Someone developed a theory and, ipso facto, it became - not speculation, but - truth. The same happened with anorexia. The parents - father included in this case - became the villains of the piece because a theory was developed that anorexia was caused by having authoritarian parents. In neither case were the real facts addressed. I'm talking about the fact that most autistic children are boys and most anorexics are girls.

This would seem to point to the fact that some physical root-cause was a possible reason for these disturbances. But the age we happen to live in dictates our views and denies us vision too often and it was the age of psychology when Freud ruled OK. Furthermore, those powerful academics who held the theory of Nurture over Nature made belief in neurological differences between the sexes into something politically suspect.

In my childhood my grandmother used to make me wrap a scarf round mouth and nose if we went out at night because, as she said:

"El aire de la noche es muy traicionero" - Night air was treacherous indeed.

A character in an old Western says, "The white man does not take scalps." And how many, many films have we seen where the American Red Indian collected scalps as war trophies. Did the Indians do this? Absolutely! It was a custom that they learnt from the white men; yet the theory that found acceptance was that the barbaric custom originated with the Indians. Hyenas were also deeply misunderstood till relatively recently. They were seen as eaters of carrion, as scavengers. Their appearance was, I'm sure, held against them and they seem to have a distorted sense of humour. Now it appears that they are highly organised and are probably the most efficient nocturnal hunters in Africa.

By contrast, the King of the Beasts has always had good press - the noble lion, the great predator with its mighty mane of gold. It's amazing what a good hairstyle will do for your image! The truth of the matter is that the lionesses are the hunters of the pride; that the lion will eat his fill before letting the rest of the pride get a look in; that he will kill any cubs that he has not fathered. Another theory bites the dust.

There's one theory in the field of art that is currently doing the rounds which justifies any production as "a reflection of the society in which we live". Such a theory surely could be used to justify something like the Snuff Movies that circulate secretly, those films where a rape is actually a rape; where torture seen on the screen is really being inflicted and where a murder is precisely that. Isn't art much more than a mere reflection of something?

Having said all that about theories, I will now admit that I'm filled with awe for the mental accomplishments of scientists on the whole. And I admit the importance of theories. We develop them to try and make sense of many facets of life. It is not surprising that we fall into error or come up with what will later seem hare-brained ideas. I mean, we are gradually moving to some understanding of the universe. Each theory provides a challenge to our perceptions and perspectives to the point that they eventually lead to the evolution of new theories.

There lies the crux of the matter. Theories constitute an evolutionary process. Anyway, that's my theory.

14th November, 2003.

ONCE UPON A TIME...

THE BOUNTY HUNTERS.

Don Narciso was a man of standing in the town: he owned a large herd of goats, two dozen cows and a bakery. He also owned a good deal of land that he leased to lesser men who paid him in kind with olives, grapes and wine - and he was the mayor of Salto Grande. To the young men he was the potential employer. To the young women he was the aging gallant with a roving eye and roaming hands; and to the old he was "El Tisnao de Pampera", for he was not a local man and when he had arrived in Salto Grande as a charcoal burner, the nickname "The Sooty One" had suited him admirably. Not that anyone used the name publically any longer. It was "Don Narciso" and "Señor" and a tug at the forelock.

As the old folk were fond of saying, he had done well for himself.

His was not the story of a man risen to great things by the sweat of his brow. He did, however, have the sharpest of blue eyes. He had seen that the town was virtually owned by the Gaviras - Don Francisco and his daughter, Paca. She, in her turn, had seen the young charcoal burner one day as he stood on his mighty bee-hive of an oven, dangerously close to the opening at the top that was beginning to smoke like a threatening volcano. He had turned and stared at her and she had seen his eyes, aquamarines in a blackened face.

It had been easy enough for Narciso after that. The fact that she was eight years his senior and that she took after her father did not put him off; and her stubbornness had its advantages. She was headstrong enough to make herself the talk of the town with her pursuit of the young charcoal burner, and he had left it up to her to win her father over. Don Francisco had first tried bribing Narciso.

Narciso was noble: "I am not for sale. I love Paca. She loves me; she is a passionate woman."

He had walked away rapidly, letting the possibilities of that "passionate woman" sink into the father's mind. Not that he had bedded Paca yet. No need to face that before it was necessary.

The father turned to Paca. He was a man used to giving orders: "You will give up this stupidity. I forbid you to see that man again. He is scum. If you even speak to him, I shall disinherit you and throw you out. You will beg for your bread."

Paca did not have her father's way with words. She stood in the middle of the room with its large windows that overlooked the town square and she unbuttoned her jacket. Then she unfastened her skirt and pulled it down. Then, off came the first petticoat and her blouse. With some difficulty, for she was a little corpulent, she set to on her stays.

Don Francisco was appalled; he had never seen even his wife undressing; she would never have permitted it.

"Are you mad? What are you doing?"

"I am taking my clothes off. I will walk out of here in my shift and I shall beg for my bread," then she added with a rare touch of inspiration, "like Saint Francis."

He caved in. Paca and Narciso were married and she was surprisingly happy, now and then. They had one child, Paquita, who took after her mother in many ways.

One day a gypsy family came to the town. The eldest son had aquiline features. He had narrow hips and a small waist. His eyes were cool grey and he noted who the wealthiest man in the town was.

The old people looked on: "He will do well for himself," they began to say.

5th September, 2003.

THE LAST SHEPHERD.

I am glad that a man of learning like you wants to take down my words. You heard me talking in the tavern, didn't you?

It must have been late in the spring because we had our flock out on the hillside during the night. Mild it was. One of those clear nights when the sky looks clean and black and the stars are like distant candles. The men were round the fire and I had been set to watch the sheep. I was still a lad and I did as I was told, but the sheep were all huddled together and there had been no talk of wolves for weeks, so it was little enough I had to do.

Then something happened. What did I see and hear that night? Well, Sir, it's hard to tell. I recall my own words, the words I used to my mother the next day, but words aren't enough. As I stood on that hillside above Bethlehem, watching the lights that still shone from some of the houses, I felt myself growing cold, as if I had plunged into a river in the early morning. And the next thing was that my whole body tingled and grew warm. I began to be afraid for I had heard of how evil could enter the body of a man and steal his soul. There was something in the air, like music or like voices singing; one long note that filled my head. The sound was very beautiful so I stood very still. I was afraid that if I moved it might all change and I didn't want it to change. My eyes were still fixed on the lights of the town and one of them began to grow brighter and brighter and seemed to be coming closer to us on the hill. It came so close that I could make out that it was a lantern hanging from one of the beams of a stable. There was a man settling his donkey for the night and a woman lying on a bed of straw. Then she opened her eyes wide and called out, though I could not hear her words, and the man was there beside her, kneeling on the ground. The light from the lantern grew brighter and brighter till I had to close my eyes, and I was filled with a feeling of calm - as if nothing could ever go wrong in my life.

When I opened my eyes, it was dark again and some of the sheep were stirring and bleating softly. The men were all standing up, wrapping their blankets round them, getting ready to move off, agitated and all speaking at once.

"Stay with the sheep!" one of them called out to me.

They went and did not return till daybreak. They had seen a child, a king, a prophet. He had been born down in the town next to Samuel of Sidon's inn, in the old stable. It had been bright daylight in the stable and the hay had looked like gold. Each one of them had something different to say. They had heard voices; they had seen spirits; the Almighty had spoken to them.

It happened some weeks before the killings began. No one knew what set the massacres off. One minute Herod was away in his palace, leaving us to lead our own lives as best we could, and the next, his edict went out and his soldiers swept through the countryside like ravening locusts, destroying our lives: every male child still being suckled was seized and put to death on the spot. You can have no idea, Sir, of the horror of those days. The only sound to be heard was the wailing of the women and the cries of the men. My own mother had a boy child at the breast and he was torn from her and his head was smashed against the wall of our house.

I was only thirteen summers old, but I swore vengeance. There was born my thirst for justice. I couldn't be happy keeping the flock for my father. It took me three years before I could leave, but leave I did. My mother gave me her blessing, though I think she had guessed that I was not going to stay with my Uncle Joshua for very long. He provided me with the perfect excuse to get to Jerusalem. I wanted to find the rebels I had heard speak of. There were men ready to fight against Herod and his allies, the Romans, and I was ready to join them. I was big for my age, with a man's strength.

For nearly thirty years I was a rebel with a price on my head. I began as the lowest and became one of the leaders, but we never succeeded in destroying either Herod or the Romans. We were like a swarm of mosquitoes that bit and irritated and made them sicken at times, but we were too few and we lacked a real leader to unite us. Then I heard tell of a new prophet who defied Herod publicly. I sought the man out; he was called John the Baptizer and I found him by the River Jordan, preaching repentance. He was not the leader for me. I had killed men, Herod's men and Caesar's men, but I did not repent of that; I rejoiced in it. Mind you, that prophet was a brave man. Brave but rash and they executed him. But he had spoken of a greater prophet who would follow him and I set off to find him.

This one was different. I heard him preaching a couple of times. I saw him drive the merchants and money-lenders from the temple. I wondered if he could be the man we needed, but he talked of the wrong things. When he was asked what allegiance we owed to Caesar, he took a coin and pointed to the head stamped on it. "Render to Caesar the things that are Caesar's and to G-d the things that are G-d's." He was no use to me. A man like that might be a good lawyer or a good rabbi, but he was not the man to lead a revolution.

And then they got me. I had grown careless and shown myself in public once too often. It was prison and, for sedition, the penalty was death. I can see that you find that hard to believe. You are thinking, "If he was condemned to death, how is he here today? Is he just spinning a yarn?"

No tall tale, just the honest truth. They dragged me out of my cell one day and took me to where a great multitude had gathered. Standing there was the prophet. Now he'd learn what Caesar would render to him! Then someone was calling out to the crowds. One man could have a pardon that day; one could be released and the other would be crucified. Which was it to be? Who was to go free?

"Barrabas!" the cry went up in reply.

When I heard my name, I felt my knees give under me. I was free. I looked across at the prophet who merely stood silent. And then it happened for the second time in my life: I felt my body go cold as if I had plunged into a morning stream and then my body began to glow with warmth. I heard a long, beautiful note in the air and the prophet disappeared before a blaze of light that made me close my eyes. I thought I was back on that hillside overlooking Bethlehem, but when I opened them again, the crowd still shouted my name and the prophet was being dragged away.

I never understood it, Sir...what did you say your name was? Ah, Saul of Tarsus. Well, Sir, that is my tale and when it is written, I will set my mark on it, for every word is true.

23rd December, 2005.

THE BEAR TRUTH.

Aesop never wrote his fables for children, in fact, to be strictly correct, he never wrote them - he *told* them and they were not written down till well after his death. And the brothers Grimm didn't write their tales for the entertainment of impressionable young minds. Do you recall the fate of some of the villains in those Grimm tales? - and grim they were. I never forgot one, the villainess of the piece, who was sealed in a barrel into which had been driven six-inch nails; it was then rolled down a long, steep hill. And folk tales from the north of Europe give their heroes and heroines almost as hard a time during the tales as the villains have at the end. There's the girl who had to wear out three pairs of iron shoes wandering around the world to find the lover she has lost. And why, pray? Because he came to her by night and she was forbidden to see his face. Be honest; if it had been you, wouldn't you have been just a wee bit curious? Wouldn't you have sneaked a candle into the bedroom and lit it when he was asleep? You, however, might have been less careless than the girl, who managed to drip a few drops of melted wax on to his chest. He awoke and deserted her. And, to cap it all, once she set off in search of him, all she had by way of an address was "East o' the Sun and West o' the Moon". No postal code, no nothing.

Heroes fared little better, but at least they were proactive and did things like fight dragons and pit their wits against witches and magicians. They met gnomes who helped or hindered them, talking animals with clues to give and had the odd magic sword or cloak of invisibility to aid their efforts. They needed all the help they could get because they sometimes had to serve for seven years before reaching their goal.

I love all the old stories, just as, from the first time I heard them, I loved the perfection of form and content of Aesop's fables. I have dabbled in the genre on occasion and have been searching high and low for those I wrote years ago. I finally found just the one, which I offer you now.

*   *   *   *   *   *

There was once a god-fearing family of bears. There was a mother bear, a father bear and several sons and daughters of varying sizes. The males were liberal-minded bears who took an interest in world and local politics. The women folk had a narrower perspective and believed that their cooking was better than anyone else's.

One day the father attended a civic meeting. The usual factions were there and the father had determined that he would speak out for the nameless, underprivileged bears who knew everything about the forest, but couldn't write it down. He spoke. Like Caesar, he conquered, to some extent at least. A rousing ovation and the consequent euphoria made him invite his most enthusiastic supporters home for a drink and a bite to eat.

Mother Bear grumbled when she saw them coming. You couldn't offer them porridge at that time of night, and there wasn't enough whisky. The daughters also grumbled as they prepared sandwiches and made Irish coffee. By the time the men sat down, the table was covered with the second-best tablecloth and the fire was blazing. The women smiled and, in a sudden glow of hospitality, served the men so that they could get down to hard discussion.

There followed many such evenings. A new pressure group was formed. It took a while to decide on a name and, by a narrow majority, they settled for "The Bear Socialist Movement". There was some dissatisfaction with the name and several bears left. The weeks ran their course; a constitution was drawn up; it was transcribed onto parchment and copies on plain foolscap were circulated to all members. The bears met often and talked late into the night. They had discussion groups to set up, surveys to carry out, and a recruitment policy to settle. They also needed to keep the public informed and they all felt they had a real aim in life. It was as well because they needed a sense of purpose when they met with adversity, which they surely did.

Mother Bear, her daughters and all the womenfolk indirectly involved with the movement, carried on their ordinary lives. They managed, just about, to feed the numerous members who attended one or another of their houses on a daily basis, and they had no sense of purpose to sustain them so they had to do the sweeping, washing and cooking without knowing they were on the side of the angels.

And when the blizzards of winter threatened, many abandoned THE CAUSE - they did think of it in capital letters - and the movement began to break up. The women were not worried by the political implications and didn't seem to care that such a force for good had been lost. They were too busy worrying about their empty storage bins and trying to find food enough to see that their families were fit for their long, hard hibernation.

The bears of the forest survived the winter very well because they knew everything about the forest even though they couldn't write it down. Months later, the members of TBSM came out of hibernation looking the worse for wear, and the womenfolk still believed that their cooking was better than anyone else's.

The moral of the story, and there has to be a moral to any self-respecting fable - well, you've got me there. One moral to be drawn is that it was all too easy for a female writing forty years ago to typecast her own sex while seeing the value of women. I seem to glimpse several other morals. When you find them, do let me know.

11th February, 2005.

MISSY - A STORY.

There was a time when I went twice a month to the dirty little house in La Linea to help her or to sit and talk to her while the sun shone outside and I avoided looking at the clock on the sideboard. It must have rained sometimes, but I was still half a child and my memories are of sunshine. Even sorrow was exhilarating in its intensity and I know I was glad to sacrifice my pleasure to visit her.

I forget the connection now, but she was somehow related to someone who was related to us. For some reason we had taken to calling her "Missy", and it made her unreal, displaced, an ageing woman with a girl's name. One of her brothers had emigrated to the Argentine and the other lived in Algeciras with his young mistress. Missy lived alone in one of the crumbling houses in a back street near the bullring. There were neighbours, but she had fallen out with them, or they with her, so when we crossed the frontier every other Sunday to visit a great aunt, I would go to see Missy.

She never went out, but spent her days squatting in an old rocking chair like an inoffensive toad. It was only when she stood up that you realized how small she was. She would prop herself up with her crutch and swing her body forward, her useless left leg making her look like a rag-doll. She was forever treating her leg with large gauze patches which she bought from a "curandero", a quack, who peddled his cures door to door; and I would watch her apply them to the brown, spongy wound that never got any better. Life in that dark house with its acrid smell of damp was of a horrific and reassuring monotony: no friends, no future, a dead present, and faint echoes of some sort of past.

Sometimes Missy would laugh at nothing that I could see. The sound jarred, as if she had never known how to be amused. One winter her brother appeared in the house. He was ill and his mistress had left him. I arrived one Sunday to find him lying on a makeshift bed in the kitchen; there was nowhere else. And he began to die there. He once spoke of his son: the boy was seven, and the father was seventy-three when he died the following spring. There was no sorrow, only a death, and the kitchen was empty once more. Sometimes Missy talked of her mother or of the brother who had gone to make his fortune: she always said the same things and we were bored - her mother had been beautiful and her father had been stern. My grandmother told a different tale:

"That man was a big, ugly drunk, but a quiet one. And her mother was," she shrugged, "just an ordinary woman."

Once or twice Missy spoke of her fiancé, long dead, and I did not know how to believe her. Then one day she showed me a faded photo of a sturdily built young man, a very young man, staring at the camera from behind large, blonde whiskers. From a drawer she took out a small bundle of letters tied with what might once have been pink ribbon.

"He was an English soldier. His hair was the colour of straw: I used to laugh at him because he had an old man's head." She laughed her hacking laugh, "We couldn't talk because he was English. An English soldier from Gibraltar. He was a 'corporal'," she spoke the word as if she were tasting rather than speaking it, "that's a 'cabo' in Spanish. His name was Yoni."

"Johnny?" I felt the need to say something.

"My sister was walking out with his friend and Yoni wanted us all to go out together, so he came one day in a horse-drawn carriage - such a fine one - and all the neighbours came out to look, but my mother didn't like us to go out alone with men so we stayed home."

I remember that her sister had died some years before, a spinster who lived elsewhere on the other side of La Linea.

"So Yoni went and got me a ring and we went out together, but with my mother so that nobody could talk. I have the ring here. It has a real stone."

She scrabbled around in the sideboard and found an old biscuit tin. Inside it was a small box: she took out the ring with its grimy stone. I tried to sound enthusiastic, but she wasn't listening.

"They sent him to England. It is a big country. He wrote to me. Here," she handed me a card from the meagre bundle of letters. "See what he said; read it; go on." She urged me, anxious that I should know how he had cared for her. The words on the card said nothing: he was happy in Aldershot; he was busy. The script was big and the words were few. "Here, take his photo; look at it over there by the window where the light is better. Read the letters." She pressed them into my hand. "Read them to me in Spanish."

I translated them, to please her, while she tried to anticipate me - "Is that the one where he says he was going to buy a car to take me out? He was a crazy Englishman! No one had a car in those days." She laughed again. "Read the other ones."

I have forgotten what Johnny wrote about in his careful, schoolboy writing. He had little to say and she had never written back.

"I never went to school," she grimaced, "and I didn't know English. He was so funny. He came from a place in England where it was very cold. He liked my hair, and he took me out in a carriage with two horses." She nodded her head, "Two horses. Then they sent him to India. It's there in that letter with the different stamp. There was a war."

She paused and began to put the letters back in their envelopes. "He was killed out there. Such a fine boy. It was so funny to hear him trying to speak to me in Spanish. Look." She handed me a last letter. "You read it. Yoni didn't write for a year. My mother had a friend who worked in Gibraltar for a captain in the navy, so she asked him to help and he wrote a letter for us. He got this letter back that said Yoni had been killed. Read it. I was eighteen. We were going to get married. Such a fine boy."

I looked at the envelope: "On his Majesty's Service" said the black print and I thought of the young man meeting with a violent death in some Indian skirmish and of Missy slowly dying in peacetime. I read the officer's words. He wrote briefly. Perhaps he had had to answer too many such enquiries - Johnny, I forget his surname, had left the army some months before; his address was not known. The officer could not help.

I looked at the woman in front of me and cleared my throat. "It must have been terrible for you to find out that he...had died," I heard myself say.

She was pleased to hear me, "Yes, it was very bad." There was no sorrow left, but Missy needed her young lover and she talked on with a coyness that repelled me and made me feel inadequate.

"That letter," I hesitated, wanting to warn her, but I found no way of doing so. "That letter...it's a sad letter."

She nodded and smiled, then put everything away carefully while I sat and avoided looking at the clock on the sideboard.

7th January, 2005.

LITTLE GIRLS DON'T.

"It'll do you good!" Miss Hedges had said bracingly; it was one of her rallying cries.

She abounded in energy and in enthusiasm for her elderly evening-class students - all of them to be chivvied along and bullied kindly into creative writing. "I want a short story in under forty words," she had beamed at them, "you can do it!" That was another rallying cry.

Rosemary typed out the words: "One firm push and he was over the low wall and into the well. They ran away, screaming in triumph. Everything would be fine now. After all, little girls don't commit murder, do they?"

It had been so hard to write. Too many images and ideas crowded her mind. After sixty years, the farm in Suffolk was blurred in her memory, but she remembered the well - and Uncle George, of course.

The offer of free holidays had been a godsend, hadn't it? With the twins - Rosemary and Poppy - and Baby George, and a low salary and so many bills and Mummy herself unfit for work outside the home because of her "condition". Yes, a godsend. Rosemary could still hear her mother's voice reciting its growing litany of complaints until Uncle George would step in.

"Come on then, Lad," he would say gruffly to Daddy. "Take that lovely wife of yours out for the day. Blow away the cobwebs; do you both good. I'll look after the girls."

And Mummy, Daddy and Baby would set off; and Rosemary and Poppy would stare after them.

The first holiday had been wonderful. It had been 1947. Daddy looked different in the country. He shed his shabby de-mob suit for a shirt and a pair of worn corduroy trousers held up with an old tie. Even Mummy looked happier and Baby had been content to lie on a blanket in the shade of the pear tree. Rosemary wished she had talked to Poppy about those holidays, but Poppy had died last year. Rosemary had visited her every day in hospital even after Poppy had stopped talking and seemed not to see or hear her. Then, one day, Poppy's bed was stripped and her body gone.

The nurse was apologetic: they had tried phoning, but there had been no answer. She was so sorry. Perhaps Miss Murray would like a cup of tea before going "downstairs"? The word "mortuary" was not used. Rosemary had let herself be led away. The nurse had been kind and reassuring:

"She slipped away quietly. Just spoke your name and a few words and then closed her eyes. It often happens like that. She said something like, 'Rosemary, we should have...' and that was all. She never finished the sentence. As I said, she just slipped away peacefully."

Yes, she wished she could talk to Poppy about it all, but Poppy had never wanted to talk. In sixty years they had not spoken of what lay between them, giving life a particular ugliness.

Now she sat and the scene pushed its way into her mind: Uncle George leaning over the wall and Poppy and herself creeping up behind him as they had planned. Hating him. Uncle George whose hands touched you and lifted up your cheap cotton dress and made you touch him. They had wanted to hear him scream as he fell down into the mossy darkness. They had wanted him to struggle in the water, battered but not quickly dead, till he drowned.

Rosemary pulled the sheet of paper out of the typewriter. It was so true: "Little girls don't commit murder," and, as Poppy had said, "We should have."

Rosemary carefully tore the sheet into small pieces.

19th March, 2004.

NATURE, NURTURE AND THE LITTLE GREY CELLS.

LEFT SIDE OR RIGHT SIDE?

No one can deny the ancient Romans their efficiency and thoroughness. They had their society pegged down firmly in sections and layers, each with different legal rights and privileges - or lack of them - and duties. The principle was that if anything moved, they categorized it. To get an idea of their approach, you only have to look at the roads they built. They built to last and they built dead straight. If there was a hillock in the way, then it was tough luck for the hillock.

They were a nation on the move and in a hurry - they conquered, organised, ruled, spread further and conquered some more, ad nauseam. They were great believers in law and order, and they were also thieves. Oh, yes, they were. For one thing, they stole their gods from the Greek Pantheon: like, they took Poseidon and called him Neptune - QED. It saved a lot of hassle and it saved time. They also stole from Greek architecture. Why waste time creating when you saw it ready-made and up for grabs?

Perhaps that explains the system of Roman numerals. They couldn't waste time waiting for inspiration to come, for the right cerebral hemisphere to kick in - an uncertain process that could not be relied on to bring quick results. So they set to ferociously with the logical side of their brains and came up with .... an incredibly cumbersome system. MCMXXVIII = 1928, if I remember my junior school teacher's explanation. Think of it: writing out the shopping list must have been hell, to say nothing of checking your bank statement. Had they looked around a bit, they might have found that Crete had used the decimal system about two thousand years before, and they might have stolen *that*.

The Aztecs might not have come up with the wheel, but they did their counting and stock-taking by tying knots in bits of string, and the Chinese came up with the most elegant solution, the abacus. You shuttled your little beads along little rods and, hey presto! the longest figures became manageable by a child. We, in the west, stubbornly refused to adopt it. I suppose we were waiting for the calculator, so we put children through the agonies (for many) of long division and equally long multiplication.

It took the Arabs to introduce Europe, still under Roman influence, to the nought, the cipher as it was called, from the Arabic "sifr", empty. And, wouldn't you know it? The word "algebra" comes from the Arabic "al-jabr"…mathematical reduction. To my lasting regret, I came to algebra too young - for me, at any rate. I was only about nine or ten and this most absorbing and entertaining branch of mathematics left me, not so much cold as shivering with incomprehension.

I suspect that something like the nought came from what has been called inspiration. After using the logical, left side of the brain hard and fruitlessly, you take a break. It is then, while logic and order are in abeyance, that the intuitive side of the brain, instead of putting two and two together, plays around with numbers, rearranges and generally messes about with them. That's when something new can emerge. Haven't we all had the experience of going to bed with some problem that defies solution, and found, the next day, that there is actually a way out of what we had seen as an impasse? Cudgelling our brains had done a lot to establish the individual and conflicting facts, but hadn't provided the solution that comes from somehow seeing the whole from a new angle.

I once took my very large dog, Humdrum, for a short walk. I had to set off for work early and could not roam around. Instead, I chose a suitable field and began to throw stones for him to chase. Now, in the field stood a fig tree and, somewhere in the back of my mind, I was conscious of the fig tree. The result was that I found myself repeatedly hitting it. I then decided to aim for it and I missed every time.

This proves that,
1. I am a lousy shot;
2. it also proves that I wasn't fit to look after a dog – the stones ruined a couple of teeth.

3. And it shows that the less rigid and less orderly right side of the brain can do better in many a situation, once the logical left takes a back seat.

In fact, I once saw the results of some practical work on the matter. It involved a group of tennis hopefuls who seemed to have developed server's block so that every service either hit the net or missed the court completely. Yet they were really concentrating and they were putting their backs into it to no avail. That was precisely the problem, said the coach. His idea was based on the fact that their brains knew all about the height of the net, the size of the court, their service technique. It had all been computed already. The left side of the brain had done its work. What they needed was to stop trying to control the process consciously.

"Aim to fail!" seemed to be the principle applied. They adopted a casual, who-cares attitude. The services began to go over the net as sweetly and sharply as anyone could wish.

I also remember an intelligent and very hard working pupil who had revised dedicatedly for his English "A" Level exam. He had even read *all* the critical stuff I'd recommended. He had also developed a slightly hunted look and the exams were still six weeks away. I advised him:

"Stop revising. Just read other stuff; read for pleasure."

He was alarmed at this, but not as alarmed as I was when I heard myself saying it.

"OK. Read other Shakespeare plays, other novels by Hardy or Dickens if you want. Or try something else - play pool. Just lay off the syllabus."

He was like a graph that had peaked and was about to shoot downhill. I believe he followed my advice and he got his well-deserved A grade.

Who remembers Edward de Bono and his work on Lateral Thinking? That was well worth following up educationally, but nothing really happened: it didn't fit in with the officially prescribed and sanctioned approach to learning and, furthermore, there was virtually no teaching material available for it. What you did was to face students with situations, questions and puzzles that the left side of the brain could not solve easily. You needed, I suppose, both cerebral hemispheres working together. Take this:

A man lives on a fourteenth floor. He goes to work at eight in the morning and takes the lift down to the ground floor every day. When he returns at six, he takes the lift up to the tenth floor and then walks up the final eight flights of steps. Why? Students could ask questions and you answered them…till one of them found the logical answer to this strange situation.

All this is about something that I often return to: the complementary validity of different approaches: sun and moon; mysticism and technocracy; female and male; logic and intuition. And you're perhaps wondering about the solution to the de Bono puzzle? Well, the man was *extremely* vertically challenged.

8th August, 2003.

BASIC INSTINCTS…AND MORE.

Two images from this week's TV viewing have remained with me. One came from Papua New Guinea. There, in the interior of the island, can be found some of the most primitive tribes in the world. No stranger dared approach them till quite recently - certainly not if you wanted to return the way you had come. The image that struck me was the one that showed the men in the tribe aiming arrows or wielding lances as they advanced, with cries and grunts of war, on the "enemy". Their faces were painted, they had some sort of large white bone contraption…I think it was bone…which went across the face, and they looked both impressive and frightening.

The second image came from a news programme. The item I am concerned with spoke of the possible fate of a football fan who had surrendered to the police. After a recent match he had landed a two-feet kick aimed at the back of another, younger, fan. The younger man died. Then followed images of the aftermath of some other recent football match where fans were shown beating up a security guard:

the picture was frozen briefly to identify one man: it was not at all impressive, but it was certainly frightening.

Two tribes, same difference?

Not at all. For the primitive tribe it was a cultural affair; the tribe was going through a simulation exercise, just to keep their hand in and to recall past wars. The football fans were out for blood. Why, oh, why? I have spent some time turning over in my mind the issue of male violence. I am not being unfair to men when I say that most of the violence in the world is generated by men. There are statistics to prove it. Just look at any news item showing riots. What do you see? You see men, youths and boys creating mayhem. I am not saying that some are not justified in their anger, what I am saying is that the sight of a woman at such events is very, very rare.

Most torturers are men; almost all violent attacks against women are generated by men; the pornographic trade involving women and children is massively in the hands of men and caters for men. There is even, and I was horrified to learn this, a trade in Holocaust Pornography that circulates film and photos taken in German concentration camps.

How do I reconcile this with men as I know them? I know labourers, doctors, plumbers, teachers; I know relatives, friends and acquaintances. I have the highest regard for some, there are some I love, there are those I am glad to know and - inevitably - those that I may not like and who may not like me. But, but, but…I am not scared of them nor do I see them as a threat to my life. So what am I talking about? How do I reconcile the extremes of a sex that has been responsible for so much abuse of power and violence worldwide, and for so many great achievements? If you look at the world of the arts, you see that the great achievers have been men and it is only now that we find women featuring more and more as their rights are recognized, education is available to them, and their range of opportunities grows wider. If you look at the world of science, architecture, mathematics…women are still thin on the ground.

And there I found something of the answer I was looking for. There and in some books I read this last year, and in questions I had been asking myself for even longer.

Let's see: I'll start with the questions. Why is the incidence of autism much higher among boys than among girls? Why are *Idiots Savants* - a technical term and not one of opprobrium, a term now being replaced by terms like "the Savant Syndrome" - why are these apparently brain-damaged but brilliant individuals generally male? Why do men keep inventing clubs to join? You can go from the American style...like "The Most Honourable and Venerable Order of the Greater Spotted Moose"...to the Spanish "Casino"...to the Modern Rotarians...to P.G.Wodehouse's creation, "The Drones", where the inept Bertie Wooster met his cronies.

No! – I have nothing against any of them. I think they serve a purpose and satisfy a need. Some do good deeds a-plenty, serve the community and set standards of behaviour. I am merely interested in The Male Club as a social phenomenon.

So, I began to gather the disparate threads I was following and came up with what should have been apparent to me long ago - I can sometimes be very slow on the uptake. I'll summarise it: look at humanity's brief life on earth and its colossal progress. Yes, human kind has gone too fast and retains the instincts of the Stone Age allied to the technical advances of the twentieth century. This is more evident in men than in women because man's role has changed drastically and woman's hasn't. In days of yore, for the tribe to survive, the woman needed to be a good breeder and carer. She was also the provider and collector of roots, berries or whatever was available locally, which task was compatible with the need to breed and care for offspring. Her role as carer has not changed and though the need for large families is not considered a priority in developed countries, it is still important where infant mortality is high or where religious belief requires it. Woman's role, therefore, remains little changed if we substitute "family" for "tribe". What has happened is that, to this role, she has added something much more rewarding than the collecting of berries - I speak of having a career.

And what of men? Well, once, very long ago, the survival of the tribe required that the man was hunter, warrior, protector and provider of seed. As primitive man, it seems, had no knowledge that the sexual act was what led the woman to conceive a child; he needed to have an instinctively strong sex urge to ensure that she did, indeed, breed.

What is man's situation in today's world? Most societies are monogamous; the birth rate is dropping in developed countries and man as the indiscriminate provider of seed has lost out. Man as Hunter - let's say that the hairy mammoth hasn't been high profile lately and Man as Protector - hand up anyone who has recently defended his family from physical attack by man or beast.

That leaves man the Warrior, ready to beat the hell out of someone as his raison d'être.

I'm sure you can see what I'm on about. The aggression and brute force, together with a powerful sexual urge - all once making a positive and essential contribution to the survival of the tribe or race - have become a liability and a danger. They obey the law of diminishing returns, not yielding the security they once did, but they are still there and they are exercised for negative ends like rape, torture and violence of all sorts.

The men I've known, with few exceptions, have been as much my friends as have women, again with a few exceptions. The situation is under control with the majority, but, oh! that remaining large minority have much to answer for.

The question of all-male clubs? I can tell you where that stems from: it was when corporate effort was a matter of necessity. Ever tried facing an attack from a neighbouring tribe or a saber-toothed tiger on your own?

17th October, 2003.

THE AGES OF MAN – PART 1: LITTLE RAYS OF WHAT?

I once passed by a nursery called something like "Our Precious Darlings". It made me come out all over in goose bumps: people who can give their nursery a name like that should not be trusted with small children.

"Precious"? - yes! "Darlings"? - of course. "Monstrous tyrants" - also, yes!

A child psychologist I know, herself a mother of three, once said that when you're dealing with little children who are determined to be awkward they are going to win the battle hands down because you are badly handicapped: you love that child (at least, you did before it went puce in the face from screaming at you); you don't believe in corporal punishment; you have a conscience, moral standards and theories about how to bring up children; you try to be politically correct on serious issues and your ethical sense is finely honed. "Of course you'll lose," she said.

In contrast to you, stands the infant. She/he is as intelligent as you are and drags no moral lumber around. It wants something and it aims to get it; it *doesn't* want something and it's damned if it's going to have it. Consider it from the child's point of view. Think, too, of the size of its head. An adult's head is around 1/7 the length of its body. With a newborn baby it's more like 1/3. That head is full of brain, and that brain has a hell of a lot to take in over the next few years. In fact, it is taking in so much that, by the time it's been processing information for over two years, it is suffering from info. saturation and no ethical framework to handle it.

No wonder we talk of "the terrible two's". Imagine all that is going on. From being a creature that lies on its back waiting to be fed, changed and burped - a creature that doesn't know where *it* ends and mother begins, it is becoming an autonomous being who is mobile, learning about bowel control, beginning to use language and heaven knows how much else. Up to now, everything has had to be tasted - picked up and stuck it in its mouth.

Now everything has to be explored, so fingers go into plugs; or objects like hammers or mobile phones get hurled about. And if an adults says, "No, darling, it's dangerous, it can hurt you. You'll get burnt and that's nasty," then what the child picks up from all that is really the prohibition - you are thwarting it's legitimate desire to investigate!

Anyway, it probably switched off after that "No" and you've been wasting your breath.

And don't we all know that "No" brings out what we tend to call "the worst" in children. The child may look at you over its shoulder, while its hand stretches out to touch the fire/pull the dog's tail/throw the car keys out of the window/scribble on the wall with your black indelible felt-tip. The child is willing you to take it on; it wants confrontation. Perhaps it just sees it as a game, but I think it is all a flexing of the developing autonomous muscles.

And if, for their own safety and/or yours, you have to intervene physically to stop them, you find yourself trying to restrain a whirling dervish. You can use your most soothing voice and your finest arguments, and you'll get nowhere. The child can handle very little of all that language you are using. Language shifts the contest into your territory and the child - short on speech but high on strategy - isn't going to allow that. So it uses one of its most powerful weapons: it screams and screams.

Damn it! What else can it do? It can hardly engage you in a good rational discussion.

Is it surprising that these early attempts at autonomy lead it to become an anarchist for a couple of years?

And doesn't it hurt when you know it's been good as gold at the nursery or with grandparents or friends and has come home to behave like a terrorist with a death-wish? What are you doing wrong? The answer is probably that you are doing no more than your best, and that you've invested so much emotional capital in the relationship that the child can easily and instinctively take advantage of this and use it against you. That's why somewhere along the line you fall. In fact, what happens is that you keep tripping over your theories and barking your shins against what is politically correct; and one fine day you become a closet briber.

"If we go now, darling, you can have an ice-cream."

You can count, on the fingers of one elbow, the parent who has never, never used this sort of ploy, because when an irresistible force (the child) meets an immovable object (parent with principles on child rearing), something's gotta give.

Then there is that determination to use environmentally friendly nappies. Not for you the disposable ones that take something like fifty years to decompose. So you spend over three hundred pounds on these wonderfully PC nappies. And you live in Northumberland. And you can't dry the dratted things in time to use for a baby suffering from a Niagara syndrome. So you give up and go out furtively to buy those dreadful disposable ones. Worst of all, probably, are the theories you are sold: "Every mother has enough milk to breast-feed her child," said a health visitor to an exhausted mother whose baby was sleepless and, clearly, hungry. Bottle feeding was not in fashion at the time. Fortunately, the need for the parent to survive took over and the mother caved in and gave the child a bottle feed one evening. He slept! So did she.

I remember a child who once got up on the narrow parapet of a balcony three floors up and trod carefully along this six-inch "path" while a horrified neighbour in the opposite block watched helplessly crying out, "Pepe!" to the child's older brother in the patio below. The brother was called Antonio so he played happily on. The child's mother came out on the balcony and froze in horror, but sensibly waited for the child to climb down before giving her hell. The grandmother nearly had heart failure.

The child's reasons for taking this mindless risk? - "I had to do it."

Was it a terminal version of compulsion neurosis? Actually, though it happened nearly sixty years ago, all I remember is the feeling that I had to do it.

My poor mother!

To quote my psychologist friend again, "A relationship with a child can sometimes be an abusive one, with the parent as the emotionally battered party." So what happens?

I suppose what happens is that we keep trying different strategies, failing, succeeding at times, having a wonderfully funny and loving child...that's the Dr Jekyll part...and the occasional lunacy of the Mr. Hyde. We lose battle after battle, but I honestly believe that we win the war in the end; and then it doesn't seem like a war any longer, but like an extraordinarily complex and fruitful development that we have helped to shape, and which has come to a satisfactory culmination thanks to our patience, efforts and ability to endure as well as to love. But, boy, can it be tough at times!

27th June, 2003.

THE AGES OF MAN – PART 2: THE AGE OF UNREASON.

One of the most famous speeches that Shakespeare put into the mouth of one of his characters is that dealing with the seven ages of man, from infancy to dotage. So why did he not include adolescence?

I suspect that it was because adolescence hadn't then been invented. Perhaps I need to clarify that. The concept of something like "Childhood" came along pretty late. Some would have it that it was invented by Dickens. And when you look at old portraits, you see that children were dressed in scaled-down versions of adult clothes. If you look at the Meninas in Velazquez's great group portrait in their panniered dresses, or at pictures of Victorian girls with their skirts looped back into mini bustles - they all depict little copies of their mothers.

Basically, it appears that children were seen as small adults. As mini adults, unless their parents were sufficiently affluent to educate them, they were expected to start work at the age of six or seven or even less. They certainly started early in the Lancashire mills and down the coal mines. And, most regrettably and deplorably, this still happens in third world countries that exploit child labour. Perhaps childhood can exist only when you have a sound economy. The same applies to adolescence: if you are struggling to keep body and soul together, the last things you are going to dwell on are your Ego, your Id and your psyche generally. So Shakespeare went from the whining, reluctant schoolboy to the somewhat ridiculous young lover. One assumes that puberty was not something that Elizabethans were too concerned about.

Yet adolescence has received massive attention in the last fifty years or so. One reason has been – wouldn't you know it - commercial. The Teenage Market was discovered in the fifties and has been exploited ever more successfully. Psychology and psychiatry also focussed attention on it; sociologists had a whale of a time with it; and now it is the neuro-scientists who are in on the act. And thank goodness for that and for their good, hard, empirical evidence on the matter.

How clearly can you remember your adolescence? I feel it was the time when I took possession of myself. It was as if I had been living in rented, furnished accommodation till then and suddenly discovered that I had the deeds to the property and could buy my own furniture. But it was also a heady, uneasy and emotional time when I often found myself weeping for no reason in particular and suffering agonies of uncertainty alternating with rushes of arrogance.

And do you know why? It was partly the fact that my melatonin cycle could not always be relied on to deliver on time; my dopamine levels went sky high and I was suffering generally from an "exuberance" of grey matter. There you are. You are puzzled? Exactly. I haven't the foggiest idea either of what I'm talking about, but neurologists have.

Neuro-scientists have been involved in long-term research that involves scanning the brains of teenagers. The brain has now been mapped in such detail that considerable precision is possible and areas have been identified that are responsible for anything from getting the point of a joke to thinking about the consequences of actions. Before I look into that research, I'd like to mention the sort of thing that we've all noticed at one time or another.

1. Phenomenally good gymnasts who seemed to get younger every year.
2. Extraordinary young musicians.
3. Amazing stories of the way teenagers use computers and hack into military software, banking or great commercial concerns.

4. The way mathematicians seem to peak before they are even twenty.
5. The lunatic element that makes teenagers take appalling and quite ridiculous risks, like - don't they realise you need a parachute if you are going to jump out of a plane?
6. The idealism of young people, when they want to give their lives for a cause.
7. The way teenagers can become antagonistic, rejecting everything you say, on principle, it seems.
8. How clothes, hairstyle, tattoos, body piercing and anything connected with appearance become a minefield for parents. Nothing you buy is suitable in their eyes and anything they want seems unsuitable to you and the twain shows no signs of meeting.

I recall a conversation with one of our daughters when we were apparently the wrong parents for her: we wouldn't let her take the last bus back from town on a Friday evening and our offer to collect her at midnight was met with anguished horror.

"But...my friends will see you!" As we knew and had taught many of her friends, we rather failed to pick up the point she was making. "They'll see you waiting outside the disco (or whatever it was); I'll feel so stupid!"

There was no answer to that. So we ended up lurking and waiting round the corner where we would not be seen. I suspect that, surreptitiously parked in every lane in the area, were other parents in their cars, all trying not to be a source of embarrassment to their children. On another occasion we were attempting reasonable negotiation in the face of mounting provocation as she deliberately blocked every suggestion. Suddenly she couldn't take it any more:

"Why do you have to be so reasonable? How am I ever going to break away from you and grow up if you act like this?"

And she was as annoyed as she was amused at what she had said.

Meanwhile, back at the neuro-scientists' camp, we discover that the brain goes through a massive process of refinement in adolescence.

There is an overload of capacity and possibility - which accounts for extraordinary feats of excellence, of maverick activity, of study. There is a heightening of experience and emotion at a time when youngsters are less than prepared to cope with it. And here Shakespeare knew instinctively what Romeo and Juliet were about, for they are surely two of the most irrational and ruthlessly ego-centred lovers in literature.

Teenagers, it also appears, suffer from a lack of formation in the part of the brain that deals with planning, which is why they can be so chaotically disorganized. Equally they are still a bit short in the area where caution and tact will later stop them being confrontational with parent and others. That dopamine I spoke of makes you want to take risks, to experience new sensations; and the melatonin will affect your sleeping patterns. So many changes, so many hormones on the loose! Little wonder that hormones are called "violent chemicals".

So let us be grateful for myelin, which also kicks in in adolescence, increasing by 100 % and insulating the brain's electrical signals so that they keep on the right paths and increase their speed, and the hyped life of the brain gets toned down and honed down.

I think that this sort of research has two particular benefits for parents who are suffering the emotional depredations caused by teenage children. The first is that it confirms your tottering belief in the importance of your role as a parent. Whatever your children may say, they still need you - damn it! your myelin did its job long ago. The second is that, in many ways, they can't help it - it's not so much personal as physiological, though they may hurt your feelings.

As someone said somewhere: "When I was fourteen, my parents were utterly impossible to live with. They had improved tremendously by the time I was twenty."

Yes, let's face it: adolescence too can be hell at times!

4th July, 2003.

THE AGES OF MAN – PART 3: WHAT MY MUMMY AND MY GRANNY NEVER TOLD ME ABOUT "IT".

They never said a thing to enlighten me about "It". I was left to find out all by myself because it was something we didn't really talk about and it's only now that I'm finding out about it from personal experience. *Of course* I'm talking about old age. What else?

You'll have noticed that I've gone from adolescence to age in one fell swoop and you may wonder what's happened to the years in between. That's just it. One does wonder what happened to them - one moment you've started your first job, the next you have a couple of children, the next they are leaving home and then you find you've reached retirement age. Those years are full to bursting with incident, change, developments and challenges. Perhaps that's why you don't know where they went: you were so busy living them that you didn't register their inexorable passage. Be that as it may, you awake to the fact, at some stage, that they have been and have gone.

What about old age? It is a well-known fact that it begins at something between fifty and twenty years ahead of whatever age you, personally, are at. When I was thirty, old age began at sixty. Now that I'm sixty, I laugh at my own naivety, as it is perfectly obvious that old age begins at eighty. And before you challenge that, let me say that I have a friend of eighty who assures me that I've got it wrong again, and it's only my neighbour, Francisco, who admits that he's beginning to grow old. Perhaps he's right: he's ninety-two.

All of us know that old age is something we'll come to if we survive long enough. Even tiny children note the signs of age in their elders:

"Why is your face crumpled?"

"Why do you walk funny?"

"Granny has toy teeth."

I know that I registered the aging process in the older people I knew - my grandmother's feet gave her trouble; old Mr. Perez walked ever more slowly; a neighbour complained of rheumatism - such things I was aware of, but they were not in any way relevant to me.

Precisely. It was the old idea of "You never think it's going to happen to you." We've all heard that expression from people who've been involved in an accident, who've had to face the unexpected loss of someone they love, or who've suddenly found themselves facing some crisis. The feeling that such things happen to other people and not to you, this irrational sense of invulnerability, probably helps keep us sane. It imbues us with a perfectly unjustified optimism that allows for a mentally healthy existence, and it's a splendid defence-mechanism against depression.

So it is that, when you begin to grow older, it all takes you by surprise - I refer to the way in which your body begins to take liberties with you which you would not permit if only it had had the courtesy to ask you about it. You are prepared for the obvious and you think yourself emotionally provident for resigning yourself to the onset of things like wrinkles and stooping shoulders. What no one ever told you about are the minor things...like the fact that your eyelids begin to sag and threaten to cover your eyes, and you feel you'll be blind before you know it; and your eyelashes stop curling up as muscles age. Damn it! Even your eyebrows start growing downwards! The force of gravity doesn't just affect bulgy bits of you, you know: it strikes everywhere.

And those brain cells that have been dying off since you hit your early twenties seem to reach crisis point and you begin to forget. It takes longer to remember the precise word you want to use; you can't for the life of you remember the name of that actor you admired last year in that new film, what was the title?

To compound the problem, the doctor informs you that the arteries leading up the back of your neck are hardening due to the calcium deposits building up around them: great! That means the circulation to your brain is getting worse so that the essential element for any physical activity - oxygen - is getting sluggish in arriving. At the same time he tells you that your bones are a bit thin on calcium, which accounts for the dodgy knee and the fact that your back has been playing up. Hey! What's wrong with your calcium supply? Doesn't it know where it should be going? Has it got *such* a lousy sense of direction? Can't it tell the difference between an artery and a bone or what?

Let me offer some reassurance: you still have all your marbles and you are not facing Alzheimer's. Your short-term memory inevitably gets worse, things just take a little longer and you feel frustrated. The time to start worrying is when you look at a spoon and think it's an armchair.

Now, some of us have always been a bit absent-minded, so perhaps we may be more prepared for it all. I know someone, a painter, who has sometimes seemed to be two sheets to the wind with regard to practicalities. He once went from one room to another to collect some paintbrushes and found himself in the bathroom, washing his hands. This happened three times within ten minutes. The picture took ages to finish, but he *was* awfully clean. Maybe that's why I married him.

I have no intention of cataloguing all the many ailments that may afflict you. There's a good reason for that - they may not. It may, indeed, never happen to you. Some lucky folk are repulsively healthy and fill the rest of us with envy, and why shouldn't you be one of them? Besides, of all the possible afflictions going, you are most unlikely to suffer from more than a couple.

I think the possibility that worries us most is the chance of flipping our lid and ending up with our mind completely gone. That makes us worry about the family and what it will do to them to have a parent/grandparent who doesn't even recognise them.

If you think about that, you are right to worry about their distress, but there is a side of the situation that can be positive. It was brought home to me years ago when a friend went to visit his aged uncle who had lost his mind and was in a home. Apparently, the uncle took him on a tour of the large Victorian building and of the grounds. The gardener, the nurses and the handyman all greeted him with a cheerful: "Good morning, Squire."

And as they stood at the top of the grand flight of steps that led up to the main entrance, the old man swept a proud hand in a gesture that encompassed building and grounds and said happily: "Best thing I ever did was buying this place."

There you go. If you think you are Napoleon or Greta Garbo or Einstein, then you are probably more than content with your lot.

11th July, 2003.

PRODIGIOUS PEOPLE.

The Mad Hatter in "Alice in Wonderland" was not simply Lewis Carroll's invention. Hat-making in Victorian England required the use of mercury and exposure to mercury can cause brain damage so, I imagine, there was many a demented hatter around at the time. And the nutty professor of my childhood comics was also based on fact. We've all heard tales of absentminded academics who are brilliant scholars but almost dysfunctional in terms of normal activities, like the one who set off to deliver a lecture somewhere and telegraphed his wife with the cri de coeur, "Am in Reading; where should I be?"

I've mentioned Isaac Newton before and spoken of his genius, distinguishing between him and the lunatic fringe. Halley, of Halley's comet fame, felt that Newton was, in terms of intellectual achievement, as near the gods as it was possible to be. But, to the average person, he would have seemed to be two sandwiches short of a picnic. He once took a long needle of the kind used for stitching leather and inserted it between the eye and the socket and rubbed it around the back of the eye - or as close as he could get to it - just to see what would happen. And what to say about Henry Cavendish who, in 1797, calculated the weight of the world and achieved a result so accurate that it can hardly be bettered today? He also anticipated the laws of at least half a dozen scientists who came later. This brilliant man was either autistic or pathologically shy. If he went to a fellow scientist's house, other guests were warned not to approach him and, certainly, not to engage in eye contact. The best they could do was to drift near him as if by chance and address any scientific remarks to the air. Even then, Cavendish was liable to bolt from such "intrusive" contact.

Mozart may not have shown any similar signs if insipient dottiness, but he was certainly a genius. And, talking of prodigious abilities, while I was in secondary school, an Indian lady on a world tour arrived in Gibraltar. She presented her show at the refurbished Naval Cinema (if my memory serves me right). She invited the audience to throw any mathematical calculation at her: she would then produce the answer within seconds while a gentleman with a calculator lagged behind. She was, apart from her bizarre mathematical ability, a perfectly normal woman. Where others learn and gradually perfect their craft, such people seem to acquire within a couple of years - or less - what it takes others a lifetime to learn. And it is often musicians and mathematicians who are thus gifted. Many of us remember "Rain Man" in which Dustin Hoffman played a mentally handicapped man whose ability to work with numbers was little short of miraculous. He was, in fact, what used to be known as an Idiot Savant. Such people are now called Extraordinary People and they are usually autistic.

I have mentioned autism before. It generally afflicts males and some few of them, with serious damage to the left cerebral hemisphere, become Savants. The Savant's memory is automatic, mechanical, concrete. Leslie Lemke - blind, palsied and intellectually handicapped - at the age of five didn't speak with his adoptive family, but he could repeat each and every single word that had been spoken in his presence throughout the day. Later he could reproduce any piece of music he had heard once, and do it perfectly even after years had passed. Once, to test his talent, a false note was introduced into a piece of classical music. He heard the piece and replayed it – complete with the wrong note. As his genius found scope, so did his normal skills improve.

Savants are incapable of forgetting anything learnt in their particular field. Perhaps the most extraordinary Savant is one who was unable to speak or walk or even eat and who subsisted mainly on milk. Tests revealed extensive scarring and atrophy of areas of the brain, especially the frontal areas. His *measurable* IQ was 8. His vocabulary seems to have comprised seven words. He could communicate with grunts, a smile for "no" and a raising of the upper lip for "yes". He had become paralysed at the age of six months. When you consider that an average IQ is 100, it is beyond belief that this man, given any date from 1915 onwards, would then listen to the days of the week being recited and would either smile or raise his upper lip to identify the right day. And would be correct.

Studies of Savants have centred, more recently, on the way the two cerebral hemispheres work. The left side is more concerned with language, speech and certain motor skills than the right side. It is more to do with logical and abstract strategies. The right side is more involved in spatial tasks and, among other things, in artistic and mechanical performance, which skills do not depend so much on verbal ability. It deals more in intuitive and simultaneous strategies. In most people the left hemisphere is dominant, even in foetal life. However, it is at greater risk in the womb and it seems that testosterone can slow the growth of this more vulnerable side of the brain. As a result, there can be a shift of dominance to the right side which helps to account for the fact that dyslexia, delayed speech, autism, hyperactivity, left-handedness and stuttering are more likely to occur in males than in females. An overdeveloped right hemisphere favours the mathematical and intuitive, and in extreme cases you get a Savant. An accident that causes brain damage may have a similar effect to such foetal damage.

Most of those studied have had highly developed numerical or musical skills, and a smaller number have dealt in painting or sculpture. When we lived in UK, we saw a programme in 1987 which featured a twelve-year-old lad, functionally illiterate at the time, whose drawings were fabulous – as in a fable, they seemed too good to be true. He had drawn St Pancreas Station from memory with everything about the elaborate building correctly placed. The only odd thing was that he had drawn a perfect mirror image. As his skills have developed in art, so have his social and reading skills. Alonzo Clemons was another such genius. A childhood accident impaired his, till then, normal development and his IQ, when tested, was measured at 40. As a man, he could barely count to ten. His talent lay in sculpture - animals sculpted from memory, figures of superb sensitivity accuracy and beauty.

There are two points I wish to make. The first concerns the accusations levelled at women as being less intelligent than men given that the greatest musicians and mathematicians have been men. Forget intelligence and think "Excessive testosterone and foetal brain damage"! Makes a difference to your perspective, doesn't it? The second point is that the dividing line between ordinary, impaired and gifted is a narrow one indeed, so you and I are a hair's breadth away from genius. Isn't that a grand thought to carry into the New Year?

31st December, 2004.

FERAL CHILDREN – PART 1.

The word "feral" comes from the Latin for a wild beast and in terms of animal or plant life it refers to life in a wild or uncultivated state. You are not interested? OK. How about we consider Romulus and Remus who were, supposedly, first brought up by a she-wolf with the assistance of - would you believe it? - a woodpecker; or let's look at Tarzan, brought up by apes; and there's Mowgli in "The Jungle Books" who was brought up by wolves.

They were all feral children. What all the stories have in common is the natural greatness of the characters. Yes, I do know that it is said that Romulus killed Remus at some stage when they were founding the city of Rome. Nevertheless, they were doers of great deeds. Tarzan has it all - an English Lord who becomes king of the jungle and whose exploits are legendary, not least of them - on celluloid - the yodelling cry that would give lesser men a hernia. And then there's Mowgli who, after being lord of the animals, moves on to become a fully socialised adult in the human sphere.

Balderdash! That's what I say - utter twaddle! Edgar Rice Burroughs, creator of Tarzan, would have agreed with me. As he himself said of such a feral child: "The resultant adult would be a most disagreeable person to have around the house. He would probably have BO, Pink Toothbrush, Halitosis, and Athlete's Foot, plus a most abominable disposition; so I decided not to be honest, but to draw a character people would admire." I don't subscribe fully to his statement, because, firstly, almost everything I have read about feral children points to the abominable disposition of *some of the adults* who tried to socialise the poor children, and secondly, I haven't the foggiest notion what Pink Toothbrush might be.

There was a newspaper item years ago about John Ssbunnya of Uganda, a child who witnessed how his father murdered his mother. The boy fled into the bush and would have died if he had not been taken up by a pack of chimpanzees with whom he lived for three years. He was spotted in 1991 and captured by humans. His tale, told by the good people who run a Christian Orphanage in Uganda, presents John's life in terms of suffering and redemption.

In the seventeenth century, however, the matter was seen as both religious and philosophical, and, in tales of such children, they constantly feature as not really human, as was the case with a Lithuanian child brought up by bears who "Had nothing in him like a man". He did manage to learn to speak a little. He was also baptised...just in case he was human after all. To train the boy, a ten-year-old, to stand upright like a "proper" human being, he was clapped up against a wall and held there "after the manner that dogs are taught to beg". It makes you wish he'd been left with the bears, doesn't it?

The same happened with another bear-child living in Poland at around 1690 who was given away by King Kasimir of Poland as a gift to someone - after all, he clearly wasn't a person, was he? Fortunately, no one seems to have tried too hard to "educate" him, and he just helped out in the kitchens and would often head for the woods to consort with bears with whom he seems to have been both safe and happy.

One of the most famous cases was that of Peter, a wild boy found near Hanover in 1725. He was about thirteen years old and naked, dirty and incapable of speech - so could say nothing about himself. He became something of a celebrity - was taken to London to St James' Palace, was seen by many - including Jonathan Swift - and was eventually given over to be tutored by a doctor who failed to teach him to speak but managed to socialise Peter's wild behaviour.

It was The Age of Reason and everything had to be given its place. Homo Feri - Wild Man - was labelled as a subspecies of humankind in at least one text. Sub-species. Think of that. I suppose it's understandable if you insist on having theories about things. You find a child who has run wild, either alone or with animals, and you fail to see that what she or he has missed out on is the whole process of socialization and acquisition of language. You are looking at just one more child, totally human, but one who has lived differently.

There is the truly appalling case that came to light in 1970, in a Los Angeles suburb, of a thirteen-year-old girl who had spent nearly twelve years tied to a potty chair by a harness that allowed her to move only her hands and her feet. At night she was pinioned in a sort of sleeping bag that stopped her moving her arms. She was beaten with a piece of wood if she called out and her father would only growl or bark at her. The girl, a prettily elfin child, was in a bad physical state, was undeveloped emotionally and had no language. She was less lucky than many a feral child who had lived rough, but lived free. She was only feral in the sense of lacking "cultivation".

How was her case seen? Well, it was the twentieth century so it was seen as a golden opportunity to study the whole question of the acquisition of language. Was there an optimum period during which it could be acquired? The current idea was that 13 was the cut-off point. And then there was Chomsky's theory that we are biologically programmed to acquire language. Funds were voted, scientists and linguists were involved, therapists were recruited. The emphasis was on learning and testing and Genie, as she was named, learned several hundred words (though without ever mastering grammatical structures).

Once, during an earth tremor in California, Genie ran to one of the cooks in the centre where she was at the time. It was the first occasion when she had turned to someone for human comfort: what a milestone! It was noted and one of the scientists spoke to the cook:

"So Genie responds well to your intra-supportive initiatives?"

"I just give her love," the cook said.

None of the scientists, linguists or therapists was unloving, but they seemed to have failed to see the obvious. What Genie had been deprived of totally was affection and normal human contact. What she needed was love and care and a process of gradually learning to adopt the sort of behaviour that would normally have come to her in early childhood.

I remember, with sorrow, a programme I saw of Genie being put through her daily linguistic exercises. She was made to concentrate. It was remarkably like other programmes I had watched where scientists worked with primates to see in what measure *they* could acquire language. It was the IN thing at the time.

Poor Genie. The fascinating question of language should have taken second place. After all, there are many people, incapable of speech, who live normal lives: they learn some form of communication, they study or they don't, they may marry and raise children. Genie, once funds dried up, with her enormous human and social problems, ended up being shunted from foster parent to foster parent. Some were reasonable, some were abusive. She regressed linguistically and socially. I believe she is still alive and living in some home for adults. Poor, poor Genie. Some theories have a lot to answer for.

18th July, 2003.

FERAL CHILDREN – PART 2.

Apart from friend Tarzan - and Johnny Weissmuller in his early films was surely the definitive popular Tarzan - I knew nothing of feral children till some time in the early fifties or thereabouts when there was a terrible story in the papers of a child who had been found living in a hen house to which he had been confined for years. It was in Ireland, there was no father, there was shame and, I believe, the mother was what was then called mentally defective. The child could not speak or walk upright and his body had become deformed.

I think it was that story that sparked off my interest in humans who could live like and with animals. In every case, if the feral nature of the child was the result of human cruelty, I felt horror and outrage. If the feral child had lived with animals or had run wild alone, I felt distress at what seemed to happen once humans "rescued" it.

The early European obsession with the question of whether or not such children were human, whether they had souls, should not surprise us when we think of Christianity's bureaucratic mind as it had developed over the centuries. Such a desire to categorize and organize was partly the result of an expansionist church and partly an inheritance traceable to the legalistic turn of mind of the Roman Empire. Why, in the sixth century, at The Council of Mâçon, the bishops voted to decide whether or not women had souls. And centuries later, at Wittenberg, the Lutherans were still working on the vexed question - were women actually fully human? A tough proposition, you must admit!

Feral children suffered too. I'm sorry to say that this obsessive need to categorize, to develop theories, to attempt to formulate even the nature of God, appears to be a masculine vice. And do you really believe that any all-powerful god to whom you attribute the creation of the cosmos is waiting somewhere, watching your every move, in order to zap you into oblivion or worse because you failed to turn up to worship on Sunday, or failed to cover your head - or uncover it - or cover your face - or whatever practices have accrued to your particular faith?

But I definitely digress.

My interest in the matter always led me eventually to the question of speech. It appeared that when a child had gone wild *after* a certain age, then speech could be recovered. If the children had barely had any experience of speech before going wild, then the best that could happen would be the acquisition of perhaps as many as several hundred words, without grammatical structures, so that they spoke a sort of pidgin.

The Savage Girl found in France in 1731, in Champagne, was given the name of Memmie le Blanc. She was about ten when found and her origins were unknown, but she did learn to speak French and was able to furnish information about herself. She may only have lived wild from the age of five so had already learnt to speak before she was separated from her family; she may have been a member of a North American Indian tribe - possibly she was a Huron - a child who had been brought to Europe and got lost somehow.

When captured, she swam like a fish, could run with amazing swiftness, had immensely sharp vision and could climb trees with great agility. All these skills were gradually blunted once she lived in human society. Her health suffered from being made to eat cooked foods. However, she managed, as she grew up, to make some sort of meagre living.

By contrast we have a bear child found near Calcutta at the end of the nineteenth century. She was about two or three when captured. She learnt to walk upright and wear clothes, but never learnt to speak. The same was the case with two wolf girls - found well south of Calcutta. They ran on all fours and lived with a she wolf and her cubs. They were taken, and they found a kind home with the Revd. Singh and his wife. These good people seem to have been blessedly free of theories and treated the girls with kindness, sheltering them for as long as they could from the press and the sort of notoriety that would have been pernicious for them. The girls, like so many other feral children, showed very little evidence of the emotions we associate with humans; they had certain highly developed physical abilities - like amazingly acute night vision - and they never learned to walk upright.

Like other feral children, they appeared to long to return to that jungle from which they had been kidnapped and where their wolf mother had been killed. They never learned to speak. Perhaps they had been abandoned in the forest as infants as was done with many an unwanted girl child. They had probably never really heard human speech till they were taken, and by then they were incapable of learning.

What's that gland that one finds in infants, but which gradually atrophies as you grow up? I will pause to check with Sam, my medical consultant. The thymus, that's the one. It is there, large and double lobed, in newborn babes. By the time the child is about six months old it has virtually disappeared. It has something to do with the immune system, but its function is not too clear. Is it there to afford extra protection to the infant at the most vulnerable stage of its life, and does it retire gracefully from the immunological scene once its work is done? No, this is not a digression. It's just that, as we know little about the thymus, so we don't yet know enough about the part of the brain that is involved in the acquisition of language.

Why is it that children learn language with an ease that is later lost? I believe it is Lower Cantonese that is diabolically difficult for adult foreigners to learn. The same sound pitched at different levels can change the meaning of what you are saying. Raise your voice a bit and you may well be offering an unforgivable insult where all you wanted was for someone to pass the salt. However, small foreign children will pick it up and get their tongues round new sounds and intonations without causing an international incident. In fact, small children will learn any language, even one with the most complex rules of grammar - as is the case with, as I recall, the language of the Bushmen of the Kalahari. So why, after a certain point in time, if they have not been exposed to language, do they fail totally to learn where even the least able adult will manage to learn. Why this total reversal or loss of the relevant faculty?

I have said nothing of Victor of Aveyron (circa 1780), nor of Ivan Mishukov who lived with a pack of dogs in Moscow after running away from home in 1996 when he was four, nor of the enigmatic Kasper Hauser. And there are others.

For me the issue with the genuinely wild children, not those abused by vicious or retarded parents, is whether to "rescue" them is not a greater cruelty than to let them be. In any case, however interesting we may find the subject, it doesn't justify treating such children as a source of material for study.

25th July, 2003.

OUR YESTERDAYS.

ALL TOGETHER NOW! - PART I.

In nostalgia warp, I recall how very community-based were a lot of our activities when I was a child. They took in all the members of a family from grandparents to the newest baby, and then all the families living round your patio or block of flats.

Because my family lived in Police Barracks, it was with all the families around us that we went on the annual pilgrimage to the "Almoraima" - the Cork Woods - with the small chapel and the unfenced land all around that filled with the faithful and the less-than-faithful every Sunday in May. It had originally been only the first Sunday, a time of pilgrimage, but it had grown in popularity as a day out. You could still, in fact, see those who slowly and painfully "walked" the stony uneven track up to the shrine on their knees either to beg a favour of the Christ of the "Almoraima" or to thank Him for a petition granted. However, for the greater number it was one of the social highlights of the year when you joined with friends and with other groups in one great communal picnic.

I suppose we each had a different agenda that absorbed us for days before the event. My mother's aim was to prepare enough food to feed a hungry regiment setting out on a week's hard manoeuvres. There would be things like an assortment of thermos flasks, stuffed courgettes and sandwiches; wonderful dark bread-pudding with moist raisins that felt both sharp and sweet when you bit into them. Then she would pack all the ingredients required to cook the main meal over an open fire...onions, garlic, tomatoes, green peppers, rice and chicken, and, once across the border, there would be a stop to buy coarse Spanish bread, water melons if there were any to be had, and olives that would be scooped out of large earthenware jars and wrapped in rough brown paper which would slowly disintegrate as it soaked up the saline liquid that the olives came in.

For the men in the family there would be the need to book the bus, and, on a different level, to find stout ropes and make some sort of seat. With these we would have a swing, designed to hang from the stout branch of some tree for the delight of all of us - young and old.

With us, the children, the priority was planning the games to be played, the clothes to be worn, and the toys to take. The best toys were things like wooden swords or guns and pistols. As for clothes: we cowboys (or pirates) knew the value of stout shoes and shorts or trousers. And there was always the excitement and the uncertainty of a possible donkey ride to look forward to. For me it was that particular treat that made the day something to look forward to with special eagerness. We might go to the country at other times, but it was only at the "Almoraima" that you could actually hire a donkey to ride.

Hiring cost money and there would be pleading and negotiations with parents, misery and accusations of cruelty if they cavilled at our demands - and then the delight when they gave in - and the embarrassment if they haggled over the price with the owner of the donkey. Ah, the joy of being hoisted up on to its back! Its coat, like silky coconut matting, would rub against bare legs and you could hold on to the stiff mane. It was only then that you discovered what sort of steed was yours: would it set off at a speed that scared but gratified you in the face of the sluggards around you? Or would you end up with one of those slow steady beasts that provided no thrills, though you might be secretly grateful for the security it offered? It was a matter of immense importance because you only had that one opportunity a year to taste the pleasures of riding. I always seemed to end up with one of the pot-belied slow ones - a "burro penco" - while my brother shot off on some log-legged, sprightly creature.

And there was always the uncertainty of what the weather would be like. It could rain; and it always seemed to on one of the weekends in question. To this day, I expect at least one week in May to bring rain - and it rarely fails to do so.

Getting to the "Almoraima" was an adventure in itself. The men would have rented a bus or two to take us there. They were the old boneshakers that were kept in working order by skilled mechanics who managed to perform miracles on cantankerous old engines with the use of ingenuity and the most basic of equipment. These rickety and rackety buses would wait for us as we all came out of our flats laden with food baskets, old blankets and everything deemed necessary to make the day a success.

Of course there was singing once we set off. Have you ever been on any sort of group outing that didn't involve the joys of singing in the company of other, equally ungifted musicians? And the whole day stretched ahead. I knew I might make new friendships, strengthen old ones, discover something wonderful. The promise of the unknown, the possible, the exciting, was in the air. Once we arrived, the adults would be busy setting up camp and cooking and talking to each other. We would be free to indulge in nameless adventures. The expectation was one of the finest pleasures of those outings.

On the home front, later, when I was a young adult, came the "verbenas" organised by the same community, or by your rowing club or some such association. What exactly is a "verbena"? Did it originate in Madrid or was it common throughout Spain? To call it an open-air dance is like saying that ice-cream is something cold - you are missing out the real, rich flavour of the event. "Verbenas" required that the chosen area be festooned with Chinese lanterns, paper chains - the "cadenetas" left over from Christmas - and, or is my memory playing me false? even the odd Union Jack might somehow find its way into the proceedings to cover the front of the improvised bar or to screen off the area where the drinks were stored. And it was an event at which you knew everyone, a communal "fiesta".

Sometimes you went in costume: the men with narrow trousers, short jackets, a white silky scarf and a cloth cap. The women wore long skirts, blouses, headscarves from under which peeped carnations securely fastened to their hair and, over their shoulders, the biggest "mantón de Manila" - embroidered shawl - they could lay their hands on.

And, even though the bar was makeshift, the folding tables and chairs rickety and in need of a lick of paint, and the dance floor something of a hazard...once the garishly coloured bulbs that swung above you were switched on and the sky grew dark, it was a magical place. I speak of that humble alchemy that invests the mundane with glory of a minor order.

27th Feb, 2004.

ALL TOGETHER NOW! - PART II

One of the highlights of those years, now long gone, was during Easter. We'd all embark on the trek to all the churches on Maundy Thursday after midday. By then, the host would have been carried in a splendid monstrance to the Altar of Repose where it would be placed at the centre of the finest and most beautiful display of flowers that the parish could produce. Each church would inevitably create a thing of beauty, and we would set off to see them all, walking from The Sacred Heart Church to The Cathedral to St. Joseph's and on to Catalan Bay. The weather could make or break these visits to what were called "Los Monumentos" – the Monuments - for they were not ordinary altars. A fine spring day would make it a joyful event, a wet Thursday could ruin it.

As was also de rigueur on Sundays, this round of visits on Maundy Thursday required that we dress in our best bib and tucker. Church-going meant dressing formally and I remember my mother's disapproval one Sunday when I set off for church wearing a simple dress with three-quarter-length sleeves: for some reason that I never understood it was the sleeves that really did it - for they were not deemed proper sleeves, just some new-fangled whim of mine.

And I seem to remember new clothes being associated with both secular and religious occasions. The fair in La Linea, when there was no fair in Gibraltar, meant a new outfit. So did Palm Sunday. And if it wasn't a dress, then you got - at least - a new pair of socks, for the saying was: "Domingo de Ramos...al que no estrene se le caen las manos," and no one wanted to risk losing both hands for lack of some new item of clothing.

For boys there was the 8th December when they had a special rite of passage. It was *the* day designated for their recognition as young men rather than boys. Up till then they wore short trousers; and it was a big event in their lives when they got their first proper pair of long trousers: "se hechaban el pantalón largo." I can recall lads whose voices had broken, who were almost sprouting moustaches and who still had to wait till December before they could cover their legs - which had been getting progressively hairier all year. What I don't understand is what 8th December, when the church celebrates the Immaculate Conception, had to do with boys' legs. And, come to think of it, when had this custom started?

We girls were more fortunate in that abandoning socks and wearing stockings was a matter for negotiation with your mother. So too with high heels and, which came later still, with make-up. In my case, I wore stockings only for special occasions from the age of fourteen till I was sixteen, and I generally wore socks to school till I was eighteen. There was a good reason for it. My mother and grandmother called me Trueno, Terremoto and Relampago (Thunder, Earthquake and Lightning) in acknowledgement of the way I tended to tear around, behaving like a storm looking for somewhere to break. I would bump into walls, knock into furniture and, on one memorable occasion, I managed to close a large cupboard door on my head - which was still inside.

The family could not afford to keep me in stockings that seemed to ladder when I just looked at them. Mind you, I kept the stocking-repair shop in La Linea in business for years. Was it "Mi Tienda", a small shop that sold a bit of genteel everything from hankies to hairgrips? High heels were also reserved for special occasions, as was make-up. And parental consent and control could extend to the way you did your hair and even to whether or not you could cut it once you had grown it long. The old idea that a woman's crowning glory was her hair was still around and it sometimes seemed that what was on the outside of your head mattered more than what was inside.

In the case of my parents, I remember a spell when they would go with a large group of friends from Police Barracks to the fancy dress dances at The Assembly Rooms, now converted into the Queen's Hotel. Their friends, Willie and Concha Tacon, bore away the first prizes with incredible but well-deserved regularity: as Henry VIII,

Pharaoh and consort, Robinson Crusoe, Mermaid and Neptune, Johnny Walker - of whisky label fame - and a host of other characters. Weeks of preparation went into these costumes and the results were magnificent. My parents and the others went as a group: as babies with bibs and outsized dummies; as Spanish peasants from the north; as anything that required only a basic costume. I remember them as I would a gang of high-spirited children out on a carefree spree.

Yet it was they who, with enviable efficiency, would organize extraordinary gatherings at Christmas and New Year when family and several dozen friends would gather for or after lunch or supper with tambourines, castanets, "zambombas" - those earthenware pot-shaped vessels with no base and a taut goatskin top pierced by an upright cane that, when rubbed, would emit hoarse thumping sounds. There might even be the occasional guitar. There would certainly be food and drink and much singing and telling of jokes. It was a marathon social and community event. At this time of year I longed to be allowed to go carol singing in the evening with a group, like my friend Christine did. They visited all their friends' houses and carried on till the early hours of the morning. How I envied her!

Does it sound as if I'm talking of the good old days? Of course I am. They were my good old days, which is not to say that they were perfect. Time can blur the edges of many things, including heartache, shortages and unpleasantness. Hindsight is a powerful rose-tinted lens. There is always the temptation to see the past as a golden age, but we all know that all that glisters is indeed not gold - but it can be very attractive.

Today's youth will have their golden memories too. And let me finish with a delightful discovery. I was in Leeds two weeks ago seeing my daughters. I walked into a gift shop and there, in a box, was a pile of newly printed "scraps"... the kind I used to dice for as a child; and more pleasing still was the fact that the printers were still using the old Edwardian designs. Wonderful!

5th March, 2004.

FERIA!

My memories of the fairs I attended as a child are like the curate's egg - good in parts. Those were the days when new clothes made an appearance only on special occasions so I think I must have been excited by the prospect of a new dress; and I do remember a pair of white shoes that, try as I might, I never managed to keep clean among the press of people that thronged the dusty fairground. How often did we cross the frontier to La Linea during those nine days in July? On one of the days I know I would be decked out in the so-called gypsy dress - blood-red spots on a white background, the hem thick with ruffles that flared out as I walked. My face would be made up, my hair pulled back uncomfortably into a bun at the back of my neck and I was conscious that this was finery. I think I strutted a little as I walked and hoped people would notice how splendid I looked.

Way back in the late forties those fairs were tawdry affairs in a devastated Spain that struggled to emerge economically from the Civil War. In the circus everything looked moth-eaten, from the sad lions to the sequined costumes that didn't quite glitter. I feared for the trapeze artists; I couldn't find the clowns funny, try as I might; and the only thing I liked, possibly because my father liked them so much, were the little trained dogs that seemed happy as they performed small tricks to our applause. And we had waited so long for the show to start! It was the same for the "Teatro Circo Chino" - a supposed theatre cum circus of Chinese provenance - with its single plate-spinning act by the statutory Chinaman to justify the name - where you queued for what seemed like hours. None of the shows started on time. They couldn't afford to. Not till virtually all the seats had been sold did the performances finally begin. And all the time you were waiting, loud music blared out and battered your ears as if it was trying to convince you of an illusory joie de vivre. If nothing else, it anaesthetised your senses.

And waiting was of the essence in the "positivas", those large stalls with gifts rising in serried ranks behind the fast-talking barker, his microphone squeaking in protest at the decibel level as he harried and hurried you into buying your tickets - numbered wooden tags to be reused endlessly. You stood and waited till sales had peaked and then reached saturation point. They too couldn't afford to start - their raffle in this case - till they had mustered all the customers they could. Then the wheel was spun. The finest prizes were the aluminium sets of pots and pans and the very large papier-mâché dolls in pink and white dresses that stood stiffly to attention in their boxes. Nowadays I wonder how many of the numbers on those prizes actually tallied with the numbered tags we bought, because the dolls always seemed to stay there, staring straight ahead, unclaimed. From there you might go to have your photo taken, sitting on a cardboard donkey or standing behind a screen depicting a plane, with circles cut out of the cockpit so that you could push your head through.

We seemed to call all the rides available "los cacharros" - the whatsits. There were the tiny wooden "cunitas", the cradles for toddlers, that swung to and fro sedately. There was the "Ta-ta-chín", a miniature Ferris wheel with half a dozen child-containers. The most exciting thing about it was the name, which originated in the clashing cymbal and double drumbeat that was used, literally, to drum up trade. "Chin!" went the cymbal, "Ta-ta!" went the drum. There was also the large merry-go-round and its wonderful painted horses with their flaring nostrils and open red mouths. Oh, the disappointment when you were deemed too young to ride them and to hold on to the gleaming metal bar that anchored them to the carousel ceiling above you and allowed them to rise and fall as you were carried endlessly round, with the sights of the fair laid out before your eyes.

And you never did get to ride on those box-swings on long chains that hung down from an umbrella-like structure so that, as it turned and gathered speed, the swings' orbit grew ever greater and they were whirling out daringly beyond their originally modest circle. Those of us doomed only to watch waited in half-hope that a swing might come off its moorings and be catapulted into space. And each year brought something new. Once it was "la Ola" - the Wave - to provide a fresh thrill with its drum-like seats that spun round and rose and fell as on a rough sea. Then "el Látigo" - the Whip - which swung gently in its orbit before lashing round suddenly in an attempt to make your head and body part company.

I think I must have been a somewhat cynical child because I was soon disillusioned with all these fairground attractions that went round.

I sussed out that they were on the road to nowhere and their charms palled. The only reason I continued to love the merry-go-round was an aesthetic one: the carved wood and the painted panels all round you were things of enormous charm. And I thirsted for rides on the bumper cars because they did not go round and could be steered in any direction. That was my idea of what a ride should be and, once more, I never felt I had had enough of them because young men, hell-bent on knocking the stuffing out of any other bumper car on the circuit, made it impossible for a little girl to be allowed a free hand in the matter by her parents. And didn't we admire the young lads who worked on all these rides? They darted between cars, rode "la Ola" confidently and leapt from moving roundabouts with balletic grace and gymnastic skill. I was too young to realise the poverty of their lives, those young men with their rope-soled "alpargatas", the cheapest footwear you could get, because, for me, they were touched with glamour in a way the circus performers never achieved.

And the humble stalls that lined the streets sold small pieces of Spanish nougat, for who could afford a whole slab in those days? Others sold slivers of coconut as they still do today; and there was candyfloss that was fascinating to watch as the stallholder spun the sugary thread into a fluffy mass of bright pink. Pink, too, were the tiny sugary figures of animals on toothpicks, "pirulines", that were impaled on a fleshy, prickly-pear leaf carried by itinerant sellers. Those leaves were also used to carry round a type of jasmine that drew moisture from the leaf and remained reasonably fresh for some young man to buy for his girlfriend.

My favourite stall was the one where they fried crisps on the spot and served them in "cucuruchos" - brown paper cones - that they would twirl into shape with expert fingers and which, thanks to their shape, only contained a limited number of those curling, crackling potato delights. Yes, you've guessed it: I never felt I'd had enough of them. When I think of all the thin slices of potato kept below the stall in a bucket of water, and the number of times the oil was used and reused throughout the nine days, I can imagine that eating the crisps grew more hazardous with every passing day. And what of the ghastly lemonade? No flavour, just killer bubbles that attacked your throat and brought tears to your eyes? No wonder our parents preferred to let us have soda water with a dash of vermouth or, which I disliked, anisette and water.

The street lighting was feeble, but I had no complaints about it, and I loved the smell of grilled octopus and, as you finally left the fairground at two in the morning after coffee and "churros" - cholesterol-laden fried batter - you might hear, from some bar, a voice that rose in the warm night air singing of love and betrayal. And, because that gypsy dress had become very, very heavy and you were only seven years old, you would end up being carried in your father's arms, your head drooping over his shoulder as you clutched a paper trumpet that you had bought from the easel-like stall covered in paper hats, little walking sticks and paper trumpets.

Innocent times. Perhaps I actually did like the fair after all.

8th April, 2005.

HOME DOCTOR.

You can no longer contract chlorasis, but a hundred and fifty years ago a young woman of refined sensibilities or of poor health might suffer from it. She might even die of it. In the first case she was probably suffering from depression and in the second case it could be anaemia, tuberculosis or leukaemia. There was obviously some complaint and what has changed is the naming of it, the science or mythology surrounding it and, of course, the treatment meted out. One can truly say that complaints are clearly not what they used to be. And talking of treatments, my friend, Sam, suggested that I mention the drilling of holes in the skull to release the devils within. Drastic, but probably efficacious: either the patients died or they were never the same again. In either case - end of demons.

Closer to home is my childhood and the home remedies typical of the period in Gibraltar. I remember vividly how my mother's belief in the need to clear your digestive system of toxins led her to dose my brother and me every Saturday morning with a ladleful of castor oil apiece. OK, it was a tablespoon, but it was a very large one. In fact, it was enormous. I tell you what; I'll revert to the ladle as being psychologically true to the experience. After we'd swallowed the noxious stuff - fighting impotently every single week against the outrage of it - we were given half an orange each to suck, to take away the taste.

How can you remove a taste that has seared its way via your taste buds on to your emotions and into your brain cells? To this day my brother abhors the taste of oranges. And on one memorable occasion when I was about four, after I had swallowed the Dreaded Dose, I found something better than oranges: I discovered a slab of chocolate and had eaten most of it before I was found out. The stuff was Brooklax, a laxative for children, and I spent a matter of twenty-four hours enthroned in the loo in near-solitary splendour. And we must bear in mind that my mother was being a good and caring parent, even though she treated our digestive tracts as if she were scouring the toilet and the plumbing thereof. Other families favoured cod liver oil. All I can say is, "Thank goodness my mother never considered using Harpic."

There were many weird and wonderful remedies we were subjected to: and I do not use the word "weird" lightly. Let me give you an example. My brother developed and earache that grew progressively worse as the days passed. It was diagnosed by a lady who treated ear complaints as "Wind in the ear". You must bear in mind that way back in 1948 or thereabouts there was no public health system to speak of in Gibraltar compared to what there is now. There was a hospital and there were doctors in private practice; there was the District Medical Officer for registered paupers - as there had been since around 1820; there was a Child Welfare Clinic for babes and infants; and there were ladies who treated ear complaints.

So for a week or so my brother was subjected to a cure that scared strong men witless. The lady, I shall call her Aurora, would light a candle and then take a piece of brown paper - "papel de estraza" - and drip bits of wax onto it. Then she would roll the paper into a cone and shove the narrow end into my brother's ear. *Then* she would set light to the other end and would watch carefully as it flamed its way down towards the ear. This, you see, was guaranteed to draw out the wind. It was also guaranteed to turn the young patient into a gibbering wreck as he waited for
- his brains to be sucked out as a mighty air current made its violent way forth;

- his hair to catch fire;
- the smell of burning flesh to assail his nostrils.

I was always there in fascinated attendance, admiring his bravery (though what I took as the stiff upper lip was a panic-induced rigidity that reached his toes). I'd watch with bated breath, waiting for Aurora to snatch the burning cone out of his ear before he went up in flames.

A week of this and of increasing pain showed how stubborn a case of wind could be. Then my father stepped in and called a young doctor recently established in Gibraltar. It was not wind, but an abscess which, with that treatment, could have resulted in some pretty nasty things happening in there, like wind in the brain or barbecued neurons and crispy dendrites.

My grandmother would cure "un empacho", an infant's tummy ache, with a tried and tested remedy. First you took the child and laid it on your lap, face up and tummy exposed. Then you rubbed the afflicted tummy with oil. Finally you took a goodly mouthful of "anís" - anisette - and spat it out mightily over the oily tum.

Sore throats and chest complaints both received a similar treatment. The ubiquitous "papel de estraza" was soaked in oil. In the first case it was wrapped round the neck and a *hot* towel/scarf/piece of flannel was wrapped over it. The oil then also heated up some, and a miscalculation could leave your singing voice an octave higher for a week. Similarly with the chest: this time the paper was soaked in *hot* oil. This was applied to the chest. It must have worked because patients were known to shriek and then devoutly declare themselves totally cured and in no need of further treatment.

And for the fevered brow there was brown paper again, soaked in vinegar this time, to draw out the heat. There were also two other treatments: the slices-of-raw-potato treatment and the slices-of-cucumber treatment. You placed the slices of the vegetable of your choice upon the afflicted brow and removed and renewed them when they got warm and began to curl at the edges. The patient, as I can testify from personal experience, felt a total wally and prayed that no chance visitor would drop by.

And there was the large key dropped down the back of your neck to stop a nose-bleed; and the gold ring rubbed on the eyelid to ease a stye. And everyone knows and still uses the standard hot lemon and honey drink for sore throats. Once, my grandmother, after a sleepless night during which my racking cough kept us both awake, brewed a remedy for me. I think she got confused because, instead of the classic lemon and honey, she concocted a brownish sludge made from boiling together prunes and dried figs. My brother noted that it was a cure for constipation. It also worked with the cough: I didn't dare cough, did I?

Given how often brown paper has made its way into this article as a standby in home remedies, I could do worse than finish on a literary note: remember that young couple who were sent to the well for water? Jack fell down and broke his crown and he went to bed to mend his head with vinegar - and brown paper, what else?

16th July, 2004.

GAMES WE PLAYED - PART I.

We played them out in the street so they were often seasonal, weren't they? Some could only be played if the weather was warm and dry. Others were suitable for both summer and winter, and many only waited on someone to revive them.

One girl would come out with a skipping rope and others would go home asking for one too. What we ended up with was not one of those commercially spawned ones with wooden handles, light rope that barely did the work required of it and the occasional bell that, inbuilt into the handle, jingled as you skipped. No. What we got was strong rope, heavy and thick, which our fathers managed to find somewhere like, dare I say? His Majesty's dockyard - and we were all set for years of hard skipping.

The game would blossom as the days passed. You did not just skip in solitary pleasure merely to see how long you could go till your foot caught in the rope and you foundered. Instead you found yourself seeing what others did and trying out each new idea; and there were so many variations to try once you got the hang of it! Or there would develop a competitive spirit.

You could skip forward, backward, feet together, one foot after the other. You could cross your arms to reduce the loop of rope and spin the rope either forward or, with growing expertise, spin it backwards. And, hardest of all, you could shorten the rope and do "Bumps" - where you spun the rope twice, very quickly, as you jumped a bit higher than usual. You would eventually do the backward variety that was a real test of skill. I think I remember the record as standing at forty-two forward and twenty-five backward bumps!

And, of course, you played "La Comba" where the rope was extra long and was held at each end by a girl who did the Cinderella job, turning it like you might an outsize mangle; and it could be very hard work that was only acceptable because we took it in turn. The rest of the group would line up on the right of one of these Cinderellas and jump in and out of the rope as it spun round. You went in individually with some falling by the wayside till only two or three remained, running round like dervishes to get to their turn in time, for to miss a turn of the rope was to be out of the game. There would be an eventual winner and, quite often, this would be the signal for the whole group to join her so that the skipping became a totally communal activity. And, naturally, there were further refinements that would develop, like jumping in from the left or using two ropes, one spun clockwise and the other anti clockwise. It would all be grand and then, one day, the rope would disappear from the scene to languish in a cupboard till someone came upon it a year later and it all started again. Meanwhile, the cause of its demise would take over as some new craze set in.

It might be cat's cradle, which had a short life span as there seemed to be a limit to the number of moves you could make before your fingers got tangled in the string, or you ended up with a pathetic single strand that was going nowhere, or you had worked out a cyclical progression that went on boringly and endlessly.

And there were "Las Estampitas" - Little Pictures - with two gender-based varieties. The boys would use those old rectangular cards that came with cigarette packets. They depicted famous film stars or football players, cricketers, cars or airplanes. The girls would use what we called "scraps", images that were printed in sheets. Each sheet might have twelve or sixteen cut-out pictures, each joined to the others by narrow strips of plain paper. The images might be small or very big. They might be little girls in Victorian costumes or small baskets of flowers or cats or cottages. They were all very shiny and highly coloured, even slightly embossed at times, and you fell in love with each new series that appeared.

I know I bugged my mother to get them for me, but there was no money to throw around so, when I *was* given the couple of pence required, it was a chance to look all the new sheets over carefully before deciding on my purchase. My aunts, Mariquita and Teresa, unearthed *their* old scraps for me and, it hurts me to say this! - I gambled those beautiful old Edwardian pictures away with the shiny new ones.

And it *was* a form of gambling. The boys would play in pairs, each staking a set number of cards. You had to "Chuar" – draw lots - to see who took first turn. One would then throw the staked cards against a wall. All those that fell face up were his to keep. They would then top up the set and the second boy would take his turn. With the girls it was very much a matter for negotiation as you staked one scrap against another. They were ranked according to considerations of size, beauty, novelty value and other criteria. Then you would roll the dice for them. Fathers also came into it because you kept the pictures in a box: an old cigar box or one of those flat Craven A tins.

As with skipping, so with "Las Estampitas". The craze would be slaked and it was autumn and, lo and behold, it was the season for spinning tops. I was never very good at this and my top always seemed to roll on its side - a small beached whale trying to do aerobics. My brother's top, I thought, always landed on its lead point and pirouetted around for extended spells like Rudolph Nureyev in his hey-day. It made me want to spit!

There was also "el piso" - hopscotch. Where on earth did we get our chalk from? Perhaps from one of those tiny shops that dotted the upper town, like María Leal's up Castle Street. All you needed was that bit of chalk, a stone to act as your counter, a reasonably quiet piece of pavement and you were off.

Marbles was another game that came and went every year. I'm a purist on the matter. Not for me the later fashion for merely rolling your marble along as if you were playing bowls. I held the marble in my crooked forefinger, tucked my thumb behind it and flicked it forward and out. This sent the marble shooting forth with considerable power and could knock an opponent's marble into kingdom come. In fact, I have known a new strong marble coming in contact with an old one that was suffering from glass-fatigue and splitting it in two.

As it had been with "Las Estampitas", so it was with the marbles. There was a hierarchy of values and at the humbler end were the plain pale-green ones that had started life as the stoppers on lemonade bottles. And there were those lovely elegant marbles with the trompe d'oeil central spiral of twisting colours. There were also very large marbles that were generally not acceptable for standard games. They were like the bullies in the playground who threw their weight about. The magic words "Piola, cruces, vá y vale" remain with me to this day. While I forget the exact part they played in our games of marbles, I think they were a formula for ensuring that what you had established became sacrosanct and could not be challenged. Grand games all! - and there were more...

13th February, 2004.

GAMES WE PLAYED - PART II.

For some reason, "Las Cañoneras" was almost exclusively a game for boys. For this all you needed were discarded metal bottle-tops that you flattened with a hammer. Then you looked for a suitable hole in the ground that was roughly cylindrical and whose diameter was somewhat greater than that of the flattened bottle tops. From an agreed distance you would proceed to try and toss the tops into the hole. The experts could use a stack of six or more tops which they would send through the air in a graceful curve so that they all went into the hole as one. I believe the name of the game arose out of the original counters – the flattened buttons off the uniforms of gunners, men who handled guns - "cañones". "Pali y Cachi" was a pavement game. You set short sticks against the step and hit the ends with a larger stick that acted as a bat. Up would fly the little fellows and you then had to be quick enough to clout them into space with your bat.

For wet days there was button football to be played on the dining room table. You raided your mother's sewing box and picked out large old buttons that were no longer wanted. They became your football team, but what was most important was the master button - big and flat - with which you pressed the edge of your ordinary players. If you pressed properly, the player would shoot forward and hit the "ball" in the centre of the table. Badly chosen players, when pressed, had a tendency to rear up and flip over without achieving anything. Too much pressure would send your player careering across the table, committing fouls to right and left before falling over the edge.

There were some games played by both boys and girls like the common game of Catch - "Tú las Llevas" - and the more exciting variant of "Catch en Alto" where you were safe if your feet were off the ground as you clung to a wall or leapt onto a bench. Another variant was "One, Two, Three Taco". The Taco was a block of wood and it spelt safety for the person being chased. If there was no Taco as such then any area or object would be designated as the Taco for the occasion. And "Toca Hierro" - Touch Iron - could entertain you all the way home from school as you ran from one piece of iron to another to be safe from your pursuer. Equally energetic was leapfrog. If you lived in the socially superior Main Street, you called it "Jumping Mula" - "Mula" being a mule - and if you lived up Castle Road you called it "Jumpy Mula". And there was hide and seek and "La Gallinita Ciega" - blind man's buff.

Probably the wildest of all games was "Chi-Chi la Hava", a game played exclusively by boys. I do apologise if I've misspelt it, but it was a part of our oral tradition and I never saw it written down. Boys used to line up with the boy at the front leaning over and placing his hands against the wall. The boy behind him would also bend over and hold on to the first boy's waist. The rest of the line would follow suit, holding on to whatever they could in order to form a chain with their backs - like a human caterpillar. Then those attacking would take a running jump at the line, leaping into the air to land on the human chain to try and break it. It was a game that appalled me, even as a child, and I still wonder that no one ever came to total grief in the course of it.

What these games had in common was the low cost involved. Also involved in them was the communal factor, and the element of health as you ran around getting a great deal of exercise and working up a terrific appetite in the process. We could play in groups on the street because there weren't that many cars to make it hazardous; and we could get together in the patios because there were still old houses built round such large, communal areas where children grew up together, played together, fought each other and made friends with each other.

What we were also doing in the process was learning social skills and testing our ingenuity. We had to learn to negotiate, to argue, to compromise, to organise. We learnt who to trust and who to avoid. We were learning what it meant to be members of a community beyond the family and outside the controlled society of the school. And we did establish rules and taboos of our own for the different activities. When things became fraught for you for some reason, there was always a respite to be gained by calling out an anguished "Purish!" – a cry for the suspension of activities. Everything stopped and you could try to renegotiate matters or attempt to call a truce.

I spoke of the low cost involved, and it was so, which meant that the games were within the reach of virtually everyone. What you needed was imagination and you developed skills and dexterity, but money gave you little advantage, if any.

Football was played then as it is now, but there wasn't, as I recall, the obsessive loyalty to mighty teams that you find today. With no television and with many families reading only the occasional newspaper, our loyalties were purely local. In fact, my loyalties were purely aesthetic and were dictated by colour schemes. The Britannia football team sported green and yellow, which was unsubtle; the Europa went in black and green, as I seem to recall, which I found dreary; the Gibraltar United was rather strident in red and white and it was the Prince of Wales in their white strip with small touches of red and green that earned my tepid support.

On a personal level were the games my brother and I played at home. Playing soldiers involved setting up an old blanket with folds and lumps and bumps for us to ensure that the soldiers could take cover. Out would come his lead soldiers, lovingly and carefully housed in their original boxes. Campaigns would be planned and forces deployed. I believe we had more joy out of organising all the preliminaries than out of the actual battles when we finally got round to them. Another of our absorbing games was the creation of a plastacine family. There were parents, children, sister-in-law, and a horse for each one to ride. There were also dogs. I think the family wore large hats - plastacine of course - and lived in the Wild West. When not being played with, we kept them in a large square biscuit tin.

Today there is an enormous amount of money made out of the children's market. It is in the interests of commerce and industry to persuade us to buy, buy, buy for our children. There are politically correct toys and there is terrible rubbish available, but have you noticed how many of the wonderfully sophisticated toys that children get on December 25th hold little interest for them by late January?

What saddens me and angers me most, however, is the gradual shift to the playing of games that require no friend, no co-operation, no socialising. It saddens me that children may relate almost exclusively to a screen. It angers me that so many computer games involve violence, destruction and a ruthless disregard for anything like ethical or moral concerns...like the plagiarised version of Monopoly that involves the player in becoming a drug baron. Some things have not changed for the better.

20th February, 2004.

A TOAST TO THE DAUGHTERS OF EVE.

A TOAST TO THE DAUGHTERS OF EVE.

Having worked for years in both single-sex and mixed schools, I have had ample opportunity to study how female and male bonding work. This could best be done during break-time or the lunch hour. The bell would go and the girls would emerge from the school buildings in couples or small groups, talking about something - it might be about homework, nail varnish, games, future career, boyfriends or anything under the sun. They would find a quiet spot to sit down and chatter away in peace. When the bell rang again, they would rise and return to the building, still talking.

What of the boys? They would erupt from the building in a kind of corporate lump, head-butting the air and shouting at each other in an act of mass bonding as they set off to play a game of football or any group game where they could run and leap on each other. For closer, more personal relationships they would grab friends round the neck or in a half-nelson and proceed to thump them. Clouting with the satchel was another option. It was all pre-verbal.

We certainly seem to belong to two different emotional species.

Women are basically loving. They are intuitive, caring, affectionate and perceptive. They are good organisers, good listeners, fine students, conscientious and intelligent…I fear I must cut this part short as the article must be under 1600 words. Do feel free to supply further virtues of your choice.

When I first came to live in Spain I was struck by the behaviour of women in offices. You'd walk in and the secretary/clerk/receptionist would be sitting at a desk piled high and the Out tray piled equally high. She would be answering the phone and filling up forms. You'd ask for whatever you needed and she'd pull out a couple of papers from assorted drawers and wave you down the passage to Room 6 or whatever it was. You'd realise that the waving of the hand was also aimed at drying her nails which she was somehow managing to varnish.

In Room 6 you would find her boss, the architect or planning officer or legal adviser. His desk would be so highly polished that a good sneeze would have sent any papers on it sliding to the floor - had there been any. He would, however, have a splendid blotter with leather corners and a drawing of Snoopy which he had just finished embellishing in green biro.

A similar insight into the way the sexes operate is captured in the joke about the Three Wise Men. What would have happened if they had been Three Wise Women? Well, for one thing, they would have arrived on time for the birth because they would have asked the way. Secondly, they would have brought practical gifts like disposable nappies and would have rolled up their sleeves and done something about cleaning up the stable. And last, as they left, one of them would have muttered discreetly, "My Dears, she may be the mother of the Messiah, but did you see the sandals she was wearing with that skirt?"

There is a good reason for the fact that we approach life differently: there is a neurological basis to the way we operate. In women it appears that the bridge joining the two cerebral hemispheres is broader than in men. Women actually draw more on both sides of the brain and men tend to stick with a single side. That's why men call themselves logical and consider it a splendid thing and they call women intuitive and don't really trust their way of thinking.

When I did a basic course in philosophy years ago, I was faced with logic and had to work my way through a series of exercises in order to assess whether the statements made were true or false. The sort of thing I had to work on was along these lines: "All geese are white; this bird is white, ergo it is a goose." I ask you. I felt it was great for playing around, particularly as some of it was a bit like algebra, but I failed to see its value as anything but an academic exercise. Consider the matter coldly: I don't know what varieties of geese exist or what colours they come in, but even if they truly were all white, I should hope I could tell the difference between a goose, an albino ostrich and a white budgie.

It's this approach to reality that makes women such first class factotums. We can tackle all sorts of different jobs at the same time. Take the Monday morning scenario of the domestic rush-hour. The woman may have to iron a shirt, answer the phone, pack the kids' lunch, find her partner's missing glasses and make the scrambled eggs. A trial on precisely these lines was carried out a few years ago with a group of men and women, all working against the clock. All the women finished the tasks in the set time. Only one of the men did. The rest had managed to iron the eggs and scramble the shirt.

I've known a number of fine men, upstanding citizens and loving husbands, who cannot respond to the call, "Darling, can you help me to shift this furniture/take down the curtains/set up the Christmas tree now?" They will happily do what you ask, of course they will. They are not being unhelpful - perish the thought! It's just the word "now" that causes them to blench. They prefer to have notice of the task to be undertaken...like being told two weeks in advance. And if you can hand them a form filled out in triplicate, all the better. You can't blame them. Their neurons are probably busy with one task and they can't change horses in midstream, as it were, without rupturing a synaptic connection somewhere in the brain. (I know you can't rupture an electrical connection, but I speak in metaphors and like to mix them.)

That's why you will get a man doing research in a laboratory and devoting twenty years of his life to a project which finally brings to light previously unidentified bacteria that dwell in the lower intestine of the common flea - and can give humans a nasty rash. His wife? She didn't have a job. Didn't work like he did. She hung about the house and brought up their five children.

It's not just scientists who profit from that linear type of thinking. Philosophers, as I have indicated, do it too. Let us glance at Descartes. He went around worrying about the nature of existence and reality. Questions like, "Does the chair still exist when I leave the room or does its existence depend on my perception or what?" Tricky one! After obsessing around and deciding he couldn't trust his senses or anyone else's, he came up with his ground-breaking premise: "Cogito; ergo sum" - I think; therefore I am. Now, I don't know about you, but I've always had a shrewd idea that I existed. My mother assured me that I did. In point of fact, my sense of being was so strong that it was clear to me that I was thinking precisely because I existed: "Sum; ergo cogito," as I said to Mum; and she agreed. Actually, before setting aside the question of scientists, did you know that the Nobel Prize for science, for decades, had only once been awarded to the same person on two separate occasions? That was to Marie Curie. I bet she was using both sides of her brain for all she was worth.

The search for knowledge is there in the Garden of Eden. Adam is quite happy to get on with the gardening and it is Eve, with more on her mind than the flora, who gets chatting to the serpent, the way one does. The thought of the Tree of the Knowledge of Good and Evil gets her going. It's actually a remarkably common tale and there are many variations worldwide. The common factor, apart from the way the woman behaves, is the fact that each tale involves an arbitrary prohibition - as if the god in question is deliberately setting up humanity for a fall:

Australia, New South Wales - god forbids humans to go near a tree where bees nest. The women go. Death enters the world.

Uganda, the Baganda people - the first man is allowed to marry a daughter of heaven, but they must not return to heaven. You've guessed it…she does and Death comes into the world.

North America, the Algonquin Indians - the first man is given a package that must not be opened. His first wife opens it and lets Death out.

Greece, Pandora - she is given a box that must not be opened. Of course, she opens it and releases all ills into the world.

All these women have one thing in common - an enquiring mind, curiosity, a desire to know. Can you honestly take these tales literally? Don't you see them as metaphors for the paradox of existence? We live and we die; we suffer and we hope; we are mortal and can conceive of immortality; life can nurture and destroy in an arbitrary manner. However, for the literal minded these tales showed how "dangerous" women were. Perhaps women were quicker off the mark with speech, were less conformist and were perceived as a threat if men were convergers - conservative and less given to breaking the social mould?

In around 1790 Jane Austen could write with irony: "A woman, especially if she have the misfortune of knowing anything, should conceal it as best she can." And in a Victorian periodical which offered advice to its readers one could read about young women who wanted to study that, "Study is likely to produce ill effects on women *and their offspring*...(and such women)...ought to accept voluntary celibacy." (My italics.)

I get the feeling that it was fear of women that led to their suppression for a couple of thousand years in the west. Now that many countries provide the same opportunities for both sexes, girls are outstripping boys in school and in some countries are even taking up more university places than the lads. It's clear to me that we Daughters of Eve have a strength and vitality we haven't been given credit for and may even be unaware of. It's wonderful to be a woman when there is freedom and a growing degree of equality. And there is one thing we can do that no man has ever managed - we can have children: and it's a mind-blowing experience.

Three cheers for us!

28ᵗʰ March, 2003.

PAPERING OVER THE CRACKS.

Think of the attention given recently in the media to the attack launched by Princess Anne's dog on one of the queen's corgis: if the princess had herself bitten the queen, the incident wouldn't have been given more space on the air or in print. First we heard of the attack, then we were told that it was the same dog that had gone for a child last year, and then came the final bulletin - it was a mistake! It wasn't the same dog at all and, anyway, the original dog was in therapy to help him with his antisocial tendencies. Those last items merely went to show that

1. there was not one, there were *two* aggressive dogs;

2. you couldn't trust the news;
3. it looked suspiciously as though someone might be papering over the cracks.

I blame it all on Queen Victoria. I truly do. Before she came to the throne, the monarchy had been in the sort of shambles that was the delight of cartoonists like Cruickshank who lampooned royalty with a vicious satire that you'd be hard put to match today in any field. The King himself, George III, suffered from bouts of what was termed "insanity" owing to a condition that was not medically identified till around 1930 when he was very dead and could not profit from the knowledge. It was well-known to the public that the sons of George III were a ripe lot. He eldest son, Prinny, heir to the throne no less, secretly married a catholic - Mrs Fitzherbert - and later had her pushed aside while he contracted a second marriage which many considered bigamous. His brothers were notorious, either for fathering many children in common-law unions or for selling military titles to the highest bidders or other equally "un-royal" activities.

You noticed that I placed the word un-royal in inverted commas, didn't you? That's because I use the word ironically for to do what the hell you pleased and to be accountable to nobody had most certainly been a royal prerogative since goodness knows when. To be royal did not mean that you were morally head and shoulders above your subjects. Well, it did for a few like Edward the Confessor and the queen, St Margaret of Scotland, but for the majority it seemed to be taken as conferring license to do as you would.

Then came Victoria and created the myth of happy families. She seems to have worshipped Prince Albert and she certainly gave birth to a lot of children, though we now know that some of them or their offspring seemed to be emotionally dysfunctional, and we always knew that others were married off for dynastic or political reasons - as was to be expected. She lived on, and on…and on and the other myth - of the upright, morally incorruptible sovereign - came into being.

Her descendants set about giving the lie to this for a time with their sexual adventures, but George VI stemmed the tide and Elizabeth II followed in his footsteps. Sadly for her, the world changed and her progeny have once more made it clear that being royal is no defence against your own passions, foolishness, arrogance and all the weaknesses that flesh is heir to.

So all this malarkey about the dog that did/didn't attack the corgi is a load of old...protectionist public relations. If the dog should be put down because it really is dangerous then - sadly - the sooner the better. Or are royal dogs to enjoy the Divine Right of Kings' status which died out centuries ago?

It seems to me that we have a similar situation with regard to a very different issue: women and the priesthood. There, it's out. Why is it similar? Principally because it's also a case of papering over the cracks: you make an ill-considered statement and then you stick to it come hell or high water, and in the face of evidence that you were wrong in the first place.

Centuries ago, the reason for women being denied ordination was clear enough to great thinkers like St Thomas Aquinas: "(As).....the female sex has the status of an inferior, that sex cannot receive ordination." St Bonaventure strengthened the argument when he explained that only the male is made in the image of God so only he can exercise this god-like office. And Aquinas clinched matters by giving scientific proof of women's inferiority: they are "a mistake" because male sperm clearly should reproduce *itself* and a boy child should be born.

Furthermore, he tells us that the problem could be that the woman's womb is defective, or there could be some "deforming interference" - like the south winds which are too wet. Biological mutants, that's us!

Let's see; he is assuming that God's intention is that only males should be born, and females only occur when there's a systems' malfunction. So what did he make of God's injunction to increase and multiply? Pause for thought...

Lucky St Bonaventure! I wish I too knew what God looked like, but I'm confused. Was he like my husband?...or my nephews Arthur or Adrian or my sons-in-law, or my uncles? They are so different, I expect my confusion arises because I'm only an inferior woman and am even incapable of understanding that bit about the humid south wind, but that's why I have two daughters. So what's the Met. Office going to do about it?

But now I know that woman is a misbegotten man and, a fact well known to the Fathers of the church, contains more liquid than man - with all the weaknesses that that entails! And, this is one there's no getting away from: woman is impure because she menstruates. Please, don't start asking me about what that says about childbirth and the holiness of the marriage union and the duty of Catholics to avoid contraception: I don't know. What I *have* read is that in 1917, Canon 813.1 (Canon Law) stated that women "may in no case come up to the altar, and may give responses only from afar"...possibly from outside the church?

Perhaps, in fairness, I should abandon such old ideas and look at the present reasons for declaring that women cannot serve God in the priesthood. As far as I can make out, it goes like this:
   - Christ made men his original apostles so women can't be ordained.
   -"A natural resemblance ...must exist between Christ and His minister." (Come back St Bonaventure, all is forgiven?)
   - The church is the bride of Christ so the priest must obviously be a man.
   - I think that's about it. But, to bring this further up to date, let's look at Sacerdotali Ordinatio, 1994:
   "The Church has no authority whatsoever to confer priestly status on women."

You could have fooled me; and there's me thinking that the church has authority over matters religious, but clearly it can only refuse ordination, not grant it. I feel I'm definitely missing something here, but be that as it may, there it is: a rationally argued and watertight case against the ordination of women, so why do I get this persistent, nagging feeling that custom - even the custom of centuries - is a different matter from immutable fact or truth?

Let me bring all this to a more cheerful end with a few facts you might be glad to have. The apostles were apostles, not priests and 1 Peter 2:5 speaks of priesthood as a communal and not an individual ministry. Saint Peter himself was married and St Paul tells how Peter travelled with his wife (I Corinthians 9:5). Maybe she was only around to wash his socks? Thanks to St Paul, we know of church ministries in the early days which involved the office of elders, prophets, ministers, teachers, shepherds and a number of others. Women could exercise all of these. Women like Prisca, Junia, Julia and Nereus's sister were missionaries with a male partner (husband or brother).

What do I think of it all? I think church or state can be afraid of admitting to error and can keep papering over the cracks. I think honourable men can make mistakes. I think priests and popes can err. I can too. But no one can stop us looking at the evidence and drawing our own conclusions.

23rd January, 2004.

MARY, ANDREA AND US.

Within a week, the papers have had to cover the deaths of the Pope and Prince Rainier, and the wedding of Prince Charles to Camilla. They must have wept with frustration: so much potential copy of the highest order all jostling together for media attention. Amazingly, they managed to cover all three pretty well. But, with so many demands on limited radio, TV and printed space, it is not surprising that virtually nothing was heard of the death of Andrea Dworkin on April 9th.

Quite! Who was she? The papers had plenty to say about her in 1964 when, after being involved in an anti-Vietnam-War demonstration, she was arrested and later made public her treatment at the hands of two doctors while she was in prison. She had also been the subject of abuse by her father and was to become a battered wife during her first marriage. A truly unenviable CV. You may consider it an exceptional, an atypical one. "Don't generalize from the particular," you say, so I won't. Let me just add that it is not surprising that she became a notable feminist.

"Burn your bras!" Remember that early feminist cry in America? All you need to do is look at the sort of bras women were wearing in the fifties and early sixties to agree heartily with this injunction on aesthetic if not philosophical grounds. The cups on those bras were conical, stitched in a spiral from base to apex so that they looked like armour plate. You could poke someone's eye out...with a bit of manoeuvring. When you wore them you looked like one of those carved prows of ancient sailing ships - female figureheads that thrust breasts of epic dimensions at the world. Who designed those embarrassingly obvious items of underwear? Who promoted and sold them? Who made decisions about marketing them? It surely wasn't women. Little wonder that early feminists picked on them as a symbol of women's subjugation.

The place of women in most societies still has a long road to travel before there is equality rather than discrimination at virtually all levels. Yes, women can have babies and men can't, and it takes real imagination to turn that fact on its head, yet it has been done. List while I tell you: there is a simple native tribe in the depth of somewhere (I do apologise for my utterly terrible memory) which, once the wife goes into labour, puts the husband to bed. He will mimic the process and when the child is born, it is placed on his chest and he will lie there recovering from his ordeal and receiving members of the tribe who come to bring him their gifts. The wife can't attend to them as she's out in the field doing a spot of agricultural work. Well, in what is probably a subsistence economy, you can hardly expect them both to take the day off, can you?

We in the great societies are not that primitive, are we? The women really do get the credit for having the babies; the men merely limit themselves to drawing up all the rules connected with the process from conception to birth and, in some places, with all the rights of parenthood which often reserves the duties for the woman and the rights for the men.

You think I jest? You feel my voice is too strident? You consider that I exaggerate? Harken to my tale, and it's not a pretty one. No one can show that the Koran, at any point, requires the faithful to practice sexual mutilation. How comes it, then, that the figures for female sexual mutilation stand, at present, at well over 120,000,000? If you're lucky, you undergo the version called Sunna where, at best, only the clitoris is removed whole or in part. Less fortunate are the women on whom Pharaonic Circumcision is carried out. Clitoris and inner labia are removed. Outer labia are sewn together allowing only an opening for urine and menstrual fluid. Marriage means that the opening is enlarged, and then fully opened for childbirth. Naturally it is sewn up after childbirth. Who drew up the rules? Not the women. Who orders these mutilations? Caring mothers, of course. How else can mothers ensure that their daughters will be considered marriageable? In a society where women have no economic power they are reduced to being a commodity that must be marketable.

I hate writing this, but how else do we learn about such things unless the information is available? It doesn't take a genius to figure out the reason for it all. Women who've suffered such sexual mutilation are unlikely to be anything other than virgins when they marry. They are unlikely to enjoy sex. Ergo - they will remain faithful and men can stop worrying about being cuckolded. We in the west don't have such barbaric practices; we just have certain private clinics where, up to around a dozen years ago, such "operations" were carried out. France finally passed a law making them illegal about twenty years ago. And in Victorian England a form of Sunna was used on young women showing "hysterical" symptoms, which generally meant that they were in the habit of indulging in what was called "the solitary vice" and were probably going to go blind, at least, if nothing was done to "save" them.

Let's get back to the particular, shall we? Specifically, to the "Mary" in the title. Mary Wollstonecraft was an early feminist, a social philosopher by inclination rather than by training. Back in the late 1700's rights went with privilege and she fought for equality for both men and women. She also wanted women to receive as good an education as their male counterparts. The rest of the world took nearly two centuries to reach the conclusions that were so obvious to her. In her time she was branded "impious" and "a philosophising serpent".

This is hardly to be wondered at when the great thinkers of the time could write things like, "A learned woman is a punishment for her husband, her children and the world," (Rousseau1712 - 1778); "Laborious study and deep reflection destroy the merits proper to her sex," (Kant 1724 - 1804); and Locke (1632 – 1704), the philosopher who championed man's right to revolution and whose thinking influenced the French and American Revolutions, believed that neither women nor…wait for it…animals were entitled to the same rights as man.

And Andrea Dworkin, centuries later, was fighting paedophilia, pornography, wife battering and the use of sex as a tool in the subjugation of women. She considered marriage as another form of prostitution where the woman got her financial security from sex with one partner rather than with many. There you are; I'm a gentleman, aren't I? I refuse to hide a fact that would prejudice my comments in the eyes of some readers. (And had I said, "I'm a lady," you might only interpret that as referring to my courtesy and breeding because a sense of honour is considered, almost exclusively, a masculine virtue.) And before you rush to condemn Ms. Dworkin's extreme feminist stand, it would be well to recall that, at that time, a woman in Portugal could not get a passport or travel outside the country without her husband's written consent; I believe a woman in Spain could not hold a bank account in her own name; and in America, Betty Friedan's book, "The Feminine Mystique", became a runaway bestseller. The main idea the book presented was that being wife, mother and housewife might not be quite enough. Women flocked to buy a book that propounded such a liberating and new idea. Goodness! How radical can you get?

Women today owe an enormous debt to all feminists: to writers like Mencia Calderón in Spain, who identified the traditional relationship between the sexes as "El juego simbiótico entre victima y verdugo" - the symbiotic game between victim and torturer. Or Christine de Pizan who, at the beginning of the fifteenth century, struggled to understand why God had created such a vile creature as Woman. She knew women were inclined to every vice: enemies of Man, avaricious, cruel and full of lust. She knew this was quoting the Fathers of the Church; and you don't go around contradicting people like St Jerome and St Augustine, among others. It took her years to decide that this image of woman was Man's construct and not God's creation.

Let me end by thanking all feminists who paved the way. Without them I couldn't have written like this today and if I had, you might be dismissing me as unhinged and ridiculous.

22nd April, 2005.

AU DESSUS DE SON GARE.

That was the punch-line of some joke, the gist of which I've completely forgotten. It's a literal rendering of that dated expression "above their station". If you were born a duke or an earl, it wasn't something you worried about, your station in life being pretty lofty. A road-sweeper's daughter and a clerk's son soon learned how surely it applied to them. Had God meant them to be other than lowly, He'd have provided the proverbial silver spoon at birth. You tampered with God's will at your peril so you kept to your own social sphere. Expressions like "upwardly mobile" had yet to be coined and, well up into the first third of the twentieth century, you were expected to know your place and stick to it.

Which, believe it or not, brings me to Switzerland. I once drove through a bit of it. It was early morning: they were shampooing the drains and polishing the pavements in preparation for another new day; the word "dirt" had been expunged from the language and a law had been passed that forbade dust to settle. Not one nasty smell, not a single bit of litter, and everyone had a recently laundered look, and if we forget the rather kitsch cuckoo clock and consider instead Switzerland's place in Europe in terms of finance, then we really have something, n'est ce pas? Can you get more advanced than all that?

Of course there's a catch in it. Let us cast our minds back to 1971. That was the year when women were *finally* granted the right to vote in Switzerland. And about time too! The Lebanon had got there nearly twenty years earlier; Austria, just next door, had instituted universal suffrage in 1907 - way ahead of others, including Britain. Sad to say, in Japan general suffrage *for men only* didn't arrive till 1928. All this reflects a world pattern: you start with might is right and no votes for anyone; along comes a powerful nobility who get a say in matters; then the wealthy or those necessary to the central power get in on the act. Eventually every man gets the vote, however intellectually challenged some may be. Only certified lunatics and women are left out, and it takes time till women are eventually granted the right to vote.

"Why aren't there more women in politics?" I was asked years ago and all I could think of were vague generalizations that failed to provide a real answer. My inability to provide that answer rankled. I eventually began to look into the matter. It soon became evident that it had been made very clear to women across the centuries that they must not go "au dessus de son gare", and that "gare" did not include politics.

If you are denied education, refused access to the professions, restricted to the domestic field, given an image of yourself - at best - as the loving bearer of children or - at worst - as a frivolous and dangerous purveyor of sexuality, then you are very unlikely to think, "It's politics for me!" Politics, medicine and the law were seen as spheres of exclusively male activity. Women were too fragile and their brains were incapable of intense mental effort. You may be thinking, "That's all very well, but decades after having the right to education and the right to vote, why are women still so poorly represented in governing bodies?" I use the term "governing bodies" because the situation obtains in everything from an educational establishment to the national government. It's all politics.

One answer is that old prejudices die hard. A woman going for a post of responsibility is still liable to be asked, if she has children, how she will cope if the kids get sick. Her husband will never be asked such a question. It's almost as if the man's role in family life is restricted to providing the sperm, while the woman must shoulder all parenting responsibility. Forgive me while I snort. Another answer is because centuries of brain-washing may take centuries to reverse. Take a country where equal pay for equal work only became law thirty years ago - give or take a year - and you realize that today's mothers and grandmothers and older single women were all paid less than their male counterparts for performing the same tasks. I am not talking about some Third World country, I am referring to the UK. I know that when I entered the teaching profession in Gibraltar I was paid less that the men I had trained with. "Men have to support families!" was the reason, which ignored the fact that all those young men were bachelors, and that there were plenty of single women supporting aging relatives. Doesn't it make you want to spit?

A whole society long conditioned to seeing the female as a second-class citizen and the male as the socially, legally, religiously and financially dominant being does not adopt new attitudes over-night, however many laws you may pass. Change will come, but sometimes very slowly because both sexes are trapped by the clichés of their cultural inheritance.

All that I'm saying now seems obvious to me, but I have been considering two other facts. Both have to do with gender, genetics, neurology - with physiology, in other words. Firstly, all politics whether with an upper case P or a lower case p have to do with power. If the first rulers - kings, chieftains, emperors - were there by right of conquest, by power of arms, because they were the strongest in the tribe or because they had disposed of their predecessors or rivals in some way, then you have started to lay down the ground rules of politics. We are not looking at strategies like collaboration, negotiation, discussion, sharing or fostering contented relationships based on co-operation. In its origins, politics seems to be about raw testosterone or nature red in tooth and claw.

Matters have been refined over the centuries and you get treaties and pacts between countries. They are grand indeed, some of those treaties, based as they may be on the fact that I agree to what you say because I'm forced to, or you accept certain terms because you have no option. We swop territories or exchange our children in marriage. Then we sit there and lick our wounds and wait for the chance to stab each other in the back as soon as we find ourselves strong enough to get back what we so reluctantly gave away. Other treaties involve mutual back-scratching. Of course I'm simplifying matters, but all you need to do is look at the catalogue of disastrous wars being waged at this moment to realise that not enough has changed. The world of governments is still one based in large measure on aggression, confrontation, power brokering and control. Even the refusal of certain governments to reduce pollution, to accept controls on over-fishing, to give third world countries a real chance to develop into developing nations has to do with vested commercial interests and powerful lobbies. Personal or corporation power and wealth are placed over the common good: the world can go hang as long as I protect my profits.

How do you enter this world if what you want to do is kiss it better? For sound genetic reasons many of women's strengths are directed more to ends like affective involvement, co-operation, negotiation and nurture. Politics looks less than appealing when what it seems to require are attitudes and strategies alien to you.

Secondly comes the crucial matter of decision-making. To take unpopular decisions is not easy, but it seems to be the case that men can decide, act and then put the matter behind them. A woman wants agreement, seeks the opposite of disruption so will find decision-making more difficult emotionally and is less likely to forget the matter even once a decision has been reached.

What might things have been like if the world had been ruled by matriarchal societies? Would politics have developed along totally different lines? Would the ground rules laid down in cultures dominated by the Goddesses of Life, of Fertility, of Growth been concerned with avoiding war and fostering collaboration? Life's not that simple, is it? Nevertheless, there is still room for hope: Burma may continue to violate human rights; North Korea may be a hereditary dictatorship; criminally political leaders may continue to bring horrendous misery to millions; but there are more women in leading political posts than in the past and there are male-driven political initiatives nowadays that are trying to rectify the balance and move towards a more equitable distribution of wealth, towards protection of the planet, towards justice for all: they are concerned for the world as a whole and are not simply fostering national welfare.

Perhaps women will begin to recognise this more humane face of politics and seek to be involved more actively in the process. Perhaps women will realize that they are as capable as men of taking responsibility and will value their own strengths. Perhaps men will acknowledge the need for women in politics and, as Zapatero has done in Spain, aim for a balance of women in parliament that reflects the fact that women are 50% of the population, and place them in posts of responsibility on an equal footing with men rather than seeing them as loyal supporters. Perhaps the Tory Blue-rinse Brigade in English constituencies will start stop favouring the male and blocking women when they come to electing their candidates. And perhaps I will live to see such major changes become the rule and not the exception - but they better hurry up because I'm not planning to live beyond the age of eighty-five.

3rd June 2005.

FRIVOLITY AND RECKLESS.

The old Spanish names that women were lumbered with have long been a source of horrified amusement to me. Names like Immaculate One, Anguishes, Dolours, Virtue, Conception and others of the like ilk can quite turn one's stomach. I wouldn't object to these names so much if boys had been christened with a similar schema in mind. They could have been called things like Benevolence, Protection, Humility, Gentleness. Get it? Good.

What's in a name? indeed! That which we call a rose we would never have called a Krebooticule. Why not?...because the sound is wrong. A rose is scented, has soft petals and delights the eye. You don't give it a name that suggests something between a carbuncle and an old shoe. I hate to disagree with Shakespeare - well, not really with Shakespeare, only with Juliet, and she only about thirteen and would have said anything to justify her love for Romeo, a family enemy - but there's a lot in a name.

It is not just a sound or two put together in an arbitrary fashion. It is a society's definition of itself, its people, its beliefs. In American films the plains Indians of North America were called things like Running Bear and Morning Sun. Fantastic names! And what of Mongol names? You don't want your beautiful child to be envied, and therefore taken or harmed, by demons so you call it "Yak-snot". It makes sense though they'd all feel a bit stupid in Clacton, don't you think?

Which brings me back to "Anguishes". The message is clear: we women were going to take our Old Testament neat, not on the rocks or diluted in any way - woman would bring forth children in pain and suffering and serve her damn well right for getting man kicked out of Paradise. What?...*Of Course it wasn't his fault.* So woman's role was clearly indicated in those Spanish names. She was to bear pain, to endure, to develop any virtues you could name, to be the long-suffering member of a partnership. What a pity they never came up with names like Frivolity, Amusement, Delights, Daring or, at a pinch, Lust.

If you're called something like Lydia or Emma or Yvonne they are not value-laden and they place no burden of moral expectation on you. Furthermore, today's girls have plenty of lively role models to follow. Just off the top of my head I can think of about five TV programmes that present women as dashing and constantly involved in deeds of derring-do. (My computer has never heard the expression and is suggesting that I substitute "herring".)

There is "Zena Warrior Princess" - which title is sufficient to give you some idea of the programme's content. There is the indifferently titled "Charmed" which gives no hint of the exciting adventures and violent encounters in which the three good witches are involved as they work to protect the innocent and rid the world of demons. Similarly with "Buffy: Vampire Slayer", in which a young woman, backed by a team, works along similar lines, complete with expertise in Karate. I know little of the new version of "Charlie's Angels" except that the three young women take on any danger, fight - physically - the most threatening male rivals and emerge triumphant. They have also, it appears, given the totally gratuitous male presence, Charlie, the boot. Praise be! That eliminates the horridly prurient feeling of Charlie's private harem that the early programmes had.

There's a fifth TV programme in which a girl of Asian descent...called Sydney, I believe...is also an expert in unarmed combat. And "Excalibur", a French cartoon programme, features a princess, as the Guardian of the Sword, and her right hand helper is another princess. That's quite a crop of female figures who are active rather than passive and who are conquerors rather than victims.

Of course it's all wildly improbable, but so are the male role models that boys have been presented with for years. Rambo and Terminator are hardly representative members of the average community. These New Wave Women, or whatever you want to call them, draw attention to the fact that women can be perceived in a different way to what was once standard practice. We know that they're all stereotypes: domestic, sexual, daring - but at least the parameters have been extended.

"Reckless Ruby" by Hiawyn Oram is a children's book in which the beautiful child heroine hates being called "Precious" and being told that her ambition should be to marry a rich man who will cosset her. So she takes to a life of wild daring and ends up with two broken legs, fractured ribs, black eyes, stitches, bruises, broken fingers and a pretty awful feeling in her stomach. She is no longer called "Precious Ruby", but "Reckless Ruby" and she is delighted. You must admit that it's a more appealing proposition to be daring than to be treated like a china doll. And, once again, though it's fiction, it offers an alternative model to consider.

It's a pity that more use is not made of real women of action. The seemingly fragile Claire Francis presents a good starting point. To sail round the world solo is no mean feat. She's part of a very English tradition, well established in the nineteenth century which was rich in idiosyncratic English gentlewomen who set out to do things like go to the heart of Africa or to the Middle East to collect butterflies or sketch flowers. Some were bordering on the slightly dotty, like Lady Esther Stanhope in her final days, but - my goodness - did they have guts!

And then there are those of great intellect like the writer and thinker Maria de Sayas y Sotomayor, whom Lope de Vega called "milagro de mujer" - A miracle of a woman. And Catherine the Great of Russia who, despite the recent film, offered the world a great deal more than a fine bosom. She was a playwright, she corresponded with people like Voltaire, she reformed the administrative system, organized the legislature and was such an active ruler that it is a wonder that she had time for the lovers that made her notorious in a world where it was only the male rulers who were allowed such license.

The twelfth century produced Hildegarde de Bingen, a genius comparable to the great Arab Avicenne in her range and originality of thought. Almost her contemporary was Maria Perez of Castille who led an army against the invading Arab forces and against Aragon. She even challenged the mighty Alfonso of Aragon, "El Batallador" – The Warrior - to a duel.

He lost.

And there's Mary Read, the pirate; there's Mencia Calderón, Conquistadora, who directed an expedition to Paraguay in the sixteenth century…so many extraordinary women. You won't have heard of them because history was written by men and such women were treated as the exceptions that proved the rule - so they could be dismissed and forgotten.

I rest my case.

15th August, 2003.

PERSONAL VICCISITUDES.

ON VISITING THE DENTIST.

Let me say from the start that I have always liked the various dentists whom I have had recourse to over the years. It is not their fault that as far as I'm concerned they are in the ruthless business of scaring me witless. Blame my father for my fears: he told us fearsome tales of his first extraction. As far as I remember, it was a pliers-in-the-mouth and foot-on-the-chest job…with him, his tooth and the dentist wrestling for supremacy.

Nevertheless, far from disliking dentists, I have found them amicable souls with whom I have enjoyed many a friendly chat. Actually, that is not entirely accurate because you can't really chat with them, can you? You sit in the chair, open your mouth and in goes the hardware: the winch to get you to open your mouth wider; the Hoover to collect the debris; the sprinkler to rinse; and the odd crochet hook and the pruning shears. This done, your dentist then talks to you.

"So, where are you going this summer?"

"Arg uungh," you reply.

"Interesting. We're thinking of Norway or maybe Finland."

"Ea-ay?" You raise your eyebrows in enquiry.

"Well, it would make a change from all the usual hot places. Yes, probably Finland."

"Uuuunghy iughin."

"Nawrince 'n spitt," he says as he clears out the hardware.

For a split second you are left wondering if they are cities somewhere in Finland; resorts near the polar icecap perchance? Then you notice that the dental nurse is trying to hand you a plastic cup full of pink fluid. You sit up with a jerk and blushingly oblige by rinsing out your mouth. The liquid goes in pink and comes out brown: the shame of it.

*　*　*　*　*　*

In point of fact, my kind dentists have made me a braver woman: fillings I can now cope with with a measure of insouciance, but it's the abscess followed by the extraction of the nerve that are the toughest tests. You spend a week on antibiotics to deal with the abscess, then you go back knowing that, whatever happens, you have left enough food in the freezer for the family to survive till after the funeral when the will is read. The dentist tells you you won't feel a thing as he takes out the hypodermic syringe.

It is about a metre long and contains several pints of anaesthetic. You feel the point going into your gum and it's followed by a tidal wave that washes round your molar before swirling up into your brain. He has injected your jaw at three different points, or was it twelve? Suffice it to say that when he finally jacks open your mouth and goes for the offending tooth, you feel absolutely nothing. That's when the sound of the high-tech drill begins. It almost drowns the Prozac music that's meant to lull you into a state of passive somnolence - though how you are expected to doze off with a possible denticidal maniac around is beyond me.

Now, the old-fashioned drills would rattle, belch and drone and make your whole head vibrate, shaking your teeth loose and thus eliminating the need to draw them. Nowadays the state-of-the-arts drills are elegant, high speed contraptions with a high-pitched whine like a bluebottle with a nasal condition. They seem harmless enough until you notice that the dental nurse keeps ducking to avoid the splinters of bone flying out of your mouth and embedding themselves in the wall behind her. The smell of burning bone fills the air and you are aware that he's been at that tooth for rather a long time. What is he up to? Is he hoping to strike oil or something? Damn it! He'll be coming out through the back of your skull at any moment. You have to stop him. He's dangerous. You won't stand for any nonsense. Right!

"Fine," he says, "Just a bit more to do. Are you all right?"

You nod and make happy little noises at the back of your throat. You coward.

Then suddenly it's over. He's mixing cement with his little trowel, is packing the cavity with wadding and generally wiping clean the scene of the crime. Only a temporary filling? Who cares? He wants to wait till the tooth has settled down before finishing things. Heck! That tooth has been there for years; it's not going anywhere. You try to tell him so, but your lips have turned into two slabs of blubber. Never mind; the important thing is that you're free to go. You sit up and give him the lopsided sort of smile the Phantom of the Opera managed on a good day. And you are grateful really.

"Unk oo," you articulate carefully.

Then you stand up - and fall over. The anaesthetic in that syringe didn't just go to your brain; it went down your left leg too. Your kneecap is loose and your toes have cramp. Somehow you manage to hobble out and set off for home. Ah! the relief of arriving, pain free and triumphant. You said that you would do it and, by George, you did. You faced the impossible whatsit and you survived. You are a heroine. On the strength of this euphoria you decide to celebrate. You pour out a glass of your favourite wine and sink into an armchair. Then you take a long swig and realize that you have a lapful of red wine and that little red drops are splashing on to it from the side of your mouth. Never mind: you are the woman who has conquered fear. At this point your eldest walks in, followed by the younger one.

"Ho-oh dah-ing," you say, smiling.

"Gosh, Mum; you look weird. Have you had a stroke or something? What's for lunch? I'm starving".

You'll change that will you made before going to the dentist; you will. That'll teach them.

26th July, 2002.

THE DRIVING TESTS.

Some people are born with ball sense: they know instinctively how and when to move, how and when to swing their rackets or when to reach out to grab a ball that is apparently travelling at the speed of light. Others can learn the requisite skills given time and effort. And there are those who after blood, sweat and tears will still play the game as if their shoelaces were tied together and they are wielding lead-reinforced rackets.

With driving it's no different. Some are born drivers, some become drivers and others have driving thrust upon them by circumstances. The first may become Formula A champions, but most of us fall into the second category; and there are the few who pass their driving test eventually but never really get the hang of the thing - like an old friend who had to plan her route very deliberately so that she avoided turning against the traffic. I am not a born driver, but having acquired all the skills I see myself as a safe and competent driver. So how come I've managed to fail my driving test four times?

I learnt to drive in the days when some cars still needed a double de-clutch action as you moved from one gear to the next (got you there, haven't I?) and, as I learnt to drive in Gibraltar where traffic crawled sedately along and parking space was at a premium, the tests seemed to concentrate almost exclusively on your parking skills - forget the highway code. There were no driving schools as such and my first tutor was my father. He had strong feelings about my tearing madly around empty spaces at a reckless ten miles an hour, putting both our lives at risk, so we agreed to dissolve the teacher-pupil relationship sooner than endanger the familial one.

I had two further teachers: a friend of the family came and taught me well and my friend Dorothy - who is a born driver - let me drive her car round and round Gibraltar while we chatted about this and that, and I developed a measure of self-confidence and a feeling for what driving was all about.

Sadly, when faced with a live examiner, I lost that confidence together with my know-how and my sense of direction. My first failure occurred in my father's Morris Minor. I remember sitting there, holding the steering wheel in a grip of steel, my knuckles white and my blood pressure rising. The examiner organised his clipboard and his fountain pen...which shows how long ago this all was...and told me to start. I made ostentatiously sure that the gears were disengaged, pulled the starter, depressed the clutch and would have put the car into first gear if it had shown any signs of life. I smiled at the examiner and tried again. It wasn't so much a smile as a contraction of the appropriate facial muscles. After the third time, when I went as far as to put the car into gear in the vain hope that it would make something happen, the examiner, a busy man, pointed out that I might achieve the desired result by turning on the ignition. I did so and we bucked off in first gear before the car stalled. I tried again and, as I rarely make the same mistake twice, this time I quite forgot about gears. I seemed to have developed a certain rapport with the examiner because we both took out our diaries at the same instant in order to settle on some distant date for my next test.

My second attempt went a great deal more smoothly and I only sank into imbecility when, towards the end of the test, I was told to hold the car on the clutch on a hill, the one below the Smith-Dorrien Bridge in Gibraltar, to be exact. Well, hold it there I did. The car clung to the slope like a well-trained limpet. I had already stuck my left arm out of the window and was waving it gracefully to indicate to the traffic behind me, which was conspicuous by its absence, that I was planning to hang on there for a while. With my mission successfully accomplished, I took the remaining hand off the steering wheel in order to pull up the brake. This display of, "Look, Mum: no hands!" led to a fresh consultation of our diaries.

Now the third attempt went like a dream. I proved myself the perfect driver. I wasn't rashly over-confident nor was I insecurely timid. In fact, it was the final manoeuvre that was my undoing. I was required to park in a reduced space in a limited number of moves. With both hands conscientiously clamped on the steering wheel as was then the fashion, I moved back and forth judging angles and distances with impressive nicety. Then I screwed myself round in my seat and fixed my eye on the wall behind me which I was determined not to touch with my rear bumper as I backed. All things being under control, I changed gear, eased up the clutch and watched the wall recede as we moved out into the road and into the path of an oncoming lorry.

However, I was soonto be officially recognized as a competent driver. I could then buy my own car - which I did, a VW Beetle. It was a car designed to test the nerve of the beginner because, as you sat there, you couldn't see where the mudguards extended to and could thus only guess roughly at the location of the bumpers. It all sloped away from you and out of sight so that you felt you were probably having a mystical experience where the extremities of the car were located in a different dimension.

You've spotted an anomaly, haven't you? There was a fourth test I mentioned early on and you know I wouldn't lie to you. I took that test in England after driving in Gibraltar, Spain, Portugal and, albeit briefly, in France. This time it was my failure to study the Highway Code that was my undoing. My husband would have it that when I was asked about double unbroken lines running down the centre of the road, I said that they indicated a no parking zone. Don't believe him; he's the man who thought our dog was a Budweiser until I put him right on the matter of Rottweilers as opposed to German lagers.

And now, after forty years of driving a selection of cars and school mini vans, I feel confident that, should I have to take my driving test again, I would undoubtedly manage to fail once more.

20th September, 2002.

THE EVIL WEED.

There's a bit of doggerel I learnt in the days when I discovered silly verse:
"Tobacco is an evil weed; I like it.
It satisfies no normal need; I like it.
It makes you thin - it makes you lean -
It takes the hair right off your bean -
It's the worst darned stuff I've ever seen:
I like it."
I was subsequently to smoke for over forty years and, while the medical analysis in that bit of verse might optimistically understate the effects of smoking, it summed up my attitude: I liked it. I smoked socially; I smoked privately; and the only time I didn't smoke was in my sleep. As I lived in England for twenty of those years, the expense

worried me. As more facts emerged about how smoking damaged your health, I worried some more. Worry made me tense so I sought relief from tension by smoking...which worried me...

I eventually decided to give up smoking and spent many happy years doing so. Sometimes I gave up smoking for six hours, or sixteen, or six days. Once I rose late, at eight (it must have been during the holidays), and resolved that that was going to be *the* day. "I must," I said with great resolution. That attempt stands out in my mind as being different to all previous efforts. I actually managed for twenty minutes before I lit up a desperate fag.

Giving up smoking became a hobby - angst-ridden, but a hobby nevertheless. There was one occasion when I gave up for two and a half years. I had made no decision about it; I just had a vicious bout of flu. While I lay in bed that first week, it would have made no difference if I'd shoved the cigarette up my nose, in my ear or in my mouth: every orifice seemed to belong to someone else, they certainly had nothing to do with me. I dragged myself around for the next two weeks, not even wanting to eat and the longer I went without my shots of nicotine the sillier it seemed to spoil the effect I'd achieved with so little conscious effort.

Conscious effort there had certainly been at other times: I read about giving up, I listened to advice about it, I discussed it with friends who were in the same boat. One of them decided on hypnosis, a remedy I hoped to try once I had saved up to pay for it, so I was particularly anxious to hear how he had fared. He told me. He had pinned all his hopes on it and - all right, I know you've guessed, but permit me to tell it my way, won't you? - the expectation was such and he was consequently so nervous about it all that he lit up the moment he came out of the clinic. When he tried acupuncture, I didn't even bother to ask.

And we all knew about changing our habits, keeping charts to identify when and why we smoked, laying off coffee or alcohol or whatever we had in tandem with cigarettes, and any number of other sensible strategies to help us. I was told that part of my strategy should be to tell everyone that I planned to give up The Habit on such and such a day: it would help to shame me into strength of purpose. Like hell it did. I felt so virtuous after informing everyone that it seemed I'd already done the job and so I sat down to enjoy a well-earned smoke. I even read many a personal testament; you know the sort of thing: "Confessions of a Teenage Nicotine Addict", "I was a Jekyll and Hyde Smoker" and "I Know What You Smoked Last Summer". None of the sound advice I read seemed to help me.

Years of failed attempts brought a dawning realization that some times had been more successful than others for reasons I couldn't fathom. On one occasion ,during the summer holidays, I woke up to a feeling that the morning felt different. I suppose it was my body that felt different, but I thought, "It might, just might, work today." I then proceeded to do all the wrong things.

I knew from experience that keeping busy, turning to some task every time I wanted a cigarette, just didn't help. Given that I thought longingly of having a cigarette about once every two seconds, I was faced with a choice of dying of exhaustion or failing to control my addiction. So that day I just sat and read and drank gallons of coffee and had wine and finally fell asleep at the end of the day without having had a smoke. Matters continued like this, with me living in a state of suspended animation in the armchair. At my elbow I kept a packet - no, you haven't guessed it this time - of tranquillisers for when the going got really hard. I took two.

By the time the third week started I didn't feel triumphant, I felt homicidal. I waited for a neighbour to sound mildly grumpy so that I could claim a legitimate excuse to kick him to death. I took two more tranquillisers and retired to bed when the children's programmes were starting on television. I was struck by the oddity that, after two weeks, I was in a worse state than when I began. It wasn't only that the novelty of virtue had worn thin, it was that the physical nature of the craving had become manifest and it obsessed me. Somehow I was also a detached observer of the process. It was a battle; "struggle" doesn't do justice to what was going on. Weeks later I was noting the fact that, without my constant input of nicotine, my mind felt sluggish and I was incapable of coping with any task that required concentrated mental effort: my attention span dropped to an uncertain twenty minutes. Only much later did I discover that nicotine dilates the blood vessels, thus increasing the supply of blood and oxygen to the brain.

In all of my many failed attempts to give up, I never objected to people round me smoking. I knew I wanted to stop, needed to stop and hoped this would be the definitive attempt. What they did was their business. One thing I did, however, was hope for some mysterious illness to strike me so that the doctor would say, "As you've only got days to live, you may as well smoke again." I also dreamt about smoking. All I wanted was *one* cigarette: about a yard long and with the diameter of a fireman's hosepipe.

And I finally succeeded when it became imperative for health reasons: my husband stopped smoking after a triple by-pass and I felt it would be unfair on him to see me merrily puffing away as he went through the process of withdrawal symptoms. I wasn't ready to give up so I used nicotine chewing gum to help me at first. Chew it too fast and you get hiccups. I spent four months with my diaphragm in permanent spasm, but I was ready eventually to give even that crutch up. I no longer fill the coffers of those who market and publicise and tax the drug and I know that I am perfectly capable, should I smoke a cigarette, of going back to a thirty-a-day habit.

I also know that when I smoked I was rewarding myself for doing some job; I also used it as a treat when I relaxed. Irony of ironies! My "reward" and my "treat" were, literally, life-threatening. Nowadays, as a non-practising smoker, I do not feel self-righteous. I have escaped the Born-Again Syndrome that can afflict one. As I watch the ban on smoking that is being applied wholesale by governments, I can see the virtues of the policy, but I also feel anger on behalf of those who smoke and are treated as pariahs, and anger at the lack of help offered to those who want to stop smoking. The vast sums of tax money from tobacco that have gone into government coffers were never employed to help such people. Smokers should be treated considerately rather than reviled and helped rather than punished. When non-smokers pontificate about the issue, my gorge rises: it's the smugness that I can't stand.

29th July, 2005.

THE POOR B'S.

Once upon a time I thought that the world was divided into two groups. The first group knew where they were going and the second lot had a poor sense of direction. Group A would end their lives in a spot of their choosing and group B might end up there by sheer chance, but were far more likely to find themselves in places they had never even dreamt of. I see things a little differently these days, but there's still a deal of truth in the idea so I will follow my original thoughts for a wee while.

The surprising thing is that it's those in group B who set out to revolutionize the world: they miss it on the way. I know. I believe I'm one of them. It's the more prosaic approach that gets you places. Imagine a busy executive who is frowning as he leaves his office and his clerk who is frowning as he settles down to unwrap the packed lunch he put in his briefcase that morning. The executive is probably frowning because he's debating the merits of having trout or steak for his lunch; it's the clerk who is going to devote his lunch hour to working on the economic revolution he plans to set in motion one of these days. The direct and straight path is more likely to succeed than the complex and tortuous one that aims for the stars. The clerk will get ulcers from irregular meals. The executive may have cholesterol problems, but I bet he'll be working out in a gym and be able to afford the occasional session at a health farm.

The people who know what they want usually know or can work out a way to get there. They also know that a thousand-mile journey starts with the first step - old Chinese saying. They also know that the first step involves putting one foot in front of the other. If the vision of eventual success should visit them, they do not let themselves be seduced by it for they know it is a succubus or an incubus (depending on their sex) sent to tempt them away from the straight and narrow. They accord such dreams a knowing glance and place their noses firmly once more on the grindstone of their choice. They dream of yachts? - they make do with watching them on television, knowing that the day will come when they will own one. They will eventually reap what they have so sensibly and assiduously sown.

Not so the B's. Their first problem is choosing from one of many goals. Their crusading and questing spirit will spoil them for choice and they will spend happy days - nay, years - considering the merits of each possibility. Once the choice is made...and I regret to say that many B's never actually get further than the short-listing stage, possibly cross referenced and carefully indexed...when, as I say, they make a choice, they know they must put their best foot forward. They try to decide the matter pragmatically and dispassionately, but ah! it's hard to know which the best foot is. Before they know it they have become emotionally involved with their feet: how can they hurt the feelings of one foot by opting for the other?

And what of the philosophical issues at stake? - What exactly is meant by "best foot"? Can such a value judgement be made on the physical appendages below one's ankle? They may eventually temper justice with mercy, or charity with ethics, and set off with both feet at once. They rarely land on them. This arouses their interest in falls, the mechanics of falls, the metaphor inherent in the word "fall", and the patch of ground on which they land, which may be of geological or botanical interest. They may even begin to consider designing protective clothing with in-built shin pads. Before they know it, they will have forgotten in which direction they had set off as they explore any one of the many ideas that suggest themselves to their enquiring and unquiet souls.

As a child, I used to have a dream that recurred with predictable regularity. I was always standing on a flight of steps and the ground was covered in what would turn out to be, as soon as I began to collect it feverishly, counterfeit money. I always fell for it: "Here's that damned dream again." I swear that I leered in my sleep, but I still bent down to collect my fool's gold. It took me a while to read the dream: I was doomed to a life of financial failure. Nevertheless, my waking dreams remained grandiose: I would write a masterpiece that would shake the literary world to its foundations; I would find the politicians' stone that would cure all ills; I would be martyred in the name of some great cause. You'll notice the common thread running through them all. Not one of them guaranteed any sort of income.

My husband might have lifted me out of this quagmire of worthy and nebulous dedication, if it hadn't been for the fact that he is also a worthy member of group B. Together we form a kind of rhesus negative combination in terms of practicalities. Take plain and simple ambition of the mundane and humdrum variety. There is a psychological game where, in answer to some seemingly simple questions, you end up revealing your innermost soul. There is a symbol for ambition; let's say it is sand. In my case there was an extensive shoreline - which had been completely cemented over. I tried the game out on my husband.

"There's a sand pit," he frowned as he visualised it. "It's tucked away in a corner, hidden among the bushes." I smiled hopefully; we were on to some secret ambition unsuspected till now. "The sandpit," he said slowly and firmly, "is empty."

I wept.

You see, it's not easy being a B. We B's suffer from doubts. We are given to exploring our motives and analysing our goals. We consider consequences and effects on others. We try to combine the ethical, emotional, intellectual and practical. That's a lot of combining to organize. The parameters we set ourselves can make or break us. The woman who decides to read a book or make an omelette will read the book and make the omelette. The one who decides to organize a feast for a hundred friends, doing the catering herself and holding the event in a marquee that she herself has knitted, is considerably less likely to do what she so gloriously planned.

Allow me to turn briefly to Einstein. After he had developed his Special Theory of Relativity he still failed where job hunting was concerned and was rejected as university lecturer and then as secondary school teacher. And, while matters eventually improved, his idea of the Cosmological Constant was treated as a pretty poor piece of scientific speculation which fellow scholars kindly forbore to dwell on and which embarrassed even Einstein. Years after his death, it would appear that he'd hit on one more piece of the puzzle and it is helping us to understand our universe.

Why this digression? I assure you that it is relevant because what keeps us B's going is the knowledge that, while the A's are succeeding and getting there daily, there are some B's who get there for posterity. Einstein, bless his unkempt hair, is a case in point. He failed to become a miner, his early ambition, and became a patent office clerk in Switzerland - I imagine he took a packed lunch with him to work in his briefcase. Failure marked a part of his life. And who failed more spectacularly than Cervantes? The poor B spent his life chasing a reasonable job, doing time in prison and generally getting it wrong in the eyes of the world.

That's the poor B's for you.

27th May, 2005.

WORDS AND WORDS AND WORDS.

NAMING OF PARTS.

This may not be the first time I mention Mis-anni-padda, first recorded king of Mesopotamia, but the name is irresistible. When you are an early, absolute monarch, your name can be as daft as you please and you can rest secure in the knowledge that your subjects can't read it or write it - and daren't mispronounce it. The name may be long or short; either carries an inbuilt guarantee that it will be treated respectfully. The earliest Chinese dynasties sound like cries of pain or the results of catarrh: Yao, Hsai, Chou. And later names suggest an early form of table tennis played with metal bats: Liu Pang, Ming and Ch'in. I'm sure they were all breathed with the same reverence as was the weightier name of Nabuchadrezzar. And, full of assured self-esteem, you could then go off and build one of the Seven Wonders of the ancient world - your Hanging Gardens of Babylon, or have a stab at the Great Wall of China.

The name *does* matter when you have less than absolute control. King Arthur's public relations department was clear on the point. That sword of his...now there was a name to rouse the blood. It conjures up a mighty horde of film extras kitted out for battle. King Arthur raises his sword aloft and it catches the light of the rising sun and the cry goes up from hundreds of throats, till the hills reverberate with the sound:

"Excalibur!"

I will now let you into the best-guarded secret at Camelot and I have Geoffrey de Monmouth to thank for this journalistic scoop. Here goes: Arthur also named the rest of his military gear. I cannot report to you on the name of his helmet or shin pads because, when I got to his lance, I lost heart. He called it "Ron". Scouts' honour. You just can't rouse your troops to valour with the cry, "Ron for ever!" No wonder they kept quiet about it.

A spot of Norse mythology makes the same point. There are short sharp names that stand proud in their simplicity, names like Eric the Red and Odin. Then it goes a bit pear-shaped with Odin's wife who is called Frigga; the first man who is called Ask and there's the Goddess of death who shows a singular lack of imagination in being called Hel. Then come the unpronounceable ones that have a certain mystery about them - Sleipnir, Skidblandnir, Muspelheim, and Yggdrasil the Cosmic Tree. So far, so good. However, for my money, I'll stick with the King of the Elves, a simple soul if ever there was one in the pantheon of gods, who goes by the name of Wayland Smith. Honestly.

Of course, the King of the Elves possibly didn't have to mind his image; the same is not the case with public figures and popular idols of the twentieth century. How far would you go to hear Ms. Gum sing? She sounds like pure stodge. Judy Garland, by contrast, sounds like the girl next door - with flowers thrown in for good measure. And if you want to scare the pants off the film-going public, you abandon the name your friends knew and loved - Willie Pratt. You opt for something both sinister and exotic and Boris Karloff does the job very nicely. And, though it pains me to say this, would I ever have felt about the rather pedestrian Archibald Leach as I did about the ineffable, the sophisticated and suave Cary Grant?

Probably not, for I've always felt that there's a magic in names. It started with my first big paint box. It was one of those enormous flat tins with lurid pictures of sunsets or landscapes on the outside. Inside were wafer-thin rectangles of paint in colours that ranged from the pasty to the pretty to the murky. Those small wafers soon developed a hole in the middle with use and the colours were always too anaemic, but oh! the magic of the names printed under them: Rose Madder, Yellow Ochre, Naples Yellow, Prussian Blue, Cerulean Blue, Vandyke Brown, Cadmium Yellow, Burnt Sienna. They opened up a wonderful world of possibilities. In fact, if anyone out there is thinking of forming a pop group of some sort and can't think of a good name for it, I offer them the most mysterious of all the names in my paint box - Gamboge Tint.

English literature is littered with wonderful names that create personality. In "Great Expectations" the hero is introduced to us as a frightened and bullied little lad with no expectations at all. He is

Pip Pirrip. His relative, pompous, self-important and stupid, is defined by his name, Pumblechook. When I first read "Twelfth Night", I felt Shakespeare had fallen down on the job. Why on earth have three characters called Olivia, Viola and Malvolio. Had the rest of the consonants in his typewriter seized up? Then it struck me that all three are chasing an impossible love. Viola, disguised as a man, is in love with the Duke who is himself in love with Olivia who has fallen in love with the disguised Viola. As for Malvolio, he is conned into believing that Olivia is in love with him, while he himself is in love with his own advancement (which never comes). He's a fake lover, hence, I suppose, the Mal at the beginning of his name.

One type of name that has always puzzled me is the one set as a snare for the unwary. I just hope I spell the first one correctly. Cholmondeley: pronounced Chumley; then there's Magdalen College: pronounced Maudlin; and there's the common or garden Mc Leod: pronounced Macloud. No wonder they tell the joke of the serious young scholar who, after years of working to master the English tongue, arrives in London, sees a newspaper headline that says, "'Hamlet', pronounced success".

And shoots himself.

But to go back to the magic of names: I loved the words of "Waltzing Matilda". Let me refresh your memories. The dramatis personae are the jolly swagman and one Matilda. He sits by a billabong, under the shade of a coolibah tree. A jumbuck intrudes at some point. The one thing that was clear about the situation was that the jolly swagman wanted Matilda to waltz with him. As far as that went, I had a fair grip on the plot, but given the other imponderables that was as far as I could go.

All I knew about a billabong was that it was something you could sit next to. The tree was foggy in my mind, but it gave shade, and who or what a jumbuck was had me stumped - but the words were grand and the idea of a lad wanting to dance in a sylvan setting had a certain romantic appeal. And the tune was awfully jolly.

Then my daughter, Gaby, broke the code. The tree is a type of eucalyptus. The billabong is a stream. A jumbuck is a sheep, and a swagman can be an itinerant labourer or a thief. Finally came the disillusion of it all. Matilda was no more and no less than his bundle. Into it he shoved the sheep and waltzed off with it. Some dreams die hard, alas!

Determined not to end this article on a sad note, I sought for some euphonious name with splendid associations. I knew what I wanted but the name evaded me so I asked my husband:

"Darling, what was the name of Alexander the Great's horse?"

He looked at me, deliberately blank: "Trigger," he said.

I don't know why I call him "Darling."

30th April, 2004.

ON MEGALITHOTELEPHOBIOMETRY.

There's not much of it about. How many people do you know who are dedicated to measuring the sense of panic generated by hearing the sound emitted by large distant stones? One reason is that such an activity does not exist; the other reason is that, should you be tempted to try it, you might soon find yourself wearing a fetching white jacket, hip-hugging, back-fastening but rather odd in the sleeve department. Yes, I cannot tell a lie; I made it up.

One of the joys of the English language is its breadth. It comes, to some extent, from being eclectic: a case of "see a word and grab it" no matter where it came from. Then you put it into the dictionary and, presto! it's a naturalised English word. The Spanish have started doing it widely in the last fifty years with regard to English words: "el camping, el burger, el footing" and the now Hispanicized "el güisqui", to name but four. The Royal Academy of Language in Madrid studies all such intruders to see whether or not to declare them legal linguistic currency. Not that they'll be able to stop the trend, whatever they do. I suppose the worst that can happen to such words will be that they are officially declared semantic forgeries of some sort, for which dictum no one will care tuppence.

The Academie Française goes further on the whole when it comes to maintaining the purity of the mother tongue. I believe that taking liberties with the French language is an offence punishable by guillotine without trial. The English have no such problems: they've been stealing words for years.

Perhaps it all started when the rest of Europe, the southern bits at least, were subject to Rome. What with being Top Dog and not having a flair for languages, the Romans made everyone speak Latin and we've ended up with Italian, Spanish, Portuguese and French which are all first cousins. If you are prone to "penser" in France, "pensar" in Spain, and "pensare" in Italy you can always close the "porte" or "puerta" or "porta" and sit down to a spell of uninterrupted reflection. In England, you may be pensive and you may have a large portal to your house, but the chances are that it will be a case of "Close the door and think."

In Britain, Old English (Anglo-Saxon) and Latin (with some Greek thrown in) and even French - when William the Conqueror came along - all jostled for control and no one won. As a very rough rule, if you have two words to choose from, the short one will be from Anglo-Saxon and the long one will be from Latin: mendacity and lie, require and need, cogitate and think. The English were spoilt for choice, weren't they? And when they began their trajectory as a colonial power, there was no stopping them. If you don't baulk at taking over a landmass the size of North America, you're not going to worry about a noun here and a verb there.

Tomahawk came from the Red Indians; canoe from the Caribbean Islanders; potato buffalo and tobacco were native words that the Spanish or Portuguese had already appropriated. India provided words like bungalow, from Hindi, gymkhana, from Urdu, Jodhpurs, named after the city of Jodhpur and patchouli - a fragrance much loved in the sixties - from Tamil. Kangaroo and boomerang came from Australian Aborigine words, banana from a West African language. It was natural that the names of flora and fauna as well as the customs of peoples colonised should have enriched the English language.

Exploration and trade added further words. The word parka for a warm hooded jacket comes from Russia via an Eskimo language, kayak comes from another - from Inuit. We all used to use kaolin powder for medicinal purposes, a word that comes from Chinese. The popular form of entertainment, the karaoke, gets its name from a Japanese word; karate, not surprisingly, also comes from the Land of the Rising Sun. And from Spain comes marijuana.

I interrupted my writing in order to check out some of my facts and spent a happy hour with the dictionary, going from one word to another and writing not a thing. I recommend it as a pastime for a wet winter's day. The two saddest words I came to were "apartheid" from Afrikaans and "jihad" from Arabic. However, what fascinated me were the roots of Old English. Before exploring these, let me just clarify one point: Old English goes from around 500 to 1000 AD, Middle English is what Chaucer was writing, and Modern English goes from Shakespeare's English to what we speak today. As for the roots of Old English, we're looking at a country that was invaded by Vikings or sacked by them for some length of time, so it'd not surprising that Old English has links with Old Norse, Frisian, Old Dutch and Germans-assorted. Let me illustrate that last one: the word "whey", as in Little Miss Muffet's "curds and whey", comes from Middle Low German. The word "wretch" comes from Old High German.

"Can one have Middle High or Old Low German?" you may ask.

I haven't the foggiest notion, but let me add to the complexity of the issue by bringing Holland into the picture - the humble weasel owes its name to an Old English word related to Old Norse, Old High German and Middle Dutch. "Wedlock" comes from the Goths who, it appears, had no Highs, Lows or Middles as my dictionary is pretty tight-lipped on the matter and merely offers the cryptic "Gothic and Old Norse". The Celts gave us "brigand" and the Welsh are responsible for "crowd", but you can bet your last dollar on the fact that if the spelling is awkward, you're looking at Old Norse or German (of one height or another): "strength, wreck, wrestle, wrong" are classics of the spelling hurdles that frustrate foreign students.

There's no way one can do more than glance at the fascinating vocabulary that English offers us. My favourite at the moment is "imbroglio", which entered the language in the eighteenth century and didn't hang around but seems to have departed pretty sharply in terms of popular use. I cherish it because it is still there for me in Spanish - "embrollo". Thank you, Italy. The word "market" comes from the Latin. I think it's "merx" and relates directly to the word my Spanish great-aunt, Ana, used for shopping - "mercar". And mention of Latin returns me to a wonderfully rich area: Latin and Greek.

When a new device, idea or chemical come along, we have recourse to Greek or Latin roots. "Kaleidoscope" comes from the Greek "kalos" (beautiful) and "skopein" (look at). Arm yourself with a few more roots like "tele" - distant, "phone" - sound, "photo" - light, "lith" - stone. Check out others like "graph, geo, mega, micro, ology, meter, phobia, ambi, bio, hemi, poly", and you have the basic tools for making up words. You may think the title of this article is bizarre, but I feel it can rub shoulders with words like "hemeralopia"…"hemipterous"… "hemistitch" - which last is not a piece of poor needle work, but refers to half a line of verse. And if you thought, like me, that "marsupial" is an Australian Aborigine word, then you are in error. It's Greek: "mar sypion", a pouch.

There is steam coming out of the back of the computer. It has taken exception to the heme and hemis above and, as I have rejected the alternatives it has offered me, I fear we will soon not be on speaking terms. Let me end by suggesting that a dictionary is a splendid present for a child if it is first used for no practical reason at all: having fun with words is the best of starting points.

20th May 2005.

ON THE NEED FOR NONSENSE.

In a world where many things are done in the name of religion and on "principle", things that defy description understanding or forgiveness, then there is something enormously salutary about the harmless anarchism of nonsense, near-nonsense and plain silliness to help keep you sane.

Take words, for example. I have introduced hundreds of children over the years to the longest word in English (excluding the names of pharmacological products) which means the running down of or dismissing things as being of no worth. The noun in question is **floccinaucinihilipilification**. At this point my computer has gone berserk and is painting the page red. You can't blame it. After all, I have never heard the word spoken, nor have I seen it in any text other than a good dictionary, but think of the joy of dropping it casually into conversation one day:

"My goodness, yes, he's always so negative, always indulging in floccinaucinihilipilification."

As an adolescent I delighted in collecting useless remarks like, "Why is this thus? What is the reason for this thusness?" and I never knew that I could have introduced a note of variety by saying, "What is the reason for this **haecceity**?"

However, for usefulness the word **scaphocephaly** takes some beating. It means having a head the shape of a boat. I am glad to say that I have never been able to find anyone to whom the word might be applied. By contrast, the word **corsned** could become part of common parlance if we amended the judicial system and simplified the whole process of minor infringement of the law where the accused has entered a plea of "Not guilty". The meaning of the word? Ah, yes - the practice of establishing a person's guilt or innocence by seeing whether or not she/he is able to swallow a large piece of mouldy cheese. Couldn't be simpler. Equally we could revive the word **bumdocdoose** - I write this phonetically as I only saw it written once, and that nearly forty years ago - which is the name of a street game clearly meant to drive the cold away. Three players stand in a circle. Let us call them A,B,C. A kicks B in the posterior, B kicks C and C kicks A, and the cycle can begin again. Hours of innocent fun for all!

I also enjoy reading what makes perfect sense to others, but is a mystery to me. In the case of chess, I can follow the general idea reasonably, but it's the hard data that really gets to me. For example, I read that Qxf3 + 41KdQg2 + 42Ke3 is a hopeless position. Frankly, I'm not surprised; I'd hate to be in that position myself when I read that the white king is so badly exposed that the black king can do just about what he likes with his rook and his queen. And I'm willing to bet that in the meantime the pawns are getting up to all sorts of shenanigans. Why, at any moment some ambitious little devil is probably scheming to become a queen too, thus rendering the king liable to prosecution as a bigamist - the shameless hussy! And swallowing any amount of mouldy cheese will probably do her no good. It's the stuff of soap operas. I know damn all about chess, but I can appreciate the pulsating human drama behind those letters and figures.

Bridge? - fascinating and mysterious. Why the North, South, East, West orientation? I'm lost before I start. There are contracts, tricks and overtricks, bidding and pressure bids. This sounds like a world of shading financial dealings to me and there is worse; there is violence when you can throw one thing on another, crash your partner's king and goad opponents. No wonder there is always a dummy somewhere along the line, probably the fall-guy who takes the rap. Nevertheless, there is some form of justice, for you can incur huge penalties. It's not a safe world to move around in, is it? I may occasionally enjoy reading of Trypenofski's raise of Callemoff's weak jump overcall of three clubs to five clubs (a primitive arms race, no doubt) in a typical pressure bid to harass the opponents into what I presume is some gardening activity involving five spades - but, personally, I'll stick to Scrabble.

Or I can turn to the reading of recipes of the esoteric variety where the writer dwells lovingly on the use of ingredients I have never even heard of. I love reading them. There is a kind of delight in the abstract nature of the whole thing - something which is totally alien to me and which I have no intention of ever cooking. Colour supplements and quality newspapers are the place to find the sort of thing I have in mind, something like:

"'Around the World in Eighty Bites' - published by Gourmet Press, £17.95 - is Edith J. Crunch's latest contribution to the cause of international cuisine. While the section on iguana and snake is a welcome corrective to the more common ostrich dishes, it is her chapter on the lesser known pastas and subtle sauces of remote mountain regions that most readers will be eager to try. Take her Intaglio with Impasto Sauce à la Marmolieri. The ingredients may be hard to find, but if impastos are not in season, you can substitute the more common lucerola which will need to be soaked overnight in a solution of water, lemon, boracic powder and a pinch of nitro-glycerine to get rid of the bitter taste so characteristic of this root vegetable. The quantities set out here will serve four large/hungry people.

45.634 ml. olive oil.
½ kilo intaglio (medium bore).
1 kilo fresh impastos.
3 tsp. each oregano, andante, parlante, salt and pepper.
13 cloves garlic and a generous pinch of staccato crushed with a marble or brass pestle and mortar (avoid the ceramic or wooden variety that tend to absorb the curative properties of the staccato).
156 gm. Sour goat's cream (if none available, then substitute curmudgeon sheep's milk).
¼ kilo grated donkey cheese.

Heat the oil over a high flame till it begins to stick to the sides of the pan. Toss in the coarsely chopped impastos and stir, clockwise, for four minutes till the impastos begin to sweat and spit. (Wouldn't you?) Cover pan, lower the heat and allow to simmer for half an hour. Liquidise.

In a separate pan bring four litres of water to boil and introduce intaglios individually to prevent them sticking to each other, the spoon or the pan. Bring back to the boil and cook for ten minutes.

Cream the garlic, herbs, cream and cheese and stir till it has reached the retroussé stage when the spoon will stand up unaided and then move to an angle of 43° from the horizontal. Gently fold into the liquidised impastos. Stirred, not shaken should be your motto!

Drain intaglios, cover with impasto sauce and serve piping hot. This dish can be served with fresh pizzicato and decorated with small palmetto radishes, sliced raw onion, turnip hearts, artichoke livers and watermelon kidneys - the pale variety."

And I shall close with a thought for the week which comes in this proverb from seventh century China: "As the tree that grows bent cannot reach upwards to approach the water chestnut, so the man who looks only at the wall will fall over his own shoelaces."

Well, it could be a proverb from somewhere, couldn't it?

2nd August, 2002.

WORDS FOR THOUGHT.

I've been reading, "The Adventure of English" by Melvyn Bragg and "Eichman and the Holocaust" by Hannah Urendt, and they confirm my long-held belief in the immense importance of the teaching of one's own language. The poorer one's command of it, the poorer one's thinking processes. I suppose stone-age man made do with the odd grunt and gesture. Nouns must have emerged pretty soon and verbs too, that's the sort of basic vocabulary that you develop early, as any foreigner in a strange country can testify. But when did conjunctions and prepositions, arise? Words like "and...but...although...in...under...because...at" and so many others that make it possible to shade meaning and create subtle connections that the nouns, verbs, adjectives and adverbs can never aspire to.

In this sentence - "He sat under the table breathing heavily" - we can visualise the table and we may be intrigued by the fact that his breathing seems out of consonance with a static pose, but the moment you prefix the sentence with the word "Although" you turn it into a mere subordinate clause and you must read on, in fact, you want to read on to discover why this pose of his is conditioned by a conjunction. What will be revealed? Why is his action being qualified? For facts we turn to nouns and verbs, but mystery belongs to the conjunction and the preposition.

The more a language develops, the sharper the tools it provides us with to analyse experience and, once the language has a written form, the more fully we can investigate meaning. You have words placed on papyrus or skin, or carved on wood or stone. You can correct and explore them. And new concepts can be created and investigated or challenged. This may sound dry stuff indeed for a Friday morning's reading, but I speak from the vantage point of having spent years hearing pupils complain of their colleagues with the words,

"Miss, he's a 'payaso'." The child so nominated did not work in a circus so the word, clown, was being used metaphorically, not literally. It told me a good deal about the speaker's sentiments, but very little about the accused. "Payaso" was a blanket term of opprobrium, just as "colega" - a good mate - was one of praise. I tried to encourage them to be specific: was the accused a liar, a cheat, a bully? Was he actually clowning about, was he foolish, was he boastful? The list could be endless, but they only had these other words in their passive vocabulary so that though they could understand them when used by others, the words had yet to move into their active vocabulary to be used in daily social exchanges. Because their accusations were not specific, they could not be considered for validity, nor could you establish dialogue between the two boys involved. "Payaso" might lead to an exchange of insults, but not to negotiation or understanding.

I recall two old ladies I knew long ago who were always at odds. The appeared to see no middle ground between being right or wrong. Each claimed the high moral ground in every encounter - and there were many - and consigned the other to the low ground of unethical action. They only moved on self-constructed "certainties". Had their vocabulary been wider, they might have attributed to each things like "error... misunderstanding...confusion...." Each might have then been able to look at the other without rancour; they might have been able to understand each other or examine and admit their own limitations. They might have lost some of their assurance and learnt about compassion or forgiveness, or the blessed plain common sense that should inform our daily social intercourse. They didn't; and they lived their entire lives in conflict. I imagine they got a good deal of pleasure out of it, but it's regrettable to get your kicks by kicking someone else.

Handling concepts requires a measure of confidence in the use of language, and this comes with breadth of language, experience and use. Furthermore, words exist, mutate and develop. Take the word "cavalry". It came to English with the Normans and their "chevals". All they were was mounted soldiers and, in carrying out William the Conqueror's policy of subduing his new kingdom, they could be termed mounted bullies. Later, with Eleanor of Aquitaine, came the concept of Chivalry, which turned them into mounted gentlemen -

compassionate, defenders of the weak, noble and courteous. Big difference! All they kept of the original model was the horse and fighting prowess.

A concept takes time to evolve and be accepted. When I was in school, it took me a long time to really understand the concept of irony in all its guises in literature, and so too with the idea of tactile values in painting. Concepts are immensely important because they take us from the concrete world we inhabit to the world of ideas with which to inform our minds. They are like stepping stones that lead you forward towards a greater degree of understanding and depth of thought.

Which brings me to Eichman. Hannah Urendt sat through his trial in Israel and listened and observed. This man had sent millions of people, innocent of any crimes, to be brutally done to death in concentration camps. He must surely have been a monster. Instead she found what she was to see as the banality of evil. In the five-part article she wrote for the "New Yorker" she explored a number of issues, but her portrait of the man himself was something she probably hadn't expect when she started.

The man who emerges was incapable of real analysis or thought of any depth. He appears to have fed off clichés and off empty phrases which *sounded* fine, like Himmler's "My honour is my loyalty," which Eichman admired as what he called "winged words" that inspired him, but which mean nothing if analysed. The judges finally summed his defence up as "empty talk", which they assumed was feigned. Hannah Urendt's view was that it was genuine. The stock phrases and self-invented clichés he used, together with the fact that he repeated his own words with little variation in court, under interrogation and in the memoirs he was writing, taken with his inability to really engage with questions, to explain or understand his own guilt, were "closely connected with his inability to *think*." She goes on to say, "No communication was possible with him, not because he lied but because he was surrounded by the most reliable of all safeguards against the words and the presence of others, and hence against reality as such." He was protected by his inability to think.

He had worked zealously on the early, enforced deportation of Jews into exile and then worked with equal zeal on the massive deportation to concentration camps. There seemed to be no difference in his mind between them: he was doing an efficient job in both cases of moving bodies around. After reading the articles, I wondered if there wasn't a further dimension to be explored in the man's inability to engage emotionally with others, with their sufferings, with their shared humanity. In fact, he seems to have had doubts about a bloody "solution", which doubts were resolved by gassing because that wasn't bloody. Such a "thought process" beggars description.

Eichman's personality is terrifying in its banality. He was a man who might have been thought rather stupid and limited had he merely worked for an ordinary commercial enterprise, but it was precisely those limitations and his simplistic linguistic mode of "thought" that made him an ideal servant of the state.

My two old ladies and the boys who used "payaso" so thoughtlessly could, like most of us, do little damage on the world stage. Even so, perhaps we need a subject on the school curriculum that is called "Vocabulary for Thought"?

18th November, 2005.

ZULUTANA.

Years ago I began to compile a dictionary.

"Why?" the question arises.

"Why not?" is my reply.

It's not a dictionary that will ever be in common use: not even I use it. But silly definitions were popular at the time and I joined the game.

Dictionaries matter, of course they do, but think of the hundreds of years...or thousands of years...when no one used dictionaries because there weren't any. I can't speak for the Greeks and the Romans, and I certainly can't speak for the Japanese and the Chinese and, when I consider the matter carefully, there's no need to speak for peoples who have stuck with an oral culture and have never developed a script.

I can, however, speak to you of the Byzantine 10th century Lexicon, of William Temple's first ever English-English dictionary, published in 1530, and of a couple of others that dealt with English - Welsh, or English - Italian.

Actually, I lie. I can't really talk about them because what I know of them you could stick in your eye and never feel. The dictionary we all tend to know of is Samuel Johnson's dictionary of standard English that didn't see the light of a printer's office till 1755. Till then, it had been every woman/man for herself/himself and the devil take the hindermost.

So Shakespeare, who was born in 1564, had no dictionaries to consult...well, nothing much. It was much more fun to invent your own words or to apply existing words in a new way or to turn nouns into verbs and vice-versa. After all, his London was a city where there is mention in documents of the period of teachers, not just of French, but of Arabic, Dutch, Polish, Turkish, Russian...for businessmen who were trading widely. Words were also coming in from The New World.

When you think that the Grammar School education that Shakespeare received was Latin, Latin and, by way of light relief, more Latin, then you can understand such a mind as his rejoicing in the freedom to do his own linguistic thing in a language that was alive and changing.

Among the accusations levelled at him was his use of words like "idiom...impression...savage...obscure...clumsy...strenuous" and "damp" – such outlandish nonsense! Some words he invented, some he picked up from others. It all went into the melting pot.

But the people understood what he was saying in his plays. They didn't need an interpreter. We're rather different in our approach to theatre. We talk of going to see a play. In those days, people spoke of going "to hear" a play. I'm sure that they enjoyed savouring the language.

No, I don't think I'm being fanciful. We Gibraltarians do it all the time when we speak Llanito, an early form of what might be termed Spanglish nowadays. Think of it: anyone queue jumping is "collating" - from the Spanish "colarse"...to slip in. And if I decide to say that I am "pensating" about whether or not to do something, then I'd be sure to be understood by a fellow Gibraltarian, even though that word, to the best of my knowledge, is not part of Llanito as it stands. But "pensar" - to think - will happily take an Anglicised verb ending.

One thing that delights me about the titles of early dictionaries is the spelling: "Shorte Dictionarie for Yonge Begynners" and "Table Alphabeticall of hard usuall English wordes". I've had plenty of pupils who have spelt like that, and their only problem has been the fact that they were not born in the fifteenth century. Five centuries ago their spelling would have raised no eyebrows - even Shakespeare kept changing the spelling of his name as he tried new versions out for size.

If dictionaries with their definitions were late on the scene, then the standardisation of spelling and the use of capitals came even later. Like so many things in life, it's all relative. Hence my boldness in offering you today this small selection from my very own dictionary. I'm afraid that I have yet to sort it out in alphabetical order: my apologies.

Warning: to understand these words you are advised to read them aloud before turning to the definitions.

ZULUTANA: warlike African raisin.
MAHAGONY: the anguish suffered in a rain forest when one is hit on the head by a falling tree.
MEASLI: red-speckled cereal of a contagious nature.
MARI-JUANA: Spanish lady who has led an impeccable life and who wishes to take this opportunity of stating that she has never had anything whatsoever to do with Indian hemp in any shape or form.
BLINQUE: what zey do en France when zey close de eyes brefly.
BROWNING: automatic nineteenth-century poet who fired off fine dramatic verse.
BUTTER FLY: but I find that it usually stay in dish.

BEDLAMB: hospital for mentally unbalanced sheep.

BENIFEET: the advantage of having legs that don't stop at the ankles.

WATS: wodents, wather like mice, notowious plague cawiews.

BISON: Australian receptacle used for washing hands and face; not to be confused with the North American BUFFALOO - a toilet for nudists.

CARRÓTTE: Spanish method of strangling vegetables.

ABIGALE: windy female servant.

SCORPEON: poisonous Mexican labourer.

WHEREWOLF: could be here or there - or someplace else for all I know.

DRAGULA: a transvestite vampire.

SAWRONG: Samistake, sanerror.

STRANGULL: to throttle a seagull.

ORGEE: American exclamation when faced with a scene of debauchery.

QUADROOPLE: four times the normal droop; a droop indicative of total exhaustion; one hell of a droop.

POETTERY: expression of elevated thoughts about ceramics.

LIELAC: to tell untruths till one goes purple in the face.

DIPTHEORIA: serious illness arising from too much philosophising.

(Well, I never said it was going to be easy, did I?)

ORKID: an exotic baby goat of monocotyledonous characteristics.

LOOFAR: the last thing you want to hear when looking for a public toilet.

AUBERJEAN: purple denims.

WELLINGTONE: the sound emitted by rubber boots.

MYNESTERY: the enigma of cabinet policies.

MATRIMONEY: marriage of convenience.

LOIN: the king of the baests (think about it.)

KRAAL: what Americans do when moving around on all fours.

NOEL: absence of twelfth letter of the alphabet.

HARANGUE-UTANG: the dangerous practice of addressing large primate in hectoring tone.

ARDOUR: the opposite of sophter.

ACKNEE: spotty patella.

AFORD: a very reliable car.

ALOOF: topmost part of Chinese dwelling.

WHYSTERIA: emotionally unstable flowering creeper.
PONSTIFF: dead pope.
VOLECANIC: exploding garden rodent.

Phew! That's it. I promise; guide's honour; that this is the end of it.
The other umpteen pages I shall consign to a bonfire.

6TH June, 2003.

WORDS ALLSORTS.

With language you enter a world that seems to have no end. The
need to acquire the right word or the right term was brought home
to me in what must have been my first day at infant school. One
little lad had sat in mounting misery till he began to weep with the
helpless anguish of that age. Below him, staining the wooden floor,
a pool of liquid began to spread to his shame and our general horror
- it could have been one of us!

Then the teacher intervened and I discovered the magic formula:
"Please, may I be excused?" It's not a question that makes any
sense to a tiny tot. Surely, you think, that's an apology: It's what you
need to say *after* you've had the accident. And once you see the
need for words, you can spend a lifetime accumulating words, jargon,
the acceptable turn of phrase, the sort of language to see you through
all the different spheres of life that are opening up to you. I certainly
set out on this road, and the only thing that slowed me down and
made be more selective was the endless educational meetings I had
to attend at one stage in my life.

Some of the people there were into all the latest buzz words and
jargon. They talked in acronyms abbreviations and initials - it showed
they were in the know. They might come out with something like
this: "The latest PEST report does advise local PND's to consider
the need for TTP at county level and coordinate all CHOK activity in
their area."

All too often I heard such in-talk from people who seemed to have
little contact with children and who were more interested in tidying
up administration and in furthering their careers than in the teachers

at the chalk-face and the pupils. It was soon borne on me that, if that's what it took to get on, I was going to fall short because I didn't want to travel that road and didn't speak SHIT fluently enough -Simply Horrendous Incomprehensible Terminology.

By contrast, you get those who, having acquired a limited number of words and structures, see themselves as equipped to handle any situation. They see life as a challenge and they are eager to meet it head-on. They give endless pleasure to their fellows when they go beyond their immediate circle and get into print, particularly if it's in a foreign language.

Like a synopsis of "Carmen" provided years ago by the Paris Opera which referred to the "tobago factory where Carmen takes a flower from her corsets and lances it to Don José (duet: talk me of my mother)," and works its way through the plot to where "called by Carmen shrieks the two smugglers interfere with her but Don José is bound to dessert," and on to the grand finale when Don José "Stabbs her (Aria; Oh rupture, rupture, you may arrest me, I did kill her)" as he sings of his "subductive Carmen".

And I love the Japanese hotel which advises guests in an admonitory tone: "If you want just condition of warm in your room, please control yourself." I should jolly well hope so! They are a polite lot, as further proven by a Tokyo car rental firm that advises drivers thus: "When passenger on foot heave in sight, tootle the horn. Trumpet hirn melodiously at first, but if he still obstacles your passage then tootle him with vigour."

Closer to home was a Marbella restaurant that stated firmly - "Cheques will not be accepted in lieu of food." And, talking of food, there was a nihilistic Swiss establishment which gloomily announced, "Our wines leave nothing for you to hope for." That's the trouble with catering for foreign tourists: you are forced to write in a foreign tongue which you may not have mastered.

A tourist brochure from Seu D'Urgell illustrates this vividly as it expounds on the city's cultural and religious heritage when the writer is moved to lyrical heights as he recalls great bishops of the past, "bishops with peninsular and European projection; Justo who dragged along Elipendo of Toledo in his adoptionist version, and Ermengol who was a remarkable European figure and stretched bridges over the Segre and to the Eternity." I know - search me! I have to stop, this is cracking me up and I can only regret all the choice bits I have no room for, as I have other points to make.

What does one make of world leaders who cannot make themselves understood? Semantically and syntactically challenged presidents may have first seen the light in the person of Gamaliel Harding, President of the United States in the '20's. Here is one splendid sentence of his...well, hardly that... let's call it an utterance, which takes off into the blue - "I would like the government to do all it can to mitigate, then in understanding, in mutuality of interest, in concern for the common good, our tasks will be solved." You can't say fairer than that, can you?

And another name springs to mind - Bush - to name but two. We have Bush Junior to thank for at least one book of Bushisms that appeared a couple of years ago with gems like... "It's clearly a budget. It's got a lot of numbers in it." And "There's a huge trust. I see it all the time when people come up to me and say, 'I don't want you to let me down again.' Well, I think if you say you are going to do something and don't do it, that's trustworthiness." What, you may ask, is his approach to the written word? Actually, he has been known to say, "One of the greatest things about books is sometimes there are some fantastic pictures."

During Perseverance Month (whatever that may be) in New Hampshire he managed this: "This is preservation month. I appreciate preservation. It's what you do when you run for president. You gotta preserve."

Mr Bush is not morally responsible for still being linguistically challenged, despite having had the best education that money could buy, but this is not reassuring when you consider that he is a world leader in the field of politics. He can deliver written speeches or memorised ones, but does he know what the words really mean? Certainly some of his off-the-cuff statements make you wonder if he always knows what he's talking about.

He is following in Gamaliel Harding and Dad's footsteps, and it surprises me that I can actually find a measure of comfort in that. It shows that life goes on despite the ineptness of leaders. It also points to what a lot of us have suspected for years - that a great deal of power does not lie with the leaders but with lobbies and the éminences grises behind them. Perhaps this should alarm me even more, but behind all those is the matter of chance, luck, accident et al which may occasionally do more to change the course of history than do individual leaders.

What the hell, you've got to think positive, as Bush Senior said when seeking re-election: "Remember Lincoln, going to his knees in times of trial and the Civil War and that stuff. You can't be. And we are blessed. So don't feel sorry for - don't cry for me, Argentina. We've got problems out there and I am blessed with good health, strong health. Jeez, you get the flu and they make it a federal case. Anyway, that goes with the territory."

Darn it - that's the kind of fighting talk one likes to hear! and I just hope he found his knees as helpful as did Lincoln with his knees when he went to them.

But, oh! a menu or a brochure is one thing. A world leader is another. If we need words in order to think, then...

24th January, 2003.

OTHER WORLDS OF OURS.

SPECIAL OFFERS.

Let's see; what can we buy for £25?...a pair of trousers, some bottles of wine, an ordinary sweater, a ten-tear-old slave, a meal at a restaurant or...

The slave? I'm afraid you'd have to go to Kanchipuram in India to find one that cheap. However, you *could* try nearer home. After all, in the year 2003 there are records of 118 countries that have dealt in slaves. To qualify for the list there had to be evidence that at least 100 human beings had been bought or sold. Yes, indeed, there were countries like Senegal, Cambodia, Venezuela and Sudan. I quite understand that it's a bit far to go, but we need not despair, because the list also includes other places like Switzerland, Sweden, Spain, Portugal and the UK. And the supply is unlikely to run out given that it would appear that there are approximately 27,000,000 slaves in the world as I write this and as you read it. Yes. Now.

Many years ago we had a friend who told us he was working for an anti-slavery organization, and I naively imagined that he was involved in a mopping-up operation just clearing a few small pockets up somewhere in Africa, all that remained of the old slave trading of the eighteenth and nineteenth centuries. Since we spoke to him, slavery has grown, not diminished, and has done so massively.

Those children in India may be sold by a desperate family which is motivated by the need for economic relief and, equally, by the need to find someone who will feed one of their children whom they themselves cannot feed. However, such children may end up working in the silk industry for fourteen hours a day till their fingers bleed and the dyes used in the silk poisons their system. Or they may work ten hours a day making bangles that will later sell for less than 30p a dozen. There are boys of five or six from Pakistan working in the Persian Gulf as jockeys in camel races. There are girl prostitutes in Thailand. There are Chinese children of Infant School age who work in a leather factory in Italy - near Florence, to be precise.

The figure of twenty-seven million slaves can be subdivided into those bought and sold as straight merchandise, and those who become slaves as a result of debts. "Slaves" is not a metaphor for the very poor, the destitute, the starving. That's a different matter and does not involve 27 million.

At the more expensive end of the slave trade are many brothels in and around Europe, from Tel Aviv to Switzerland, and brothels in The United States that use young Ukranian women. They are bought for under three thousand pounds each. For an investment of forty thousand, a brothel owner can make an annual profit of about a million pounds. That's the more expensive end of the market. There is a Greek academic, holding a chair of sociology in Athens, who has studied in depth the importation of prostitutes into Greece from Bulgaria. A phone number in Moscow will put you in touch with the network that will take your order and deliver these women to your doorstep. It's a lucrative trade and each woman costs a mere £700.

These young women are tricked into leaving their country with promises of employment. They are transferred from one place to another with promises of work and are told that they owe for transport, maintenance and fake documents. They are then beaten, raped and intimidated into prostitution and moved again before the "debt" is paid, so that they can be told that they have incurred a new debt. What has happened is that they are being re-sold. The system ensures that they remain enslaved for as long as they have any value on the "market".

A similar system operates in the East - in Nepal, India and Pakistan. Poverty will make people turn to money lenders in times of crisis or because of a family event like a funeral or a wedding, which require an outlay of money. The exorbitant interest rates can mean that the debt is never paid off and even that it increases as the debtor fails to pay back the interest, never mind the capital. The end result can be that whole families, including small children, are doomed to work for life for whoever lent them the money. They will be paid a pittance that ensures that they can never pay off what they owe. It is a way of recruiting what is effectively a slave labour force.

Anyone living in our part of the world knows about those who cross the Straits of Gibraltar in open boats, having paid heavily for the transport, such as it is. We have also read of illegal immigrants found dead - suffocated - in container lorries that were intended to smuggle them into some country of Europe. One thing that makes such a trade in humans possible is the restriction on immigrants. Where restrictions get more stringent every year and there are desperate people, these will be prepared to accept that they must pay heavily for illegal entry into a country which they believe will offer them a new and better life.

The dumping of cheap subsidised American maize and rice in South America has beggared many families. They look north for work, to the land of wealth and plenty. Young women crossing illegally into the United States may be offered work as waitresses. Soon their employer will report them to the police as illegal immigrants. The women are arrested. They are then bailed out by that ex-employer who will tell them they have to work off the debt they have unwittingly incurred: it is another road to slavery. Similarly, given the stricter controls established at entry points since September 11th, those who traffic in illegal immigrants have doubled their prices and those who buy their services are at the mercy of employers waiting to exploit them: another route to slave labour. A woman now resident in the USA was born into slavery in Mauritania. Her parents were slaves as her grandparents had been. The law in Mauritania may not recognize slavery, but it exists.

I said earlier that this 27,000,000 was not a figure that applied to the very poor of the world. For anyone interested, I should say that the number of people worldwide who survive on an income of less than £1.3 a day - and on as little as 30p - adds up to three thousand million. And it's that kind of poverty that will keep the supply of slaves going.

What can we do about misery on such a vast scale? The answer is simple: absolutely nothing to remedy the existing misery at this precise moment. But we can certainly do something about one or two or more people specifically. And that "something" can be the total salvation of those individuals. They would not think that it is "absolutely nothing" to be redeemed from a life of misery. We are talking, among others, of children like our own or like our grand children.

So if we don't want to buy a young slave for twenty-five pounds, we can consider rescuing one. Why not contact anti slavery organizations? Try

www.antislavery.org/ or any of those you'll find on the internet.

The information for this article comes from a special investigation carried out for, and the information subsequently published by, "National Geographic" magazine.

10th October, 2003.

DOOM, GLOOM AND A LUNCHTIME BEER.

Somewhere, sometime, I saw a picture of the Thames frozen over. People were skating on it; stalls had been set up on the ice and were plying a lively trade with the crowds; and a hefty fire had been built over which a whole ox was being roasted. It was Elizabethan London, as I recall.

I am willing to make allowances for a Thames that was once less wide and shallower than it is today. That still makes the event extraordinary, and what is even more amazing is that it happened twice. So, what was going on with the climate? Consider how thick the ice would have to be for that fire to be built on it. Let's assume a bitter cold of the kind that is still common in parts of Russia - remember the hairy mammoth found somewhere in Siberia that, deep frozen, was still edible? I'm willing to bet that the Elizabethans must have had something to say as they watched the Thames turn solid. For the sake of art rather than in the interests of verisimilitude - lovely word, that - I shall imagine them speaking in blank verse, in iambic pentameters - the rhythm that Shakespeare, my hero, employed in his plays.

1st Citizen: And so our Thames doth freeze and we can walk
          And sport upon its waters now turned hard.
2nd Citizen: 'Tis so, a pleasure for us all, but woe
          Is me and woe is you for toes do freeze
          And nose and fingers too. The world will end
          If this continue for the gods have spoke.
1st Citizen: Oh sorrow fierce! Thou sayest true, my friend.
          Mayhap we have but days to live and this
          A judgement from the gods that deal with man
          As sport and care not how they're messing us about no
end.
(Yes, I know I broke the rhythm, but I have the rest of this to write;
that rhythm is very seductive and you don't want pages of the stuff,
do you?)

I know how they felt because eighteen years ago the media were full
of the Ice Age that was threatening the world. Experts appeared on
television programmes and wrote in the papers; they calculated and
predicted with awful certainty and my husband and I considered are
rather basic central heating with fear in our hearts. Pardon? Oh, you
want to know what happened to that Ice Age? So do I. It just vanished
from everyone's agenda. What was really coming and they had
apparently missed, or they misread the signs, was global warming.
This is now a proven fact: there is research and we have figures to
make this latest threat a matter of concern for us all. That's the
frightening difference. What hasn't changed is that experts have been
wheeled on who calculate and predict. The worst do it with an
unjustifiable degree of certainty that you are tempted to dismiss.
The best give us parameters that are wider and all the more frightening
for being that much more convincing. They are aware that, at the
moment, the hole in the ozone layer is not behaving quite as predicted.
First it grew, now it's shrinking somewhat. One is thankful for small
mercies, but that doesn't solve the problem and we can't ignore what
is happening.

What an American poet called "The United beautiful States of terrible
America", has a government that, defender of democracy and purveyor
of sanctimonious platitudes about values and virtues, is not co-
operating with other countries over the question of toxic wastes being
released into the atmosphere. It is, however, not indifferent to

conservation issues, no indeed! It has done a sound job of criticising Brazil and others who are decimating the rain forests of South America - the Lungs of the World.

Other nations too are failing to subscribe to or reach agreement on issues like whale protection - not just Japan, but also the Scandinavian countries. In fact, when our interests are the ones threatened, we will ditch principle and go for expediency or national interest or our culture or whatever euphemistic label we can dredge up that will sound acceptable as we set to destroying some part of the world. Depressing, isn't it? And there are disasters aplenty to consider. We hear that this century will see a gradual rise in temperatures. Estimates I have read range between 1° and 6° depending on what part of the globe you're looking at. Experts say that even one humble degree in the Arctic will cause havoc with the icecap. And here's a vindication of those who predicted an Ice Age - there is reason to believe that over eight thousand years ago the cold spell in Europe followed a flood of glacial water into the Atlantic.

And there have been so many natural disasters since "el Niño" - that incredible current which we believe began to cause climatic mayhem a couple of years ago. And now it appears that vital Atlantic currents are slowing down dramatically and could seriously affect the climate from the Amazon to Asia. And pollution and global warming could cause the monsoon to lose strength - all of which has its domino effect while we sit here feeling safe because our part of the world is little affected as yet. Geographically we appear to be privileged, but that leaves the rest of humanity at risk. With tragic irony, it is the Third World that suffers most...or perhaps it is because of their location that such nations are precisely the disadvantaged world.

Dare we consider other horrors that afflict them presently like leprosy; or the new variety of pneumonia that has arisen in the last few months, or the terrible Urundi ulcers - a latter-day leprosy, or the horrendous figures for AIDS sufferers which has reached pandemic proportions in a little over twenty years?

Wars come into the picture too. Ethiopia would not now be the land of suffering it is if it weren't for the war that has been waged there for so many years. There is the loss of 4,000,000 lives in a war the west has forgotten: the war in Nigeria where marauding militia from neighbouring countries seem to have gone in to rape, plunder and pillage. And there's Afghanistan and Iraq. Where will Bush's "crusading" spirit lead America into next? And there's North Korea to concern us all, and the scandalous regime in Burma with its horrific record of human rights' abuses. What else will emerge when you get the spread of religious, political and commercial fanaticism and fears?

Bears. Yes, bears come into it too; bears held in captivity that "dance" for tourists, whose cubs are made drunk on beer so that they stumble and stagger clownishly to amuse people. And in some countries the paws are a delicacy, but only if they are cut off while the bear is still alive.

You want to know something? I feel quite ill writing this.

There's no rhyme or reason or end to the horrors and fears one can compile. Nature, luck, human greed, stupidity, cupidity, accident, deliberate cruelty, chance - I really can't believe in Fate. It may be a vaguely consoling concept at times, but it saps your will power. It just seems like another attempt to give shape and meaning to the chaos that we keep at bay by organising our lives in nations, villages, religious groups, tribes, communities.

Just as there is no accounting for the horrors around, there is always the goodness of so many people, the happy accidents of life and the incredible humanitarian and intellectual achievements of which the human race is capable. And the lunchtime beer is the one I shall have when I've finished writing this article. How dare I? How can I when the world is in the state I've been detailing? After all, you were perfectly happy before you started reading this. What right have I to pour out a pre-lunch beer, open a tin of olives and sit down with my dog on my lap to enjoy a lifestyle that others can never aspire to?

You're spot on target, of course. I have no right. I was just born in the lucky side of the world. I can contribute to all the charities I choose and it will not alter that fact. To live with the guilt of having been so blessed by chance is something that will constantly nag me into awareness of misery and is, to my mind, a kind of necessary hypocrisy. No, I can't explain that. How can I explain something which leaves me so confused? Perhaps it's what T.S.Eliot phrased neatly when he said that human kind "cannot bear too much reality". That is the cowardly truth for most of us.

I have a life which I live. I suppose it's a choice between living it in one way or another, devoting myself body and soul to relieve poverty, or committing suicide. It may help if I say that one of my favourite stories about saints is the following. The saint in question was riding his horse. It was winter and very, very cold - as on that frozen Thames, no doubt. He saw a beggar in rags and he immediately took off his warm, lined cloak and, here's the odd part, he cut it in half. He gave the beggar one piece and kept the other for himself. Why didn't he give the beggar the whole cloak and go on his merry way till he fell off his horse in one solid, frozen block? I like this saint because...because – am I afraid to put it into words? Perhaps it's because it represents for me the dilemma we all face in the rich countries. We have far more than we need. We have to give, and we really can and should give - probably a great deal more than we think. After all, since I began to write this article, about 26 children have died of hunger somewhere - a child every seven minutes.

But it's only the few of us who give their all. What of the rest of us? Perhaps the real reason I like the story of that saint is because I think it exonerates me somehow and gives me an excuse to hang on to my privileged situation. I really don't know. If anyone has a better answer, I'd be very grateful if they'd tell me.

23rd May, 2003.

IT'S A MAD MAD WORLD.

Among 200,000,000 people you'd expect to find the occasional dentist or surgeon, an atomic scientist here, an author of world renown there, musicians, teachers, civil servants, parliamentarians, and you might even stub your toe against a genius. You wouldn't expect every last one of them to be doing things like sweeping streets and cleaning out toilets. But you would if you are talking about the Untouchables in India.

As far as I can make out, Indian society was divided into four main castes about two thousand years ago. Those castes were further subdivided. At the top were the priests, the Brahmans. Then came the nobles, warriors, traders, farmers and servants. At the bottom of the bottom were the Untouchables. Such was their lack of any kind of standing that if the shadow of an Untouchable fell upon a Brahman, the said Brahman would need to purify himself of such defilement. Other castes are polluted if touched by an Untouchable, and, in some cases, even by the sight of one. Gandhi called them Harijan - Children of God - and discrimination against them was declared illegal in 1947, but what is sixty years against the prejudice of two millennia? You can't legislate so easily against entrenched attitudes, and legislation alone will not easily eliminate a slave mentality.

Things are changing. Once, though animals were tolerated if they wandered into a temple, the Untouchables were forbidden entry. They have fought against that. They have also fought against the ban on their owning land and have occupied tracts of land supposed to be used only to pasture animals. They have planted and reaped and tried to be more than the landless millions they have always been. Their lot is still dire. A day's labour in the fields can earn them a euro a day. Many emigrate to cities like Mumbai where they may or may not find work. Ten hours of back-breaking labour breaking stones may bring in two euros. Fourteen hours a day spent collecting and sorting out rubbish can earn them fourteen euros a month.

Isn't it appalling that so enormous a source of skilled labour, of potential professionals, is going to waste because of laws established two thousand years ago for some reason or other. It probably seemed like a good idea at the time to someone…and I bet that someone was not an Untouchable.

Something else that has caught my attention this week is maize, and it's another instance of a topsy-turvy world. I've been viewing a TV programme I taped about a year ago and which I put away in a safe place. It suffered the fate of all things put in safe places - oblivion. But it now sees the light of day once more and I watched and listened, bemused, at a huge industry that I didn't know existed. I'm speaking of Food Aid. You know the sort of thing: there's threatened starvation somewhere in the world and tons of food are rushed in. It sounds laudable, pragmatic and efficient as well as munificent. (You couldn't expect me to miss an opportunity of putting those words all together in one sentence, now, could you?)

I hate to disabuse you, but all is not what it seems. You see, American farmers - who are heavily subsidised - produce a surplus of maize. Were this maize to be destroyed, there would be a national and international outcry. So it is stored, not by the farmers, but by the government. That's all quite clear. Now cast your mind back to post World War II Europe. Things were very bad for many people in a devastated land and the Americans came out with the Marshall Plan in 1947 to send food to the worst affected areas. You can't send aid on that scale without a pretty elaborate infra-structure to collect, store, transport and deliver the aid which is going from one continent, across an ocean, to another continent. So the necessary structures were all elaborated and were thus available for later use – in our time now.

And then we come to a serious difficulty. No matter how efficiently you organize things, it will take weeks or months to assemble, load, ship, transport from port to devastated zone and then distribute bulky sacks of that maize you've stored away. You therefore employ people whose job it is to forecast where the next crisis is going to happen so that you can ship the stuff over before it happens. You may be right in your assessment, but, there again, you may be wrong, in which case you may be flooding North Africa with maize when the need arises somewhere in South America. You think I exaggerate? Well, several years ago Zambia found itself with one province in dire straits where basic food production was concerned. The other provinces could have, between them, made up most of the shortfall, but the machinery for Food Aid got under way. Reports exaggerated the crisis so that it seemed as if the whole of Zambia was going to starve, and maize began to pour in by the ton. About 80% of the aid came from the United States. There was no stopping it. In fact, you may remember the furore that arose at some point when Zambia refused to accept the maize that was genetically modified. The fact was that they didn't need it and, though Americans might be happy to have a modicum of GM maize for breakfast or a bit some lunchtime, Africans, for whom it is a staple food, would be making it the mainstay of three meals a day - and they didn't feel enough research into genetically modified crops had been done. The maize was shunted on to Malawi.

I was impressed by the lucidity with which one particular Zambian minister, the one for agriculture, argued the case. He objected to the way supply and demand had been created: you store your surplus maize so that there is a constant supply. A country with food problems is encouraged to demand. That country is cast in the role of victim and is not helped to find its own solutions. Furthermore, it would make better sense for the rich nations to provide money and with it to buy maize or grain from other countries in Africa. This would speed matters up and would give a boost to local agriculture. He spoke forcefully about the need for aid programmes to be determined by Africans instead of having them imposed by Americans or Europeans. As he said, "Zambia is a land of plenty and we are being turned into beggars."

I am not an expert on the matter and I hope you will forgive any ignorance I'm betraying, but one thing became abundantly clear because the figures speak for themselves. In America, a million citizens are employed in the shipping, storage, collection, and every other stage of what I shall call the Maize Mountain. Vast warehouses in Louisiana are crammed with sacks of maize awaiting the next crisis. The farmers are happy, those employed in the massive infra structure are happy and the executives running it were, a couple of years ago, seeking an increase from 1200,000,000$ to 5000,000,000$ to finance the whole operation. There is, naturally, a powerful lobby as the private sector and the aid sector work on a mutual back-scratching policy. A lot of vested interests around, wouldn't you say?

It's a bit like Frankenstein's monster. He started off with the best of intentions and created a creature that he was unable to control.

31st March, 2006.

- BUT HOW MUCH DID IT COST?

I came home well pleased with myself yesterday bearing two bead curtains for which we had paid the princely sum of 30 €. We've been in need of them for ages. You see, we have two doors that give out onto our small patio; we keep them both open for much of the year and they're an invitation to wild life to enter. Flies of assorted sizes and degrees of unpleasantness zoom in. We have enormous black insects with small iridescent blue wings that come bombing in and, after the briefest of looks around, fly out again into the greener world of creepers and flowerpots. I like them. The large bluebottles, however, have no sense of direction and, once indoors, will barge and blunder around when they finally decide to get out. I don't like them: I've seen them in the great outdoors settling happily and greedily to feast on putrid bits of food and excrement. I bear them no ill-will. I understand that a fly's got to do what a fly's got to do, but I want them to do it elsewhere. To have them hovering over the food I'm trying to prepare is not on. I'd taken to swatting them - nothing personal, but a woman's got to do certain things too.

However, the bead curtains are working a treat - not a fly in sight in the kitchen, air circulating and strings of varied beads making a pleasant pattern in earth colours against the sunlight.

On closer examination it becomes clear that the beads are strung on rather thin cotton thread and I foresee a future when I shall hear a soft twanging noise as the thread gives way, followed by the gentle pattering of dozens of beads falling to the ground. Oh, horror! I shall be forced to re-thread each string. Which nightmare scenario brings up the question of how the beads got strung in the first place. Considering that we bought them in a Chinese supermarket, that each strand is a slightly different in length to its neighbour and that the pattern is a weeny bit out of kilter, I think I can detect the hand of woman/man behind them. But what if they came from the hand of child? And who on earth would want to do the job anyway? How long does it take to complete one miserable curtain? How much is each worker paid if, after production and transport costs they can sell such curtains at 15 € apiece in Europe where they've bought premises and paid staff - and still make enough profit to make it really worth their while?

I'm not so happy about my curtains any more. What am I to do? I belong to a generation where the word "frugal" had real meaning and where one of the virtues of a Girl Guide, as a friend reminded me, was to be thrifty. My mother's reaction was always - "I can get it for half that price!" and she was a woman who converted haggling into an art form. I have a cultural, personal and economic history that pushes me towards the Bargain, the Sale, the Flea Market. You want I should give you an example? My small dog has just had two big stones removed from her bladder. No bargain to be had; it's cost 400 € to test, ecograph and remove the damn things. I now have two thumbnail-sized pinkish lumps that are not going to go to waste. I intend to hang them on a chain round my neck: they certainly cost more than I've ever paid for a piece of jewellery.

So what do I do about all the cheap goods to be had in street markets? goods from Thailand, China, Cambodia, India? If they're cheap, then I know the workers were paid peanuts to provide me with my bargain. To get down to concrete examples, let us consider that a small family can live in Delhi for thirty pounds a month. Even allowing for a six and not a seven-day week, that would mean earning about one pound a day. That day could be anything from nine to twelve or more hours long. I've mentioned in a previous article how, when I went to India with Popri, we subsidised our ill-paid driver - who might have been on the job from dawn till the early hours of the next day - but how do I make it up to my anonymous and distant curtain makers?

It's now a known fact that companies like Gap, Levi, C & A, Nike and others, all use or have used factories in places like Cambodia. You pay sixty pounds for a shoe that cost less than two pounds to produce; you pay thirty pounds for a top for which a worker earned twenty-two pence. Our welfare in any working environment is safeguarded by law; with them there are no such guarantees. We sleep in ample bedrooms while they sleep on straw pallets, perhaps four to a room in, probably, unhealthy districts lacking basic facilities and sanitation. They may work up to fourteen hours a day. They are workforces with no possibility of alternative employment, no trade unions and no voice. Improvements are very slow to come.

The Cambodian rag trade has only been around for about ten years and in that time it has grown massively. In a country devastated by twenty weary years of war with its consequent economic depression, any job may be welcome. That does not excuse the West for profiting from the misery of thousands of workers. One of the western contractors visited the factories it employed and said it found nothing wrong when it interviewed workers - workers who needed their jobs and who had, no doubt, been told what to say and what not to say. Another company saw some problems that it intended to take up with the management and, as it conducted no interviews with the work force, it encouraged them to send e mails in confidence with regard to complaints about or problems at work. That was truly a stroke of genius. Workers who may be under the legal age of fifteen, who are earning about thirty pounds a month, who are paying rent and sending money home, who live in a one-room hovel will, of course, be rushing home from work to sit at their computers.

What can I do? If I buy from such large concerns, I can write to them, find out about their policies, insist that they pay higher wages. As this means asking them to reduce what must be hefty profits, they will only listen if the voice of consumers becomes insistent. I can buy goods that carry the Fair Trading stamp/label. I can contribute to charities that set up commercial enterprises which pay just wages.

A living wage is a relatively recent concept in Europe and the basic minimum wage in UK is a paltry £4.85 pounds an hour if you are over twenty-two years old. That makes you realize what a long way we have to go worldwide. I accept the fact that where the cost of living is low, the wages can be proportionately low without compromising the meaning of "a living wage"; but low does not mean overtime at 15 pence an hour. So if my curtains fall to pieces, perhaps I should do some restringing. It would be part of my education in how others live.

1st July, 2005.

NEST OF VIPERS?

I'm very conscious that reading the papers becomes ever harder for me. One reason is that the buzzwords keep changing and it's hard to keep up with it all. Remember when "ethnic" hit the scene? Everyone in the media was using it and I didn't really know what it meant. And what about the ozone layer, when it was news to anyone without a scientific turn of mind? Why, when AIDS first appeared, even the people who were sent to schools in Sussex, where I lived then, to inform staff about it - so that we could answer pupils' questions - weren't able to answer our questions!

And now it's "Globalisation". As I felt pretty ignorant about it and as there was an immensely important conference about to come off in Mexico, at a place called Cancun, I decided to settle down to inform myself.

I was trying to get to terms with statistics, concepts and terminology that were made all the harder by the use of initials. What do you do when faced with WTO, EU, CAP, OEDC, IMF? I know that a bit of thought would help because I *have* heard of the International Monetary Fund...IMF to its friends, and of the World Trade Organization ... which is clearly WTO, but it does make it all uphill work and that is very worrying because the issues at stake in Cancun concern all of us.

Globalization? - world trade is what it is all about: you sell me your stuff and I'll sell you mine. It sounds fine. Furthermore, we'll sign international agreements. The poor nations of the world outnumber the rich so they can out-vote them. Great! It's what the world needs to get a bit of economic equality going. Correct?

How wrong can you be? Facts rather than theory help to clarify matters. We want to help developing countries? Let's do some sums of what is needed:
1. $ 20 bn to set up universal education.
2. $ 5.5 bn to provide universal access to sanitation and water.
3. $ 10 bn HIV/AIDS protection, treatment and support for a year in other than developed countries.
4. $ 2.7 bn to eradicate polio.
5. $ .6 bn TB control in the 22 countries most devastated by it.
All right, all right; I'll stop there. After all, where are these huge sums to come from? Damn it! That list adds up $44.2 billion dollars. We're not made of money in the developed countries, are we?

We in the West cannot really afford that because...well... because. Let's take concrete examples: America spends $4 bn a year on cotton subsidies. What? How many farmers are involved? Actually, it's 25,000. And Japan spends $2,555 dollars on subsidising cows.

Let me be specific: that is the annual subsidy per cow. Anyway, it's not the cows' fault that the national income per capita in Ethiopia is only $100, is it?

And this is one of the main problems where world trade is concerned: rich countries will subsidise their farmers. Poor countries can't afford to. The result is that the rich countries can flood third world markets with cheap products that then drive the poor countries out of business.

The American cotton subsidy is ruining cotton production in West Africa. Cheap European tomatoes are doing a like job in Ghana. Rice from the USA has severely damaged the rice growers in Honduras, and so on with onion growers in Senegal and oil seed producers in India. In other words, the wealthy are contributing directly to the growth of world poverty.

And tariffs and quotas are another of the huge problems facing developing countries. If you live in Europe, you establish tariffs to protect your own goods. You know the sort of thing: an imported car costs X % more than the national variety. You slap an import tax on meat or booze or cigarettes or whatever item in your particular economy might be at risk from cheaper imported goods. You can also establish quotas for the amount of X or Y that you allow into the country. In this way you protect your own.

So why don't developing countries do the same?

Ever heard of twisting someone's arm? There's the fact that western-controlled institutions like The International Monetary Fund, as I read in the papers, insist that their Third World clients drop all protection of local products in order to qualify for loans. Pretty neat, eh?

And that's the sort of thing that is expected to happen at Cancun next week. The developed nations, particularly the US, will be going in for hard bargaining, for extreme demands, for throwing their weight about with implied threats to reduce existing assistance, for wheeling-dealing behind the scenes. And Europe is expected to follow where America leads.

The World Trade Organization aims to offer "special and preferential treatment" to poor nations. That's the theory and the intention and they are good, but we've all heard the saying "Might is right." It doesn't just apply to physical muscle. Economic muscle is much worse.

And, yet, the WTO (I can do it too!) could be a great force for good if the poorer nations were allowed a real voice in it and if the protectionist attitude of the developed nations were to change. It is an organization that could help redress unfair trading policies in a world where 20% of the world - and that includes me and you - enjoy 86% of the goodies. Turn it round and it sounds appalling: I have over twenty meals in five days to someone else's one meal in the same time.

Like so many things in life, the protectionist policies of Europe made sense once upon a time. The now pretty-well infamous subsidies were something that arose in a Europe facing the threat of starvation after World War II. Governments needed to ensure that they had adequate food supplies in countries where industrialisation had been the cause of a drastic drift away from the land. The same sort of economic help was also offered to industries that had been laid waste by a war economy - when everything is directed at the War Effort, then all else suffers, from the textile trade to the manufacture of furniture to the production of domestic appliances.

So, it certainly made sense - once. But, where other industries and endeavours gradually ended up standing on their own feet, agriculture has continued to receive ever-heavier subsidies. America has followed a similar pattern and subsidises its farmers even more generously: The aid which rich countries give to the whole of Africa in one year, is less than the Western producers receive in subsidies in a *fortnight*. It is hard to believe, but it is true.

Even at a purely selfish level, the west should be in revolt. When you realise that only 1% of the population of Great Britain works on the land, and that French agriculture produces only 2.9% of the gross economic output of that country, then the 86.8 billion dollars of farming subsidies in the European Union means that the average taxpayer is paying massively for the few. (And don't forget that it is $42.2 bn that would resolve so many huge problems in the Third World.)

There seems to be a choice between two extremes:
1.   The world is mine because I have the economic clout.
2.   The world is ours and we are all entitled to share the benefits.

The title of this article? The original name of Cancun meant, "Nest of Vipers"; I hope it's not prophetic.

26th September, 2003.

The talks broke down largely due to *Europe's* hard-line attitude; and China and India began to emerge as the potential champions of the poorer countries...We have been warned!

August, 2006.

SHOES AND SHIPS AND SEALING WAX.

WHAT'S SO FUNNY?

I wonder who the first human to laugh was; and I wonder what caused that laugh. What was the joke? Was it the classic slipping on the Palaeolithic equivalent of a banana skin? It seems unlikely that it was verbal humour at work because, if you look at babies and small children, they find much in life that is funny long before they react to their first joke - which they will then tell you repeatedly and expect you to laugh at each time. With one of my daughters it was: "Why does a bear have a fur coat?" and the answer, which cracked her up, was: "Because it would look silly in a mackintosh."

There appears to be an age at which verbal skills are such as will allow children to respond to word play, situational humour and the pleasurable fun of the unexpected. Actually, someone once said that an omniscient god couldn't have a sense of humour precisely because knowing all precludes a spontaneous response to the unexpected. Sad, isn't it? I think that in that case, I'd rather be mortal.

I did once read a book on humour that brought me close to tears of boredom, for what is extraordinary about humour is the fact that it defies analysis. In a way it resembles music in that it reaches us directly at various levels - emotional and intellectual - and that we have an untutored response to both. There are, of course, levels of appreciation and understanding, but one can be responsive to both music and jokes without any form of tuition other than that provided by our general socialisation. However, different societies have different musical scales and different instruments; and so too they have different forms of humour.

Slapstick is pretty basic humour: the custard pie in the face. Then you refine it when the person it is aimed at happens to duck and the pie hits an innocent third party. Or the person throwing the pie slips and ends up with *his* face in the pie. Further ideas will develop in any such situation that depends on physical humour. I think it was

Charles Chaplin who said that slipping on a banana skin was mildly funny, but much funnier was *not* slipping on it, turning round triumphantly to look back at it and, consequently, falling down an open manhole.

And from such humour I move on to the sort of situation when things go physically wrong for you on a grand scale. We've all experienced some form of this cumulative disaster. Imagine the scene: you are carrying parcels; you are in a hurry and have a dozen things to do. Suddenly one of the parcels starts slipping out from under your arm. You clamp your arm down to try and hold it, which action tips your body over to one side and disturbs the whole balance you had originally established. The other parcels then begin to slip too and you instinctively and unadvisedly clutch and grab and fail miserably to keep a hold of things. They start to fall; you manage to catch one parcel - clamping it firmly between your hands...it's the half dozen meringues which were so carefully wrapped for you at the confectioners. At this point you drop your keys and, as you make a dive for them, you hit your head against a car that's parked strategically for the keys to disappear under. And you start to laugh; and it's a real belly laugh; and you don't know where it came from! - particularly as you felt murderous or suicidal just seconds before.

My grandmother had a talent for feeling that response in the face of disaster. I remember once when we were walking down one of Gibraltar's steeper hills and her foot slipped. She shot off and ended up under a car with her head and shoulders still out on the road. She was a very small woman and I should have had little difficulty in fishing her out. However, she was rendered paralytic with laughter at her own predicament, the speed at which it had happened and my vain attempts to rescue her. Wonderful! Is such laughter a form of self-defence? Is it a way of breaking a build-up of tension? Frankly, who cares? What I know is that it seems to be an immensely healthy reaction that leaves you feeling good.

Quite a different sort of response comes when you are faced with something like parody: that is when you take a style of speech or manner or form of some sort and imitate it, using exaggeration. You are invited to see what is ludicrous about the original. If you take the type of soap which relies on strong emotion and on an over-dramatised plot, your parody will take it all to extremes with hysterics, wild protestations of love or hate, the most villainous of villains and the death of half the cast, the director and the man in charge of the lighting. The American actor, Leslie Nielsen, has enjoyed a grand career late in life as the star of a series of films that parody disaster movies, spy films and any genre the producers could think of.

By contrast, we have satire that employs a bitter form of that humour which parody uses so light-heartedly. Parody aims to entertain, but satire has a more serious purpose in that it is aimed - as a weapon is aimed - at a target. It will attempt to make us see the ills and the follies and the evils of human behaviour. Jonathan Swift wrote his satirical "Gulliver's Travels" in 1726, though it has too often been treated as if it were merely a wonderful and imaginative children's story. Three years later he produced the most vicious piece of satire I know. He wrote "A Modest Proposal" - for the alleviation of near-famine, poverty and misery in Ireland. In an extended article he developed the idea of having the poor Irish family kill, salt and eat one of their own children. Terrible? Of course it was, but it was less so than the reality it was pointing to where England deliberately turned a blind eye to the horrific poverty and suffering of the Irish.

Most satire is nowhere near as drastic as this. Is it humorous? It is, but irony - it's main ploy - is something that appeals to the intellect and which will amuse without necessarily making you laugh. The humour can often be black. It's a far cry from the custard pie!

The varieties of humour cover much more than I have touched on. There's the absurd, the bizarre and much else. What always delights me is the degree of sophistication that people in general display when they are told a joke which they enjoy. Theory is all very well, so let me end with the reality of one piece of humour.

A man walks into a bar and stands at the counter silently looking at the bartender who eventually says:

"What will you have, Sir?"

"A double whisky, thank you," says the man. He drinks it and then starts to walk out.

"Excuse me," says the bartender, "You haven't paid for that!"

"Of course not. You invited me. I never asked for anything;" says the man.

Another customer who has heard the exchange chimes in: "That's right. I'm a lawyer and I'm a witness to the fact that *you offered* the drink."

The furious bar tender tells the original customer never to darken his doors again.

Five minutes later the man walks in and goes up to the counter and stares at the bartender, who glares at him:

"I told you never to come here again!"

"I've never been here in my life," says the man coolly.

"Then you must have a double," snaps the bartender.

"That's very kind of you - make it a whisky!"

12th December, 2003.

HISTORY AND US.

When I was in college training to be a teacher, we were given an article to read that bore the intriguing title "The Sabre-Toothed Curriculum". It dealt with Bronze or Iron Age schools where pupils were taught how to hunt the sabre-toothed tiger, how to capture a mammoth and which dinosaurs to avoid...when all of these had become extinct. It was a satirical piece, a parable to encourage us to question the validity of the subjects we ourselves had been taught or were due to teach in our turn. It was a useful corrective to accepting the established curriculum blindly. Once upon a time the only things thought worthy of study were Greats - your Latin and your Greek were considered the best possible preparation for life that a gentleman could have. Mathematics? Geography? What kind of new-fangled nonsense was that? And the sciences, now being plugged so assiduously, were very latecomers indeed on the educational scene.

Nowadays, Latin and Greek have virtually disappeared and some of the arts need to justify their existence. I have known of or worked in schools that were trying to establish a high degree of academic credibility. Schools like this are likely to sacrifice subjects like drama, music and art. It's as if the only things worth studying must be those tackled with a pen and paper - the intellect at the expense of the emotions - and considering how few people out in the world spend their lives writing and reading, it sometimes seems that it's the intellect of the few that is served at the expense of the development of the many.

I do believe that every subject should justify its place in the curriculum and I remember one of my history lecturers saying that history gives us a sense of our own identity whether it's our nation, our city or our family that is involved. To this I would add that the history of other societies can teach us to exercise our judgement, to respect their achievements and can lead to an understanding of their actuality. History also provides us with a source of wonder and entertainment.

Let's take 1776. It seems remote and one might be excused for seeing it as a period of basic medicine, short life expectancy, poor to non-existent sanitation and a quality of life not worth the having. Yet that was the year of the American Declaration of Independence and, while such political freedom was being exercised, Gibbon was publishing the first volume of "The Decline and Fall of the Roman Empire". Meanwhile, back in Vienna, Mozart was busy at work and an English housewife, Mrs Constable, had just given birth to a boy, John, who was to become one of England's great painters. And perhaps little of this was of interest to Captain James Cook who was into his third voyage in the Pacific.

One can try the same thing with the recent past. A look at 1954 shows us Queen Elizabeth and Prince Philip finishing their tour of the Commonwealth by stopping at Gibraltar; the Supreme Court in America is ruling that segregation in public schools - government funded schools - is illegal and violates the 14th amendment to the Constitution; "Lord of the Rings" and "Lord of the Flies" hit the bookshops; the hydrogen bomb is tested by America in Bikini; the anti-polio vaccine comes into use; Morocco is devastated by a plague of locusts; the four-minute mile becomes history as Roger Bannister sets the amazing new record of 3 minutes 59.4 seconds. And the composer, Furtwängler, dies - and I only mention him because I can't resist the name.

As you may have guessed, I'm having a happy morning buried in "The Timetables of History". It's a wonderful book if you enjoy history, facts and drawing comparisons. It also lets you enjoy the weird and wonderful.

There are still some of us who remember Edmund Purdom in the film "Sinuhe the Egyptian". It came at a time when Hollywood had discovered the bible and ancient history. The epic production became fashionable with exotic locations and casts of thousands. The point that interests me now is that the story of Sinuhe had been written in Egypt, in what was possibly the earliest form of the novel, at some point between 2000 and 1500 BC. And, possibly in verse, the Babylonians had produced an epic five centuries earlier and the Sumerians had brought out their first epic about five hundred years before that. Sinuhe's story was being written during the 18th dynasty that brought Egypt to the height of its power and achievement - think pyramids, hieroglyphics, paintings and contraception too. And in England they were building Stonehenge in Wiltshire.

As a woman, I find much to be learnt about the role woman has played across the ages. Three thousand years before our calendar came into operation, the chief deities in Sumeria were Mother Goddess Innin and her son. They even had a goddess of chaos. The situation with regard to the gods was similar in Egypt, Scandinavia and among the Hittites. Women ruled OK! 1500 years later women musicians entertained people at festive gatherings in Thebes - the first female professional bands? And around 800 BC a woman reigned in Thebes as high priest; and the clothes worn by women and by men in Assyria were almost identical. Equality? A hundred years later we encounter the Greek poet, Sappho of Lesbos, a literary figure who preceded the great male dramatists and poets by about a hundred years. At around 450 BC Pericles' mistress ruled Athenian society.

Another thing that is fascinating when one reads history is the reality behind the appearance. Let's see. Where democracy is concerned we know we have the Greeks to thank for it. Rule of the people, by the people, for the people. Yes! Yet at around 420 BC the population of Greece seems to have consisted of three million of which one million were slaves; and in Athens itself the slaves outnumbered the citizens two to one. A similar picture emerges from Thomas Moore's "Utopia". The perfect society he envisaged also depended on slave labour.

While we are talking about the reality behind the appearance, let's look at the American Myth. I was weaned on Hollywood and there is a land of dreams in my mind where there are only clapboard houses, white picket fences round tidy gardens with lawns, and small towns inhabited by people like Myrna Loy and Walter Pidgeon. Judy Garland can be heard singing from an open window and people bake wonderful blueberry pies. Whole families gather for Thanksgiving meals. Parents speak wise words and children listen to them and act on them; they do, honestly. It's a wonderful land that, like the Big Rock Candy Mountains of song, never existed.

This returns us to 1954, to an America that contained only 6% of the world's population but had 60% of the cars, 58% of the phones, 45% of radio sets, and 34% of railroads. It was the country of affluence which has, over the years, become so wedded to industrial and commercial expansion that its representatives, attending international gatherings to discuss the effect of greenhouse gases on the atmosphere, toxic emissions and the growing fears of climate change, refuse to tie themselves down to any targets, dates or goals despite the fact that they are already responsible for appalling damage to the life of the planet. No, the charming, small-town lifestyle I loved to see on screen existed only on celluloid, just as the sylphlike figures of the female stars of today are the dream that has nothing to do with the widespread problem of obesity in America.

I said that history provides us with a source of entertainment so I shall leave you with two choice items. In 1676, Le Grand Vatel, chef to the Prince de Condé, committed suicide. It appears that he had prepared a sumptuous meal for the King of France, Louis XIV, which meal did not come up to the king's expectations: tactless king or deranged chef? And, finally, unable to resist another funny name - or two - let me recommend to you that you investigate the life of King Essarhaddon who rebuilt Babylon after the depradations caused by Tiglath-pileser, founder of the Assyrian Empire.

4th October, 2002.

THE IMPORTANCE OF FEET.

Last week I caught a bus that was full of women in the main. When I sat down, I found myself bemusedly looking at all the feet around me. They were, almost without exception, shod in trainers of one sort or another. It made me think of the days when it would have been high-heeled shoes.

High heels are still around, of course, and this last year has seen a resurgence of the spindly heel allied to the pointed toe. There's nothing new about them for those of us who remember the winkle-pickers of the early sixties. They too seemed new at the time, but they were only a revival of a fashion that was current with *men* in the Middle Ages when the part of the shoe meant to house your toes got so ridiculously long that you couldn't possibly walk - so some bright spark made the shoe terminate in a long strip of stiffened material which rose up an arched back so that it could be tied to your leg, just below the knee.

It was not the sort of footwear to use if you went into battle or were mucking out the stables, but if you were indoors in my lord's castle and you thought you had a nice leg to display then you wore your tunic short so that folk could get an eyeful of your legs in their tight-fitting hose, and you completed the ensemble with those daft shoes that drew the eye to your calves. But run in them, you couldn't.

Such a fashion was a matter of vanity, and good luck to those who chose to enjoy it. Less fortunate were the women in China who were caught up in the practice of foot-binding. I had heard of it and knew that it accounted for that shuffling walk that seemed to go with elaborate hairstyles, wonderful costumes and graceful movements.

I didn't know the half of it.

Look at the print on this page. The width of a line is about ten centimetres. Now imagine a line that's just short of eight centimetres long. Now imagine a foot that length...an adult woman's foot. It just isn't possible, is it?

Well, it is, after a fashion - pun intended. Such feet were called "three-inch golden lilies" and it was considered erotic to see a woman teetering along and taking tiny steps. The custom arose, it is said, when an emperor's concubine who had tiny feet became a favourite. Gradually it was considered essential for any well-bred woman to have tiny feet. Foot-binding came in because most women have normal feet. I mean, mine are quite ordinary at size five and a half and they are twenty-four centimetres long. In that China of the past I would have been lucky to marry a goat.

In the book "The Wild Swans" you are told how the process worked. At the age of two a girl child would have all except her big toes bent down and under the foot. The foot would be bound with yards of white cloth, then a large stone would be placed on the foot to crush the arch. The child was gagged to muffle her screams of agony and would often faint repeatedly from the pain as the bones were broken. The whole process took some years to complete and the feet could never be free of bindings as, left to themselves, they would try to recover. We are talking of years of excruciating pain. And imagine the psychological damage of having this torture inflicted by your mother. Yet mothers felt they had to do it to ensure a good marriage for their child. And those white socks the women wore? They were necessary to hide the rotting skin and unlovely sight of those deformed feet.

All because one concubine may have been a bit of a freak and one man had had a foot fetish and was the emperor. And because, dammit! people followed like sheep where the mighty led. A side effect of this appalling custom was that such women - of social standing and education - were rendered physically helpless. They were strictly controlled as a result of what was seen as their greatest charm.

It's what you can call the politics of clothes. Louis XIV of France had this sussed out and made use of it. He had every intention of ensuring an absolute monarchy and he didn't want interference from the potentially powerful nobility. He inveigled them somehow into a belief that to be in favour at his court in Versailles was of paramount importance in their lives. They were kept dancing attendance on him and the business of life became the clothes and jewels they wore. They squandered fortunes and all their energies in outdoing each other…with ruby-studded heels to their shoes, pearl encrusted dresses and suits embroidered with gold thread. Louis had succeeded in emasculating them politically. Instead of worrying about the state of the nation, they worried about the design of waistcoat or a new line in petticoats.

And while I'm on the subject of personal display, I think we can attribute to one man, at least in great part, the way male extravagance in attire of the eighteenth century gave way to the sober dress that had become standard male uniform by the late nineteenth century. In the eighteenth century, wealthy men favoured brocades and lace, wore jewellery, painted their faces and wore wigs. They must have looked like birds of paradise. What fun! Then along came Beau Brummel in the Regency period and decreed that a gentleman's clothing should be impeccably tailored, his linen perfectly crisp and neat, and all unnecessary additions and decorative touches should be eliminated. Farewell birds of paradise and welcome elegant undertaker's assistant.

I exaggerate, of course, but it did leave men in elegant and sober dress and women were the ones left to decorate their person with satins and velvets and lace. They also tortured their figures with corsets that had whalebone inserts and were made of the sort of tough material that would make a really long-lasting tent for a polar expedition. You could do precious little in terms of physical activity in that sort of gear so we can thank Mrs Bloomer for designing those liberating, baggy trousers in which women were able to cycle.

When trainers came into fashion, I thought of *them* as wonderfully liberating for girls. Gone were the sort of narrow shoes with high heels that would lead you to sprout bunions in later life. Then I watched the trainers get bigger and bigger, with immensely thick soles and yards of laces. These laces were decorative and were usually undone so that the only way to walk was by shuffling along, dragging those huge clod-hoppers. We do make our own prisons!

My daughter, Gaby, once went out in flat lace-up shoes, a long grey coat that nearly reached her ankles, a black skirt that was fractionally longer, a prim white blouse buttoned high to the neck and a grey hat of antiquated design. As she entered the underground in Brixton, the ticket collector - a large West Indian lady - greeted her with a broad smile:

"Hi, Honey; you off to convert de heathen, then?"

As Gaby explained, that day she was wearing costume not clothes. But both my daughters, whatever they wear, always opt for comfortable footwear - like Susy's special, white Doc Martens that she wore on her wedding day.

31st October, 2003.

OUR FAMILIES AND OTHER ANIMALS.

Many years ago, I remember watching a slick American comedy about a young married couple. When I consider how many indifferent films I watched - and I'm a sucker for a story, any story - I can think of only one reason why this one has lodged in my memory. Actually, I have forgotten the cast, the plot and the ending, but I do remember the premise on which the young bride operated her marriage: train your husband well from the start. Her training manual was an owner's guide to a well-trained and happy hound. She would ask her husband to do things for her and when he did, she would thank him fulsomely, and though she couldn't pat him on the head and give him a dog biscuit, she could and did praise and kiss him. As far as I remember, it worked a treat and they were blissfully happy - till he discovered the book…but that's as far as my memory takes me.

The point is that the husband responded to praise and emotional stroking. Do the same with a child, a colleague or anyone else and you are likely to get positive results too. Schools in Gibraltar have run courses on Positive Reinforcement in the fairly recent past. Your praise and approval will encourage a particular type of behaviour. Sadly, most of us were brought up in the school of Negative Reinforcement and it's very hard, I found, to change the habits of a lifetime.

However that may be, you can see the sense of it. Just compare two possible responses to the same situation where you have two children in a restaurant and one has started to sing loudly. You can go for "the little monster" with something like,

"Now stop that this minute! How many times have I told you that you have to behave properly when we go out? If you don't stop that I will never take you to a restaurant again. You're embarrassing me in front of everyone. Wait till I tell Daddy/Granny/Grandpa."

On the other hand, you can turn to the child who is sitting quietly and try this approach while you ignore the singer:

"It's really nice to take you out, Sweetheart. I'm enjoying sitting next to you. Shall we look at the menu and see what you'd like to eat?"

And you have to be sincere when you say it; you really need to educate yourself to value positive behaviour. If your praise of one is merely a one-in-the-eye ploy for the other, then they will both see through you. Children are young, but they are not fools.

With the first approach you are devoting yourself entirely to the bad behaviour of one child and you are ignoring the good behaviour of the other. You've also made a threat that you all know you won't carry out. Your remarks have also made the child important by bringing in absent members of the family who will all learn about the confrontation when you bruit it abroad. You have, in effect, made the child feel powerful. Fame at last! If that's the way the cookie crumbles, the child will be encouraged to repeat aberrant behaviour. With the second approach, you are taking note of and praising the behaviour you want to encourage and you are sending a clear signal that your attention will go towards whoever acts that way. I know; I know. It's easier said than done and it may not always work as easily as you hope, but it's a long-term strategy that's worth training oneself in.

Like the young bride in the comedy I mentioned, I have found that dog behaviour makes human behaviour all the clearer. Take Dogo. He is a small black and white creature with a jutting Hapsburg jaw and what could be taken for an aggressive streak. He sits on a small balcony and spends the day hurling abuse at passing dogs - barking and telling them precisely what he'll do if he gets his paws on them. It's another kettle of fish at ground level. While he performs the same act, any dog who decides to approach him will get a fine view of Dogo's hindquarters as he turns tail and scuttles under the nearest car. He is timorous, that's what he is, and all that bravado does not indicate a self-assured beast, but a devout coward who is fearful of the world, like the magician in "The Wizard of Oz".

The rest of the animal kingdom also provides parallels with human behaviour, but the thing about humans is that we can adopt just about any system of social organization and behaviour while animals tend to stick to one style per species. With ants the survival of the species matters over and above the welfare of the individual ant. You won't find sick ants taking time off or seeing a counsellor. The individual is expendable - and so it is with totalitarian societies. They may be Fascist, Communist, Monarchist, religious or something else, but what they will have in common is a willingness to sacrifice individuals or whole sections of society for what they will term "the common good". And when we see the dominance of the queen bee in her hive, it's more like a kingdom where the ruler dominates as did the emperors of old. By contrast, you get the near-democracy in animal packs like those of hyenas or wolves.

The way animals feed can vary tremendously too. Lionesses will hunt, but the lion will feed first. The cubs can get a pretty raw deal - no pun intended. I suppose the hierarchical approach ensures the survival of the provider of the sperm and, among the cubs, the survival of the fittest. And a new male taking over a pride can kill all those cubs sired before his arrival by his predecessor. This ensures the dominance of his sperm. On the other hand, there's the communal approach I have observed among some stray cats I feed. It began with one who was later joined by a lady friend. She, in turn, brought along another lady friend. They were later joined by a hungry kitten with an insatiable appetite and deplorable table manners who at first snatched at everything. I had, consequently, to increase the amount of food I took, but even before I did so, the older cats accepted the newcomer with equanimity and shared their food: there was no fighting, no pulling rank or attempts to establish a pecking order. By contrast, I have found dogs can be much more possessive or aggressive over food.

And there are birds to be considered. The cuckoo's idea of a childminder is really to abandon parental responsibility completely. Look at the result: a juvenile delinquent capable of avecide as soon as he registers the competition. Then there are those creatures that spawn thousands of offspring of which most will die. There are species that will mate for life and where shared parenting is the norm; there are some who will mate indiscriminately; those dependent on the female for nurture, those depending on the male, those depending on both. The king penguin is one of those where the female, having laid the egg, can waltz off into Antarctica while dad has the tough job of hatching the egg which he has to keep warm at sub-zero temperatures.

You find polygamy and polyandry, the single parent unit, group parenting - each within a particular species. There will be extended families that will accept members from outside, just as there are species that will attack any alien presence attempting to gain entry into the group. Gorillas, once assured of your harmlessness, will even tolerate the presence of humans in the family group, which says something about these huge pacifists.

Each mode of operation has to do with survival strategies. It makes you understand what evolution is about. Consider the seagull that decides it's about time that sea birds took to walking the motorways of the world: it wouldn't last long enough to pass on its genes to anyone. And so a promising line of jay-walkers is nipped in the bud. That's why those with the most effective strategies are those that survive and genetically mould the ones that follow.

I am sadly conscious of creatures whose efficient strategies break down in the face of change. I am thinking of flightless birds. It's easy to imagine them living in islands where there were rich pickings on the ground and no natural predators…so said birds took to feeding on the ground to the point where their wings no longer served any practical purpose and became merely decorative appendages. Along came man and made the placid Dodo a thing of the past.

While animals develop and stick to particular survival strategies, we humans will try just about anything to satisfy a ruler's ego, a dogma, a philosophical construct or a political schema. In the name of these we can establish the strangest and most self-destructive types of behaviour. I remember reading of a religious movement in Russia at a time of crisis where men castrated themselves and women cut off their breasts. It died out pretty quickly.

There is also the environment to consider when developing your approach to life. A recent documentary on the Amazon showed a tribe that were so laid back that they were, literally, horizontal for much of the day. They had all they needed for survival without having to work hard for it and had turned leisure into a mini-art-form - relaxing, chatting slowly, holding the baby and dozing. Yet, on the other side of the Equator…what makes for head hunters and cannibalism? Why have some groups developed fiercely rigid sexual prohibitions while others see sexuality as something to exercise almost casually? Why are some tribes warlike while the Hopi Indians in North America had no word for "war"? In fact, anthropologists working with the Hopi had their research interrupted by World War II. They tried to explain why they had to leave, but the Hopi language failed to provide the words they needed and the Hopi accepted, bewildered, the fact that these people had to go far away because they were having a difference of opinion about something with someone who didn't even live next door, but at a great distance. "A pretty weak excuse for dumping us," they must have thought.

Looking at the animal kingdom makes us understand survival strategies behind patterns of behaviour, but given the human being's perverse capacity for creating weird social patterns, one feels the truth of the old saying: "There's nowt so queer as folk."

27th September 2002.

PREJUDICE.

Anyone who is around sixty or so will surely remember the film "The Day the Earth Stood Still". It wasn't just another SF film like "The Plague of the Killer Tomatoes" or the one about giant homicidal carrots. It was a film with a serious point to make, not about spacemen but about the human race.

In the film a spacecraft lands in America and a single spaceman in a nifty silver suit steps out to approach the population in peace. Meanwhile, back at the Pentagon, at the first whiff of extraterrestrial activity, orders have been issued and the armed forces have gone into mega-defensive warp and are waiting for him with the latest weaponry at the ready and a strategy that considers that attack is the only form of defence. One trigger-happy goofball fires a shot and wounds the spaceman. The spaceman, played by Michael Rennie - remember him? - survives and spends the film looking noble, walking tall and speaking in a beautifully modulated voice. He also spends it trying to evade capture and eventually leaves planet earth as a sadder and wiser spaceman. Naturally, there is an attractive girl who helps him - Patricia O'Neal if you must know - but that was only of peripheral importance.

At the time I thought, "That which is different is seen as threatening; that is what prejudice is all about." And it was precisely that sentiment that I heard voiced over the radio recently by some church leader in England. However, I have learnt over the years that prejudice is something rather different. I had mistaken a symptom for the illness. Prejudice is like rape in one respect. Rape has little to do with sex (bear with me) and it has everything to do with domination, humiliation and control. In other words, it has little to do with the victim and everything to do with the aggressor. Most rapists are recidivists: they will keep repeating the crime. Presumably it gives them a degree of satisfaction that nothing else will produce, otherwise you could introduce them to other potential sources of self-esteem like rock climbing or macramé and deflect their attention into healthier channels.

The same happens with prejudice. There are no special characteristics in blacks, Indians, Jews, women or Christians to provoke prejudice.

What such targeted groups do is provide an outlet for negative feelings, and any accusation will do. There will develop a weird psychological consistency about being inconsistent. Contradictory accusations will happily rub shoulders: "They are all cowards," will be uttered in the same breath as, "Exhibitionists one and all; they fight hard just to show off."

It also appears that the qualities for which people are vilified arise in the accuser. It works something like this:
1. I have a fear of weakness;
2. I compensate by acting tough;
3. I can then look down on group X by attributing weakness to them.

And there is another common one:
1. I can't cope with my own sexuality;
2. I repress my interest/desires;
3. I attribute all sorts of sexual license, perversions and general goings-on to group X, which allows me involvement while I condemn them for what I am vicarious enjoying.

It is also significant that a prejudiced person is likely to hit out at more than one group. I suppose it increases your self esteem in a vitiated manner because the more people you can look down on, the better you can feel about your own lifestyle and sense of self-righteousness. Your self esteem will increase in direct proportion to the degree of contempt and rejection you can generate. No wonder it's so hard to root out prejudice - when you attack it, you are attacking people's sense of self-worth, however warped it may be, so they will resist reason and persuasion.

I know that a short article like this cannot hope to deal with such a complex issue in any real depth, but it's worth taking a long glance at the matter at least because we're all prejudiced about something in some measure...or am I judging by my own limitations? I mean, there will be many Gibraltarians who remember hearing, in the past, this sort of remark about a prospective son-in-law: "Es inglés, pero es muy bueno" - He's English, but he's very good. And in the conjunction "but" lay a small world of prejudice. Pretty harmless stuff really?

And how harmless or harmful is national stereotyping? You know the sort of thing: perfidious Albion; you can't take Italians seriously; Scandinavians are progressive, and so on and so forth. For years I resisted such ideas. Then one day, as I was teaching English to a group of German students, the issue arose when we were reading a passage in which the Scottish were represented as being tight-fisted. One of the students asked what the German stereotype was. I paused and thought of the old joke where the sergeant lines up his men and barks at them:

"Ze English von ze last var becauss zey haf a sense of 'umour. Ze captain vill now tell a joke and you vill all laugh!"

So I told them, as tactfully as I could, that Germans were considered somewhat humourless. They heard me out, exchanged serious looks with each other and then one of them said solemnly,

"Ach, so, but we *haf* a sense of humour."

And the rest all nodded agreement.

This from a group that had kept trying to find the socially relevant content in a piece of nonsense by the Canadian humorist, Stephen Leacock. Since then I have watched German films or programmes on TV and have found German humour to be simple, obvious and, for me, not particularly amusing. I'm sorry, but so it is. It has forced me to acknowledge that there may be something in the idea of a national character. If you think about it, the climate, accidents of history, the local terrain and a myriad of factors will affect the way societies develop in different countries. It is knowledge of these factors that can lead to understanding rather than to stereotyping.

As an example - there is a polyandrous society in India in some mountain region. To us the idea of one woman with several husbands - running concurrently, as it were - may seem bizarre. Do we take it that all the women in the region are raging nymphomaniacs? Or do we consider the terrain and the consequent economy of a region where survival depends on extremely hard physical labour for poor returns? A woman with three husbands, usually brothers, will not really produce more children than if she were married to only one;

and three men will thus be able to produce enough food for what is basically a single family unit.

With stereotyping, the danger arises when you find yourself indulging in it across a broad spectrum of life, becoming rigidly authoritarian, being over-concerned with power and weakness in your own terms, and being generally unable to appreciate subtleties because you see life in black and white. Beware! That is perilously close to the profile of a seriously prejudiced person. Fortunately, most of us do not fit that profile, but we do catch ourselves out saying things like, "They're all the same, those X, aren't they?" And it's only when the words are out that the crassness of such a sweeping statement may strike us.

I suppose the solution to this lies, initially, in acknowledging our own prejudice: doing a sort of Bigot's Anonymous declaration. And I think part of the succeeding process must involve learning to separate the particular from the general. So, I may think that So-and-so is a stingy/foul-mouthed/self-centred daughter/son of a camel. I might be right and my criticism be richly deserved. The fact that she/he is a pygmy or a Finn or a Gibraltarian is neither here nor there. The attitude and behaviour of one individual does not present a profile of a whole race.

I know that I should wish to be judged for what I am, warts and all. What I should hate would be to have someone else's failings foisted on me, defining me and misrepresenting me. And I bet you feel the same.

6ᵗʰ September, 2002.

YES, BUT IS IT "ART"?

"The difficulty with abstract art," said a friend, years ago, "is deciding whether or not a picture is any good."

I felt that I knew just a little about art and had got beyond the I-don't-know-anything-about-art-but-I-know-what-I-like stage, though I was still trying to decide what I did like. I had seen people look at a Picasso and say; "I could do that." But I had seen a reproduction of an early picture of his and I knew the man could already draw and paint like an angel when he was in his teens. If he distorted, it was because he chose to. And to clinch matters for me, I attended an exhibition of abstract paintings where I saw that many a conventional painter who could produce a landscape or still life with some skill had come a total cropper when faced with a blank canvas and only her/his own imagination for guidance.

I also met the other end of the abstract continuum when I talked at length to a very intense young man who was studying at some London art college. He was looking for purity of form and content, as I recall. He certainly wanted to purge his pictures of whatever smacked of representational art, of commercialism and of any kind of message or approach to the verifiable world about him. As I listened, I grew to an awareness of what would then be left, and he confirmed it - a blank canvas painted in one colour was what he was aiming for. I think he had also eliminated the frame.

Years later came the abstract pieces that made monkeys out of some critics. They were asked to judge a couple of pictures and each had to submit an analysis. They spoke of the vigour of execution, the daring colours, the composition and a last one talked about it all being a load of rubbish. The artist, as was then revealed, was a chimpanzee.

I know that I've read art criticism that has sent me into a literary stupor. It happened with a beautifully illustrated book on Picasso. The text itself was an excellent example of subjective, pretentious self-indulgence - passionate and completely unhelpful to the reader. And such writing is at its worst with abstract art because your reference points are things like proportion, balance of shapes, colours, line, tension between masses, composition and such matters. You are dealing with ideas rather than with the empirical world that can be checked out - an apple is not a sofa; an elephant is not something you'd mistake for a hair brush; a cloud is easy to distinguish from a frankfurter. You know where you are with representational pictures... well, more or less.

Personally, I blame Vasari for a lot of the trouble about deciding whether or not something is a piece of art. Before he wrote his famous "Lives of the Artists" in 1550, an artist was like many another artisan. Artists were commissioned to paint or sculpt and they got on with it. Michelangelo did not look up at the Sistine Chapel ceiling and decide that the best way to spend the next fifty-three months would be flat on his back, way above ground, with paint dripping off his brush and onto his face. No. You painted what your patron wanted. He might say:

"I want a last supper with my son Giovanni as St John, myself as St Peter and my neighbour - that son of a skunk who owes me a fortune and refuses to pay - as Judas. And use plenty of gold paint, and that blue stuff that's so expensive. I want people to know what I'm worth these days. Oh, yes, it has to fit into a space that's four feet by ten. And my wife wants it to match the curtains."

Such patronage had its advantages and disadvantages. The good news was that you had a job and weren't piling up canvases that no one wanted, and you didn't starve in a garret as virtually happened to Modigliani. The bad news was that you were working to other people's specifications. But the irony is that the setting of such parameters may have made life easier. You had something definite to work on so you then used your imagination and genius to produce of your best.

Of course there were many ordinary and mediocre artists and there were some who, working in a major artist's studio, never got beyond a particular item. "Call Carlo, we need some clouds here. He's very good with the fluffy ones." Or, in Rubens' case, "Hans, my lad, there are a lot of naked thighs in this picture. Get on with them and call me when you've blocked them in, and I'll give them that luminous touch everyone loves," and Hans would go off to do the job for there was no way Rubens on his own could keep up with demand.

The case with all the great Renaissance painters and sculptors from Giotto to Leonardo to Caravaggio to Raphael to Titian - the list is impressively long and the paintings are wonderful - was that they worked like craftsmen though they might be geniuses. If we think pre-Vasari, we are looking at great painters and sculptors, perhaps working on illuminated manuscripts or cathedrals, whose names are lost to us. He treated painters as artists; he enhanced their status. It seems to have given birth later to the idea of the artist's *vocation* to be creative, of art for art's sake and not art at the beck and call of even second-rate men with first class purses or positions. It's all down to language at times. A painter paints paintings, but an artist creates art.

And now, with the twentieth century still in view and the twenty-first stretching ahead, what are we to make of art? You read of one artist whose exhibition features dehydrated human bodies and you learn that he has a waiting list of people who have willed him their bodies so that he may use them in future exhibitions. You learn that some national art gallery may have paid fifty thousand pounds for an unmade bed with stained sheets. You hear on television that a grant of ninety thousand euros has gone to help an artist create a statue of Political Power to be made out of fibreglass, cow dung and copper wire. And you don't know who is the one in need of brain surgery.

Do not despair. It may simply be a matter of thinking in terms of upper or lower case letters. If you think of ART as something of immense value and importance then you may end up having a coronary in this world where, it seems, anything goes. If you think of art simply as something that artists produce, then you have no problem. All you need to do is decide whether or not it pleases you. If it does, then enjoy it, discuss it, analyse it, buy it. If you try to see its merits and fail to find any, then pass on to someone else's work. You are entitled to like or dislike. So is everybody else - you can't expect to find everyone in agreement.

Perhaps the key to enjoyment is a willingness to see with fresh eyes - which I don't always do. However, I do know I once spent six hours in the Centre Pompidou in Paris seeing all sorts of fascinating things from what most of us think of as normal paintings to wonderfully entertaining pieces of three dimensional work. I have no clear idea as to which were ART, art, fun, jokes or anything else; I just know that I had a splendid day there. Happy viewing!

11th May, 2005.

The printing of this book
was completed at the worshops of
Tipografía la Nueva,
Tarifa - Cádiz (Spain)
on 27th October, 2006.